# The Shorter Strachey

# The Shorter Strachey

Selected and Introduced by
## Michael Holroyd
and
## Paul Levy

*Oxford New York Toronto Melbourne*
Oxford University Press
1980

*Oxford University Press, Walton Street, Oxford* OX2 6DP

OXFORD    LONDON    GLASGOW
NEW YORK    TORONTO    MELBOURNE    WELLINGTON
KUALA LUMPUR    SINGAPORE    HONG KONG    TOKYO    DELHI
BOMBAY    CALCUTTA    MADRAS    KARACHI
NAIROBI    DAR ES SALAAM    CAPE TOWN

British Library Cataloguing in Publication Data
Strachey, Lytton
    The Shorter Strachey.
    I. Title    II. Holroyd, Michael    III. Levy, Paul
    082         PR6037.T73S/         79-40997
    ISBN 0-19-212211-8
    ISBN 0-19-281285-8 Pbk

*Printed in Great Britain by
Hazell Watson & Viney Ltd, Aylesbury, Bucks*

# Contents

❧

## Literary Criticism

## Biography

## Four French Subjects

# Introduction

❦

Giles Lytton Strachey was born in 1880. To celebrate the centenary of his birth the editors, his current literary executors, have brought together this selection of his shorter prose works. In our opinion, these pieces are not only representative of Strachey's work, but many of them show him at his literary best, for Strachey's greatest gifts are displayed in his shorter work.

*Queen Victoria* is a good book; but *Eminent Victorians* is a better one, for the latter consists of four essays, and the essay was the form most congenial to Strachey's talents. His literary virtues were those of the miniaturist: close observation of detail and exquisite care in its selection and presentation. The limitations of the smaller canvas brought out his strengths – concision and precision. His natural length was under ten thousand words, and his best subjects were biographical, historical, or critical. None of his attempts at fiction or verse can be counted a success.

His dissertation on Warren Hastings, which he submitted, un-successfully, for a Trinity College Prize Fellowship at Cambridge, was his first attempt at sustained writing. The length demanded of a dissertation was wrong for him; and the relative failure of the whole work (which remains unpublished) is in contrast to the excellence of the short introduction to it, which we print here for the first time.

Our selection has been made on grounds of literary merit, but at the same time we have tried to choose pieces that are representative of the several stages of his fairly brief career as a writer (he died aged fifty-two) and of his catholic interests. Though some of Strachey's most characteristic pieces are among those printed here, they have never appeared before in a single volume. Two of them, a paper read to the Cambridge Apostles as well as the Warren Hastings introduction, have never been published before, and the essay on Asquith is uncollected.

The 'Apostles' paper is typical of the seventeen he read to that famous secret society in his ten years of active membership of it. His ties to the Society were as strong as any bonds he formed in his life, and the paper itself captures well the tone of voice, informal, witty and *louche*, with which he captivated the group, and replaced as their chief member the philosopher G.E. Moore. The subject of the paper is one he was to return to again and again – art and indecency. The specimen autobiographies in this section are equally informal in structure, and were also written to be read aloud to an audience; though only 'Lancaster Gate' was written expressly for it, both papers were read to a Bloomsbury Group institution, the Memoir Club. With 'Asquith', which is also auto-biographical in form, these make up our first section.

Strachey was only twenty-two when he delivered his first paper to the Apostles, yet it has a maturity of style remarkable for so young a man, and its subject-matter and his treatment of it were nicely calculated to startle the broad-minded Apostles of 1902. 'Lancaster Gate' and 'Monday June 26th 1916' were much later works, the former written in 1922, the year after his stunning success with *Queen Victoria*, when he was regarded as the greatest lion of the Bloomsbury pride. 'Asquith' is of some historical importance, for it substantiates, in a first-hand account, what Asquith's biographers were led to suspect from the letters he wrote to Venetia Stanley during Cabinet meetings: that the Prime Minister was obsessively susceptible to women. Surely Strachey would have been delighted by the furore that followed publication of this essay in *The Times* exactly fifty years after his death, for the letters of protest that it provoked were as outraged, and expressed in tones as strident, as the pained howls that greeted *Eminent Victorians*.

The next three selections are pieces written in wartime, and they show a different side of Strachey. In these reviews and essays he is not always a subtle ironist: sometimes, as in 'Militarism and Theology', his good humour leaves him altogether; he writes with a pen dipped in a darker ink, and in a mood that borders upon despair. 'A Diplomatist: Li Hung-Chang' shows Strachey writing upon a subject unusual for him, but it is a subject that is possibly even more interesting today than it was when he published the review in 1918, and it has the added bonuses of touching on General Gordon and on topics and people connected with Lord Trevor-Roper's *The Hermit of Peking*. The superb 'Voltaire and Frederick the Great' shows Strachey feeling apprehensive about the civilized traditions of Europe that are the ostensible subject of this long essay. It was written in October 1915, when what he and his friends most feared was the introduction of conscription, and with it, the loss of that liberty the war was supposedly being fought to defend. The moral he drew from the clash of Voltaire and Frederick was frank propaganda against war hysteria: 'Nor, it is to be hoped, need any Englishman be reminded that the consequences of a system of government in which the arbitrary will of an individual takes the place of the rule of law are apt to be disgraceful and absurd.' What we have here is a glimpse – though not, it must be admitted, an absolutely clear view – of Strachey the political radical, the anti-war activist who wrote near-seditious pamphlets for the No Conscription Fellowship and who dared the Hampstead Tribunal to send him to jail because he would not agree to aid the prosecution of the war.

The wartime section provides a necessary and salubrious rebuttal of the common view that Strachey and his Bloomsbury friends disdained – if they did not despise – politics and everything in life that did not afford aesthetic or emotional experiences. But it does not, perhaps, show Strachey at full stretch as a writer of English prose; the next section remedies this. *Six English Historians*, written in his maturity from 1928 to 1930, is a most satisfying series of reflections on historians and their craft. Today we are better informed about Hume and, owing to the labours of Professor John Clive, we know that Macaulay's emotional life was far more complicated than Strachey could have guessed. But though many new facts have emerged about Carlyle, and many volumes have been written in consequence, Strachey's vignette is hard to fault. Strachey entertained ambitions as a dramatist. These were for the most part unfortunate, though his play *The Son of Heaven* has been performed. But perhaps it was the youthful desire to be a playwright that made it possible for him to write, aged only twenty-four, the brilliant 'Shakespeare's Final Period'; and if so, we can only applaud the boldness with which he built his biographical

edifice upon foundations of Shakespearean scholarship. His obi-
tuary of Sarah Bernhardt is Strachey on the art of acting, and
shows that he could convey the impression of particular performances so well that he might have been a first-rate theatre critic.

His own shortcomings as a practitioner of verse drama did not
blunt Strachey's critical sensibilities when he came to write, in 'The
Last Elizabethan', about the recently rediscovered work of
Beddoes. He was severe about Beddoes's faults of construction, but
praised him because 'his mature blank verse is perfect . . . And, with
Beddoes, maturity was precocious, for he obtained complete
mastery over the most difficult and dangerous of metres at a
wonderfully early age. Blank verse is like the Djin in the Arabian
Nights; it is either the most terrible of masters, or the most
powerful of slaves.' This wonderful amalgam of biography and
criticism was published when Strachey was twenty-seven, and
shows that he had learnt the difficult lesson of how to turn his own
failings to profit: it may well have been his own lack of skill in blank
verse that gave him so much insight into Beddoes's mastery.

Strachey was invited to give the Leslie Stephen Lecture for 1925.
He took as his subject the genius of the other iambic form, the
heroic couplet, and produced his critical masterpiece, his essay on
Pope. The contrast with the essay that follows, on Matthew
Arnold, could not be greater. Pope's 'poetic criticism of life', says
Strachey, 'was, simply and solely, the heroic couplet', with which
he 'turned his screams into poetry'. Pope understood the sense in
which poetry really was 'the Criticism of Life'; Matthew Arnold,
who embodied 'the essential and fatal weakness of the Victorian
Age – its incapability of criticism', mistook his own critical
touchstone and gave comfort to the 'Philistines' he had himself
named. Strachey's fondness for paradox, so devastating when
applied to Matthew Arnold, could also be illuminating, as when,
earlier the same year, he saw in the author of *Crime and Punishment*
'a humorist of a remarkable and original type'.

Strachey's literary criticism, even his more 'technical' pieces such
as the essays on Pope and Beddoes, depends upon biographical
considerations, and it is as a biographical essayist that he excels. 'A
biography', he wrote, 'should be either as long as Boswell's or as
short as Aubrey's. The method of enormous and elaborate
accretion which produced the *Life of Johnson* is excellent, no doubt;

but, failing that, let us have no half-measures; let us have the pure essentials — a vivid image, on a page or two, without explanations, transitions, commentaries, or padding.' As a writer who believed his own biographical method to be linked to Johnson's *Lives of the Poets*, Strachey admired Boswell; but he admired him for all the qualities they did not share — in particular the huge energy that, while destroying his own life, created the *Life of Johnson*.

Strachey's own talents, though more polished and sophisticated than theirs, lay in the direction of miniaturists and diarists such as Aubrey and Thomas Creevey, 'whose function it is to reveal to us the littleness underlying great events and to remind us that history itself was once real life.' His studies of obscure pedagogues, eccentrics and antiquaries show the other side of the man who had begun by trying to rehabilitate Warren Hastings and went on to pull down the eminent from their high places. Here it is the victims of life he celebrates, men and women pulled into dreadful shapes by the pressures of their lives: Lodowick Muggleton, the incom-prehensible prophet with his tiny band of crazed disciples; that caricature of academic learning, poor forgotten Dr North, Sir John Harington, led by his sensitive, impudent nose to become the inventor of the water-closet; and the uptilted aristocratic nose of Lady Hester Stanhope, 'a nose of wild ambitions, of pride grown fantastical, a nose that scorned the earth ... a nose, in fact, altogether in the air' that she followed through Arabian Night adventures until she died 'inexplicable, grand, preposterous, with her nose in the air'. Such miniatures display Strachey's feline skill at storytelling, and a humorous tenderness and sympathy, not associated with the iconoclast of *Eminent Victorians*, that seems at the same time to reveal and to excuse the absurdities of life.

Max Beerbohm, while not certain that Strachey was a warm-hearted man, said: 'A tender-hearted man he assuredly was'. Beerbohm's gifts were so like Strachey's that in his Rede Lecture of 1943 his modest appreciation of Strachey is almost a reflection of his own modesty: 'Lytton Strachey was not a great writer, not a great man, and not old enough to have become a Grand Old Man. But his gifts and his repute amply sufficed to ensure reaction against him very soon after the breath was out of his body. I think it was Ben Jonson who spoke of ''the backward kick of the dull ass's hoof''. That is not a pretty expression. But it is neither silly nor vulgar. The vulgar term, "a debunker", the term that the average writer or talker curiously applies to Strachey, is not only vulgar, it is also silly.'

When Beerbohm wrote this lecture Strachey had been dead only eleven years. His reputation had inevitably been clouded by advances in historical scholarship and by the disservice done to his biographical innovations by the near-parodies of them produced by a whole tribe of pygmy imitators. But it is too seldom remembered that by his insistence on 'biography as an artistic whole', as Robert Gittings writes in *The Nature of Biography* (1978), he 'headed a long line of writers – David Cecil, Harold Nicolson, Cecil Woodham-Smith, to name only a few – who have produced miniature masterpieces'.

There is a unity to be found in all Strachey's work which he points to when, in his preface to *Eminent Victorians*, he wrote: 'The art of biography seems to have fallen on evil times in England. We have had, it is true, a few masterpieces, but we have never had, like the French, a great biographical tradition; we have had no Fontenelles and Condorcets, with their incomparable *éloges*, compressing into a few shining pages the manifold existences of men.' A passion for the tradition of French literature informs all his writing, and his essays on French subjects have had a largely unacknowledged influence on the study of comparative literature. These, in our view, constitute Strachey's own most cherished achievement, so it seems appropriate to conclude our selection with four of the best of them.

*Three Autobiographical Memoirs and a Cambridge Apostles paper*

# Lancaster Gate

❧

The influence of houses on their inhabitants might well be the subject of a scientific investigation. Those curious contraptions of stones or bricks, with all their peculiar adjuncts, trimmings, and furniture, their specific immutable shapes, their intense and inspissated atmosphere, in which our lives are entangled as completely as our souls in our bodies — what powers do they not wield over us, what subtle and pervasive effects upon the whole substance of our existence may not be theirs? Or is that all nonsense? Our fathers, no doubt, would have laughed at such a speculation; for to our fathers the visible conformations of things were unimportant; they were more interested in the mental and moral implications of their surroundings than in the actual nature of them; and their spirits, so noble and oblivious, escaped the direct pressure of the material universe. They could understand that it would make a difference whether one spent one's life in an ancient family seat in Gloucestershire or in a red-brick villa at Tooting — the social, personal, and traditional distinctions were obvious enough. But the notion that the proportions of a bedroom, for instance, might be significant would have appeared absurd to them; and so they were able to create, and to inhabit, South Kensington almost unconsciously, as if such conduct were the most natural thing in the world. Our view is different. We find satisfaction in curves and colours, and windows fascinate us, we are agitated by staircases, inspired by doors, disgusted by cornices, depressed by chairs, made wanton by ceilings, entranced by passages, and exacerbated by a rug.

In my case at any rate the impression caused by a house has been profound and extraordinary. I say impression, because as to more remote effects — such is the subtlety and complexity of the question — I hardly know what they may have been, or even whether there

1

were any; but a memorable impression is beyond a doubt. Of all my dreams (and I am a confirmed dreamer) there is one alone which persistently recurs, only slightly varying in its details, with a curious iteration. For some reason or another – one of those preposterous and yet absolutely satisfying reasons which occur in dreams – we are back again, once more, just as we were, in Lancaster Gate. We are in the drawing-room, among the old furniture, arranged in the old way, and it is understood that we are to go there indefinitely, as if we had never left it. The strange thing is that, when I realize that this has come about, that our successive wanderings have been a mere interlude, that we are once more permanently established at number 69, a feeling of intimate satisfaction comes over me. I am positively delighted. And this is strange because, in my working life, I have never for a moment, so far as I am aware, regretted our departure from that house, and if, in actuality, we *were* to return to it, I can imagine nothing which would disgust me more. So, when I wake up, and find myself after all at Gordon Square or Tidmarsh, I have the odd sensation of a tremendous relief at finding that my happiness of one second before was a delusion.

Apart from my pleasure at it, no doubt it is hardly surprising that Lancaster Gate should haunt me. For it was a portentous place, and I spent in it the first twenty-five years of my conscious life. My remembrances of Stowey House are dim and sporadic – Jim Rendel[1] with a penny in a passage – a miraculous bean at the bottom of the garden – Beatrice Chamberlain[2] playing at having tea with me, with leaves and acorns, under a tree. But my consecutive existence began in the nursery at Lancaster Gate – the nursery that I can see now, empty and odd and infinitely elevated, as it was when I stood in it for the first time at the age of four with my mother, and looked out of the window at the surprisingly tall houses opposite, and was told that this was where we were going to live. A calm announcement – received with some excitement,

---

[1] James Meadows Rendel, Chairman of the Assam Bengal Railway and an expert on Poor Law administration, who married Lytton's eldest sister, Elinor.

[2] The eldest daughter of Joseph Chamberlain and his first wife Harriet Kenrick, she was a half-sister to Neville Chamberlain.

2

which was partly caused by the unusual sensation of extreme
height, as I peered at the street below. The life that began then – my
Lancaster Gate life – was to continue till I was twenty-eight – a man
full grown – all the changes from childhood to adolescence, from
youth to manhood, all the developments, the curiosities, the pains,
the passions, the despairs, the delights, of a quarter of a century
having taken place within those walls.

A portentous place! Yes, but exactly how portentous it is not
easy to convey. Its physical size was no doubt the most obviously
remarkable thing about it; but it was not mere size, it was size gone
wrong, size pathological; it was a house afflicted with elephantiasis
that one found one had entered, when, having mounted the steps
under the porch, having passed through the front door and down
the narrow dark passage with its ochre walls and its tessellated floor
of magenta and indigo tiles, one looked upwards and saw the
staircase twisting steeply up its elongated well – spiralling away
into a thin infinitude, until, far above, one's surprised vision came
upon a dome of pink and white glass, which yet one judged, with
an unerring instinct, was not the top – no, not nearly, nearly the
top. Below the ground-floor there was a basement, above it there
was a drawing-room floor, and above that there were four floors of
bedrooms; so that altogether the house contained seven layers of
human habitation. But that was not all; all the rooms were high,
but the height of the drawing-room was enormous; so that, if one
had the courage to go up the stairs, one found, when one had
surmounted the first floor, that one was on an airy eminence,
surrounded by immeasurable spaces of yellow marbled wallpaper,
and alarmingly near the dome; its pink lights seemed to glitter
almost within one's reach, when, abruptly, one's course deviated;
one turned to the left up six strangely broad steps, and came upon
quite a new part of the building – the bedrooms, piled two and two
on the top of one another, connected by quite an ordinary, small
staircase, and forming a remote, towering outgrowth upon the
monstrous structure below.

The house had been designed extraordinarily badly. The rooms
that looked on to the street (one on each floor) were tolerable; all
the rest were very small and very dark. There was not a scrap of
garden, not even a courtyard; and so lugubrious was the outlook of
the back rooms that the windows of most of them were of pink and

white ground glass, so that one never saw out of them. In a London winter, very little light indeed came through those patterned panes. My mother, taking a hint from my father's office in the City, had 'reflectors' put up – huge plates of glassy material, slightly corrugated, which hung opposite the windows from chains. The windows themselves were so large that it was almost impossible to open them. Little circular ventilators were cut in them, working by means of cords. All this presented a peculiar spectacle, as one sat in the schoolroom – at the end of the passage on the ground-floor – or in 'the young ladies' room', behind the dining-room; a tiny apartment, far higher than it was either long or broad, with a gigantic mahogany door, and the vast window, pink and frosted, with its string and ventilator, and a dim vision of filthy yellow bricks, chains, and corrugations looming through the fog outside. And besides the height and the darkness there were other strange inconveniences. There was the one and only bathroom, for instance, perched, with its lavatory, in an impossible position midway between the drawing-room and the lowest bedroom floors – a kind of crow's nest – to reach which, one had to run the gauntlet of stairs innumerable, and whose noises of rushing waters were all too audible from the drawing-room just below.

Then, in spite of its gigantic size, the house, somehow or other, seemed to have very few rooms in it. My father was the only person who had a sitting-room to himself. In the miserable little 'young ladies' room', Dorothy and Pippa, and Pernel, and later on Marjorie, led an oddly communal existence; privacy there, I suppose occasionally there must have been, but privacy arranged, studied and highly precarious. But, strangest of all, my mother had no room of her own. There was a large writing-table in the dining-room, and at that writing-table, amid the incessant *va-et-vient* of a large family, my mother did all her business – and she was a busy woman, with a multitude of outside interests, a large correspondence, and a curiously elaborate system of household accounts.

No doubt, in all large families, there is very little privacy; and one might say that Lancaster Gate was, in essence, the crowning symbol of the large family system. The one implied the other. The same vitality, the same optimism, the same absence of nerves, which went to the deliberate creation of ten children, built the crammed, high, hideous edifice that sheltered them. And so it was inevitable that the most characteristic feature of the house – its centre, its summary, the seat of its soul, so to speak – should have been the room which was the common meeting-place of all the members of the family – the drawing-room. When one entered that vast chamber, when, peering through its foggy distances, ill-lit by gas-jets, or casting one's eyes wildly towards the infinitely distant ceiling overhead, one struggled to traverse its dreadful length, to reach a tiny chair or a far-distant fireplace, conscious as one did so that some kind of queer life was clustered thick about one, that heaven knows how many eyes watched from just adumbrated sofas, that brains crouched behind the piano, that there were other presences, remote, aloof, self-occupied, and mys-teriously dominating the scene – then, in truth, one had come – whether one realized it or no – into an extraordinary holy of holies. The gigantic door, with its flowing portière of pale green silk, swung and shut behind one. One stepped forwards in the direction of the three distant windows covered by their pale green limitless curtains, one looked about, one of the countless groups of persons disintegrated, flowed towards one, one sat and spoke and listened: one was reading the riddle of the Victorian Age.

I only mean to say that the Lancaster Gate drawing-room was, in its general nature, the concentrated product of an epoch; for certainly it was too full of individuality and peculiarity to be typical of anything. For one thing, it was too intelligent. I believe that it was not absolutely ugly; the decorations were undoubtedly, for the time, slightly advanced. But it is almost impossible for me to come to an impartial judgement on it. I know it far too well. To the entering stranger, puzzled and alarmed, the impression it produced may well have been one of mere confusion; to me, all was clear, all was articulate, every one of the innumerable details was accurately, intimately, and unforgettably known. At this moment I am perfectly certain that I could reconstruct the whole complexity, complete and exact in every inch. The details were indeed literally innumerable, but there was a climax – immediately obvious – in the arrangement of them. This climax occurred at the more distant of the two mantelpieces – on the right-hand wall, near the window end of the room – a very large high structure of a most peculiar kind. But I cannot hope to describe that bulk of painted wood with its pilasters and cornices, its jars and niches, its marble and its multi-coloured tiles. Designed by Halsey Ricardo, it combined, with an effect of emasculated richness, the inspiration of William Morris, reminiscences of the Renaissance, and a bizarre idiosyncrasy of its own. Guests, finding themselves for the first time face to face with this colossal complication, nearly always exclaimed 'What a magnificent mantelpiece!' It is difficult to see what else they could have done, for to have remained silent before an object so peculiarly conspicuous would have been decidedly marked. Standing by that mottled hearth, one had reached the citadel of the great room. Surveying it from that vantage-spot, one could see that it was a room that was utterly unromantic. It was a mere rectangular parallelepiped — a large ill-shaped box, crammed in between a whole series of exactly similar boxes, ranged on each side of it up and down the street. And yet, though there was no romance in it, there certainly *was* something that was not quite analysable. Was it the effect of its size or its ugliness or its absurdity? — I don't know; but familiar, incredibly familiar as it was to me, who had spent my whole life in it, there was never a time when I was not, in the recesses of my consciousness, a little surprised by it. It was like one of those faces at which one can look for ever without growing accustomed to. Up to my last hour in it, I always felt that the drawing-room was strange.

Strange indeed! Is it conceivable, after all, that I ever was really there? Is it conceivable that Dorothy [Strachey], evening after evening, in that room, kissed me a hundred times, in a rapture of laughter and affection, counting her kisses, when I was six? that, in that same room, perhaps twenty years later, sitting on a sofa alone with Andrew, I suddenly kissed *him*, much to his surprise and indignation — 'My dear man! Really! One doesn't do those things!' — And that — but never mind.

It was a family room — (Andrew, I may mention, was my nephew) — and the family combinations and permutations in it were very various. Apart from the ordinary domestic moments, it was on Sunday afternoons, when my mother was invariably at home, that the family atmosphere, reinforced from without, reached its intensest and its oddest pitch. Then the drawing-room gradually grew thick with aunts and uncles, cousins and connections, with Stracheys, Grants, Rendels, Plowdens, Battens,

Ridpaths, Rowes. One saw that it had indeed been built for them — it held them all so nicely, so naturally, with their interminable varieties of age and character and class — from Nina Grey in her faded airs of Roman Catholic aristocracy to Fanny Stanley and her lodging-house garrulity, from Uncle George, bent double with age and eccentricity, hideously sniffing, and pouring out his opinions upon architecture and Tasso to anyone who ventured within his reach, to Black Pat, youthful, horribly snouted, absurdly mendacious, who had come, it was clear, by arrangement, to meet Millie Plowden, and overdid his surprise when at last in yellow feathers she giggled into the room.

The crowd was at its largest at about six, and then it gradually thinned away. But somebody very often stayed on to dinner — Sir William Ward, perhaps, who, besides having been Governor of the Straits Settlements was an executor, of astonishing brilliancy, on the pianoforte. Pressed to play, he would seat himself at the piano and dash into a Chopin waltz with the verve of a high-stepping charger, when suddenly a very odd and discordant sound, rising and falling with the music, would make itself heard. It was something between a snore and a whistle, and nobody could think what it could be. But the mystery was at last explained — the ex-Governor suffered, in moments of excitement, from a curious affection of the nose. While the family listened, a little hysterically, to this peculiar combination of sounds, all at once yet *another* sound — utterly different — burst upon their ears — the sound, this time, of rushing water. There was a momentary shock; and then we all silently realized that someone, in the half-way landing upstairs, was using the w.c.

There are various ways of 'seeing life'; but it seems to me that, in one way or another, I saw a good deal of life in the drawing-room at Lancaster Gate. And of course my experience then was not limited to an enormous family: there was a constant succession of callers, there were repeated dinner-parties and at homes. The preparations for an afternoon party I have a queer vision of — a vision, as it happens, that can be accurately dated: The room was bared, the chairs ranged round the walls, and in the middle, walking up and down and showing themselves off were Dorothy and Pippa dressed from head to foot in white muslin with full flowing skirts, and black satin sashes round their waists, tied in immense bows. They were in mourning – for the death of the German Emperor; and that afternoon party must have been in the third week of June 1888. Often, there were musical parties, and, in the days when trousers were even more unfamiliar to me than they are now, I heard, to my intense excitement, that Grossmith – the almost mythical Grossmith of the *Sorcerer* and the *Pinafore* – was coming to sing and play. 'I know what'll happen,' I whispered to Marjorie, in a great state of agitation, as we waited for the guests. 'Just as Grossmith comes into the room, my knickerbockers will fall down.' The grandest of the musical parties was much later, given in combination by my aunt and my mother, with Joachim and Piatti playing in their quartet. I can see at this moment, in my mind's eye, the Olympian features of Sir Frederic Leighton, flushed with anger, as he entered on that occasion. I can hear him explaining, in heated accents, that he had made a mistake, had gone to the wrong house, and had been driving over half London in consequence.

It must not be inferred from these entertainments that we were fashionable or smart; on the contrary, if anything we were dowdy; though on the other hand, we were not in the least Bohemian. Our conventionality, slightly mitigated by culture and intelligence, was impinged upon much more seriously by my mother's constitutional vagueness and immateriality, and by a vein in her of oddity and caprice. Her feeling for what was right and proper was unsupported by the slightest touch of snobbery; and, while it was very strong and quite unhesitating, it was surprisingly peculiar to herself. That her daughters should go into mourning for the German Emperor, for instance, appeared to her essential; but her own dresses were most extraordinary, designed by herself, quite regardless of fashion. She had all her children christened, but she never went to Church – except in the country, when she went with the utmost regularity. She was religious in the payment of calls; but the arrangements of the household, from the point of view of social life, were far below the standard. We kept up the mere minimum of an appearance. Our butler, Frederick, the promoted gardener's boy of Stowey House, uncouth, simian, with a great mouth, ill-covered by a straggling moustache, was one of the most unpresent-able of figures, and must have cast a chill upon the visitor to whom he opened the door for the first time. 'Why do the Stracheys allow their man to wear a moustache?' Marjorie, in hiding in the dining-room, once heard a military visitor inquire of another as they went down the passage together. Why did they indeed? But in truth my mother would no more have dreamt of ordering the unfortunate Frederick – one of the most excellent of creatures, in spite of his ugliness – to shave off his moustache than she would have dreamt of going without a butler altogether and having a parlour-maid. A butler, but an unpresentable butler, might have stood for the symbol of the Lancaster Gate establishment.

No doubt a contributing cause of our dowdiness was that we were only precariously well off. But, whatever the explanation, I think, as I look back, that the fact that we *were* dowdy was one of the redeeming elements in the situation. Few things could be imagined more terrible than a *smart* Lancaster Gate. As it was, there was something human in the untidyness and the dirt. It was a touch of nature that, in the hall, by the stairs, two bicycles should be grouped together, incompletely covered by a rug, that the dust was too thick on the red velvet in the alcove behind the cast of the Venus of Milo, and that, in the dining-room, my mother's writing-table, littered with papers, stood out obvious and unashamed during the largest dinner-parties. To the children, at any rate, nosing into corners, the full incorrectitude of the place stood revealed. Visitors, perhaps, might not particularly notice, but *we* knew by heart all the camouflaged abysses, taking a sardonic delight in the ruthlessness of the introspective realism with which we plumbed and numbered 'filth-packet' after 'filth-packet' – for such was our too descriptive phrase.

What had happened was that a great tradition – the aristocratic tradition of the eighteenth century – had reached a very advanced stage of decomposition. My father and my mother belonged by birth to the old English world of country-house gentlefolk – a world of wealth and breeding, a world in which such things as footmen, silver, and wine were the necessary appurtenances of civilized life. But their own world was different: it was the middle-class professional world of the Victorians, in which the old forms still lingered, but debased and enfeebled, in which Morris wall-papers had taken the place of Adam panelling, in which the swarming retinue had been reduced to a boy in livery, in which the spoons and forks were bought at the Army and Navy Stores. And then, introducing yet another element into the mixture, there was the peculiar disintegrating force of the Strachey character. The solid bourgeois qualities were interpenetrated by intellectualism and eccentricity. Our family dinners expressed the complicated state of things. They were long and serious meals; but, unless there were visitors, we never dressed for them. At the end, the three mystic bottles of port, sherry, and claret were put at the head of the table and solemnly circulated – the port, sherry, and claret having come from the grocer's round the corner. The butler and the liveried boot-boy waited on us, and the butler was Frederick, or, later, a figure even more characteristic of our subtle *dégringolade* – Bastian[i] – a fat, black-haired, Italianate creature, who eventually took to drink, could hardly puff up the stairs from the basement, and, as he handed the vegetables, exuded an odour of sweat and whisky into one's face. He disappeared – after a scene of melodramatic horror – to be replaced by Mr Brooks who, we could only suppose, must have been a groom in earlier life, since all his operations were accompanied by a curious sound of *sotto voce* hissing – or, of course, he might have been Sir William Ward, rather thinly disguised. Peering into the drawers of the sideboard, we discovered tangled masses of soda water-bottle wires, broken corkscrews, napkins, and the mysterious remains of disembowelled brushes. We took note of another filth-packet, observing at the same time, with gusto, that the glass stopper of the brandy decanter had been removed by Mr Brooks, and that a cork had been rammed into its place.

Disintegration and *dégringolade*, no doubt, and yet the total effect, materialized and enormously extended, was of a tremendous solidity. Lancaster Gate towered up above us, and around us, an imperturbable mass – the framework, almost the very essence – so it seemed – of our being. Was it itself, perhaps, one vast filth-packet, and we the mere *disjecta membra* of vanished generations, which Providence was too busy or too idle to clear away? So, in hours of depression, we might have unconsciously theorized; but nevertheless, in reality, it was not so. Lancaster Gate vanished into nothingness, and we survive. To me, that that régime would inevitably, someday, come to an end was a dreadful thought – one not to be dwelt upon – like death; what would, what *could* happen, when we went away from Lancaster Gate? Circumstances – a diminished income – brought about at length the unspeakable catastrophe: but I see now that, whatever had happened, however rich we might have continued, Lancaster Gate was in fact doomed. The disintegration would have grown too strong for it at last. Indeed the end, I think, had really come before we actually left it: Dorothy, with extraordinary courage, married a penurious French artist,[3] and Lancaster Gate was shaken to its foundations. The new spirit was signalized by the omission – under the feeble plea of the difference in nationality – of a wedding service in a church – an omission which would have been impossible ten years earlier; but a family party to celebrate the occasion it was out of the question to omit. Once more the drawing-room was flooded by those familiar figures: even Uncle William in his coat and waistcoat of quaint cut and innumerable buttons – the very same that he might have worn in the forties in Holland House – even Mabel Batten, with that gorgeous bust on which the head of Edward the Seventh was wont to repose – were there. When the strange company had departed, something – though at the time we hardly realized it – had happened: it was the end of an age.

The actual events of life are perhaps unimportant. One is born, grows up, falls in love, falls out of love, works, is happy, is unhappy, grows old, and dies – a tedious, a vulgar, succession; but not there lies the significance of a personal history: it is the atmosphere that counts. What happened to me during my first twenty-five years of consciousness may well be kept to the imagination; what cannot be left to the imagination is the particular, the amazing, web on which the pattern of my existence was woven – in other words, Lancaster Gate. To imagine *that*! – To reconstruct, however dimly, that grim machine, would be to realize with some real distinctness the essential substance of my biography. An incubus sat upon my spirit, like a cat on a sleeping child. I was unaware, I was unconscious, I hardly understood that anything else could be. Submerged by the drawing-room, I inevitably believed that the drawing-room was the world. Or rather, I neither believed nor disbelieved; it *was* the world, so far as I

---

[3] In 1903 Dorothy Strachey married Simon Bussy. As Dorothy Bussy she became well-known for her translations of André Gide. She was also the author of *Olivia* by 'Olivia' (1949).

was concerned. Only, all the time, I did dimly notice that there was something wrong with the world – that it was an unpleasant shape.

Of course, it would be absurd to pretend that I was permanently and definitely unhappy. It was not a question of unhappiness so much as of restriction and oppression – the subtle unperceived weight of the circumambient air. And there were moments, luckily, when some magic spring within me was suddenly released, and I threw off that weight, my spirit leaping up into freedom and beatitude. Coming home in the night in the summer once from the Temple with Clive,[4] parting from him, excited, faintly amorous, opposite the sentry at St James's Palace, walking on in the early morning opalescence through sleeping Mayfair and down the Bayswater Road, where the County Council carts were sprinkling the pavements with pale blue disinfectant water – I arrived at last at number 69, a little weary, but not too weary to face with equanimity the long climb that lay in front of me before I reached my bed. Up and up I went, curling round the great dim ochre well, round and up, until the dome loomed over me, and, looking over the banisters, I hung high in mid space, then turned, went up the six broad steps, then passed bedroom after bedroom, up and up still, leaving the nursery floor behind me, until I reached the bedroom, which, for the moment, was mine – almost at the very top of the house – at the back – overlooking, from an incredible height, a mews and roof and chimneys. I opened the door and went in, and immediately saw that the second bed – there was invariably a second bed in every bedroom – was occupied. I looked closer: it was Duncan;[5] and I was not surprised: he had lingered on, no doubt, till it was too late to go home, and had been provided with the obvious accommodation. I undressed, oddly exultant, in the delicious warm morning. As I was getting into bed I saw that all the clothes had rolled off Duncan – that he was lying, almost naked, in vague pyjamas – his body – the slim body of a youth of nineteen – exposed to the view. I was very happy; and, smiling to myself, I wondered why it was that I did not want – not want in the very

[4] Clive Bell, the art critic.

[5] Duncan Grant, Strachey's cousin, was the son of Lady Strachey's brother Bartle.

least – what the opportunity so perfectly offered, and I got into bed, and slept soundly, and dreamt no prophetic dreams.

June 1922

# Ought the Father to Grow a Beard?

Cleopatra   If it be love indeed, tell me how much.
Antony      There's beggary in the love that can be reckoned.
Cleopatra   I'll set a bourn how far to be beloved.
Antony      Then must thou needs find out new heaven, new earth.

To this great first colloquy, to these triumphant chords opening an immortal symphony, I wish, for the moment at any rate, to give a meaning which I can hardly imagine was Shakespeare's. These are words, I wish to think, falling from the lips of no mortal Antony, no mortal Egypt; nor do I hear them as the symbolic utterances of the eternal man and the eternal woman, the lover and the beloved. They are for me fraught with a strangely different significance; for they bring before me an image of the unending conversation of the artist and of life. Beneath the mask of Cleopatra I seem to see the infinite complexity, the untiring movement, the voluptuous fascination of human existence, and from Antony's mouth the voice of the poet and the painter and the musician strikes upon my ears. 'What!' says Life, alluring while she seems to repel, 'you say you love me, but how much do you love me?'; and the Artist, in the fervour of his ecstasy, replies that his love is boundless. 'Nay', answers Life, 'you shall not go too far! Somewhere, you must stop at last. I'll set a bourn how far to be beloved.' And the Artist, searching, struggling, achieving, declares that he has embraced all, that he who would surpass him must create the heavens and the earth anew; and Life, smiling mysteriously, is silent.

The limits of Art! The bourn set upon the artist in his love of life! Can such a thing be? Or shall there be no end, no limit to his adoration? Strange and pregnant speculation, yet now for the first time stirring us, for the first time bringing us to doubt! . . . .

In all ages, and among all nations, art has for its object the representation of Life. In every work of art – from the earliest pipings of Arcadian shepherds to the latest of Huysmans's novels – the artist has for his theme some part of human passion, or human action, or human thought. But if it is true that the whole of art draws its inspiration from Life, it is equally true that no form of art however wide, no artist however great, can press into his service the *whole* of Life. Art, therefore, depends on a process of selection, and the question which every Artist must ask himself as he surveys the world is 'Which of these innumerable phenomena of Life shall I choose for my material?'

Different ages have answered the question in different ways. To the Greek sculptor Rodin's Baptist would have doubtless appeared a monstrosity; the eighteenth century regarded Shakespeare as a barbarian; the early Victorians turned with horror and disgust from the profanities and audacities of Shelley and Byron. Perhaps the Greeks of 400 B.C. and the great age of the Renaissance in Italy and in England produced the widest artistic conceptions, the most embracing adoration of the infinite allurements of Life; but even to these a bourn was set. For who can doubt that the great artists of our own almost putrescent generation might teach much in a thousand directions of subtle discrimination to Aristophanes, to Michael Angelo, and – may one hazard the conclusion? – perhaps to Shakespeare himself?

But what is especially worthy of notice is the certainty with which every age is filled that it has, as a matter of fact, exhausted the possibilities of artistic treatment. 'What we don't express', is the ever-recurring cry, 'isn't worth expressing.' 'What!' says the Greek, 'make a statue of a starving religious maniac? Disgusting!' 'What!' says the Eighteenth Century, 'talk about knives and blankets at the very height of Tragedy? Ridiculous!' 'What!' says Early Victoria, 'deny the existence of God? Make jests about adultery? Very shocking indeed!' and then all together they exclaim 'No! You've got no business to treat of those things at all; they're outside the domain of Art! *We* only care for what is essential, for what is, in reality, the whole. Follow us, we are the true Antony, and we alone love the true Cleopatra! He who would outdo us must create the heavens and the earth anew!'

And Cleopatra smiles, because she knows, after all, that Antony is right. That new heaven, that new earth which he thinks so impossible to be discovered, is, precisely, what *is* found out by his successor. The old order changes, perishes, gives place to the new. The glory of Apollo fades before the face of the pale Galilean, who in his turn vanishes beneath the glance of some subtle and sterile Dolores, some obscure Venus of the hollow hill. As in the mystic rite which was once performed under the shadow of the golden bough, the old king is slain by the new king, the new king by the newer still; and at every turn of the wheel, at each death, and at each resurrection, the world is heard to exclaim with undiminished and unfaltering loyalty, 'Le Roi est mort; vive le Roi!'

But although it is clear that the parts of life with which Art chooses to deal are continually changing from age to age, the question remains as to whether there may not be *some* parts of life with which art should never deal. It is obvious that there have always been certain subjects particularly favoured by artists, while others have been only occasionally touched upon or altogether neglected. Can we, after our 2000 years of experience, formulate a rule? Can we say to the artist 'within these limits you may select as much of life, and reject as much of it, as you will; beyond them you cannot go'? Can we say to Antony, 'you may enjoy the limbs and the head and the breasts of Cleopatra as much as you like, but there are some parts of her which you shall never enjoy; for with these you have nothing whatever to do'?

Since the institution of Christianity and fig-leaves, there has been a remarkable unanimity as to which these parts precisely are. With an outer limit at the extreme top of the stomach on the one hand and at about the middle of the thighs on the other, the forbidden zone gradually deepens in intensity, enclosing within its boundaries the whole region of the bowels and most of the essential parts of the human economy, until it reaches the culminating and central point of the sexual organs. Here indeed is the undiscovered country, the North Pole itself. The eyes of our Antony, baffled by a thousand veils, turn away in despair. The instrument which would penetrate here must be infinitely more delicate, more gentle, more insinuating, than any with which nature has endowed him; he must be content with reminiscences, with allusions, with dreams; what is he that he should cry out for the real thing?

– But why the dickens shouldn't he, and get it too? –

– I wish to give an illustration.

Suppose tomorrow morning nursery-maids in Kensington

Gardens, clerks on buses, ladies and gentlemen driving in their carriages and cabs to the shops and to the City, were to notice that an extraordinary change had, during the night, come over the central figure of the Albert Memorial. Suppose their astonished eyes were to perceive that that imposing golden form was no longer in the sitting posture, had risen to its feet. But that is not all. Imagine they saw too that it had discarded that princely robe, those knee-breeches, those stockings which we have all admired so, that it stood there in the garb of nature, in the garb in which Augustus and Hadrian and Marcus Aurelius thought fit to appear before the millions of their subjects, thought fit to be remembered when they had long since ceased to walk the earth, had long since passed to the abode of the immortal gods. Imagine this, and imagine the accumulated force of horror and disgust and fury in the breasts of the passers-by. Imagine the indignant rush up those sacred steps, the blind fingers tearing, overturning, destroying... but to contemplate our late beloved Prince in such a situation is too painful; I draw a shuddering veil.

It is only into the minds of the onlookers that I wish to gaze more closely. What is the reason for this horror, this disgust, this rage? Or is there, after all, no reason? Or is the only reason a blind hatred implanted in the human breast of the bare truth in any shape whatever? – Dear madam, why do you turn away your eyes from what, if you come to think of it, is merely a more or less exact image of one entire half of the human race? – Sir, why do you wave your umbrella so frantically at the sight of what is, after all, not very much more than a rough representation of your own appearance as you step into your morning bath? – Alas! My questions receive no answer – unless it be a sneer or a scowl; and I, sir or madam, am for my part unwilling to analyse the confused mass of prejudices and stupidities and vulgarities, which, on such a question, lie at the bottom of your hearts. I shall be content to examine what I conceive to be the truly fundamental grounds of your position.

It appears to me that the objections against the artistic treatment of any subject whatever are of two kinds – objections on the score of morals, and objections on the score of art. Of course these two sorts of objections are constantly confused in practice – an instance being the word 'nasty' so often applied to certain kinds of books, which may either imply that they are morally vicious, or

17

artistically bad. I have not at the present moment an ardent desire to enter into a discussion of the relations between art and morals, but perhaps others have, and an elucidation of the point would of course be necessary for the solution of the whole question. If it can be proved that the treatment of certain subjects in art is definitely immoral, I think that *might* be a good reason for discontinuing the treatment of those subjects. I say *might* because it is quite possible that the immorality caused by art in this way – either to the individual or to society at large – may be purely temporary, and that the best way of preventing it may be by educating the individual and society up to a level at which art could no longer exercise demoralizing effects.

But what interests me more is the question whether there is *any* subject which is *per se* incapable of artistic treatment? Is the presence in anything of ugliness, or dirt, or any disgusting quality, or any quality at all, a sufficient reason for its exclusion from artistic presentation? Can Baudelaire be artistic when he describes with minute detail the processes of animal corruption? Or Wagner when he makes sensuality audible? Or Hogarth when he depicts the sordid and disgusting phenomena of the dissecting room?

– But what do you mean – the fearful question must now be put – by Art?

My brethren! Do not imagine that I am less aware than you of what quicksands I am setting foot upon, what 'Rocks, caves, lakes, fens, bogs, dens, and shades of Death' I am hurrying past like the Devils in *Paradise Lost*. I am quite aware of it; but I am bold, and I proceed.

I think that everyone would admit that what is beautiful is always capable of artistic treatment; and also that what is good is always capable of artistic treatment. The difficulty arises over what is ugly and what is evil. If it is asserted that evil cannot be treated artistically, the asserter is at once brought face to face with Tragedy, which it would surely be impossible to exclude from the domain of Art. If it is said that the evil in tragedy is heightened into the sublime and thus made beautiful, it is then admitted that it is only in combination with ugliness that evil is unfit for Art. But in the works of such a realistic painter as Hogarth and such a realistic writer as Flaubert instances of evil and ugliness treated artistically separately or in combination abound. It may be noticed that it does not alter the question to assert that the *form* of all art must be beautiful, for the question is only concerned with the subject; and I think it impossible to doubt that innumerable instances of artistic production exist which treat of subjects which are evil or ugly or both evil and ugly at the same time.

I am, in fact, forced to the conclusion that *anything* is capable of artistic treatment; that the function of Art is to treat of *everything* whatever its qualities may be.

I now venture to hazard a suggestion as to the meaning of Art. Personally I have always found it impossible ever to consider any one thing apart from everything else – apart, as it were, from its context. It appears to me that the relations borne by anything to other things are nothing more than a part of itself; and reality is thus not only made up of everything in existence, but of the relations between all these things and each other. What I consider that Art does is to put everything it treats of into its proper position as regards reality; and what that position is it is for the Artist alone to discover – the Artist who works not by rules but by genius and an invisible flame within him. .

An instance, which I think illustrates my point, occurred lately in conversation. How is it possible to treat such a subject as forthing artistically? – There is only one way – by finding out what relations it bears to reality. When you have done this you can treat it artistically, but only then. For me at least that mysterious and intimate operation has always exercised an extraordinary charm. I seem to see in it one of the few last relics of our animalic ancestry – a strange reminiscence of the earth from which we have sprung. The thought of every member of the human race – the human race which has produced Shakespeare, and weighed the stars – retiring every day to give silent and incontestible proof of his matinal mould is to me fraught with an unutterable significance. There, in truth, is the one touch of Nature which makes the whole world kin! There is enough to give the Idealist perpetual pause! There – in that mystic unburdening of our bodies – that unanswerable reminder of mortality!

And the Father? . . . .

Michelet has a wonderful passage in his introduction to the history of the Renaissance on the position of God the Father in the Middle Ages. He was deserted, he says, worshipped, forgotten. No altar was raised to Him, no shrine; the vows and the prayers of men were turned towards the Son, and the Saints, and the Virgin Mary. What is more the Father had no beard. Unlike the Ormuz of the Persians, the Jehovah of the Jews, the Zeus of the Greeks, the soft and melancholy God of the Middle Ages was 'imberbe', was hardly a man, was unendowed with the generative force. With the Renaissance, indeed – for so we may continue the allegory – the beard of God sprouted for a moment into a magnificent growth; and so we see it in the Sistine Chapel depicted by the hand of Michael Angelo. But today? What can we say today of the Father's beard, the generative force of the World? It is gone, it is vanished, it is shaved! And that rounded chin, that soft repletion of flesh and fat, is it not more hateful than ever was the bristling and curling hair? More base, more vile, more loathsome, more incomparably lewd?

1892

# Monday June 26th 1916[1]

❦

To come close to life! To look at it, not through the eyes of Poets and Novelists, with their beautifying arrangements or their selected realisms, but simply as one actually *does* look at it, when it happens, with its minuteness and its multiplicity and its intensity, vivid and complete! To do that! To do that even with a bit of it – with no more than a single day – to realize absolutely the events of a single and not extraordinary day – surely that might be no less marvellous than a novel or even a poem, and still more illuminating, perhaps! If one *could* do it! But one can't, of course. One has neither the power nor the mere physical possibility for enchaining that almost infinite succession; one's memory is baffled; and then – the things one remembers most one cannot, one dares not – no! one can only come close to *them* in a very peculiar secrecy; and yet . . . there remains a good deal that one can and may even perhaps positively *ought* to give a fixity to, after all!

I had already had some vague, half-dreaming thoughts about the Piero della Francesca portrait downstairs, and whether what Duncan had said about the goodness of the composition was really true,

---

[1] Rejected as a conscientious objector, Strachey was also rejected as unfit for any kind of military service. On 26 June 1916 he was staying at Wissett Lodge, a remote Suffolk farmhouse where Duncan Grant and David Garnett had set themselves up as official fruit farmers under the National Service Act. His description of this Bloomsbury colony gives an authentic picture of a matriarchy presided over by Vanessa Bell. To read this essay in its true context, one should also have read a letter Strachey wrote the previous month to Maynard Keynes: 'It is horrid to sit helpless while those poor creatures [those fighting in the trenches] are going through such things. But really one would have to be God Almighty to be of any effective use.'

and whether Norton's[2] exclamation about both his and Nessa's[3] self-delusion ... when I was woken up properly by Blanche putting my breakfast-tray down on the table beside me, and pulling the curtains. It was eight o'clock. I was happy – as usual – to find food before me, all ready to be eaten; I certainly wanted nothing else in the world just then; but, having put on my eye-glasses, I saw two letters crouching under a plate, and realized that I was very glad to have letters too. One was some damned bill, and the other was a huge affair from Ottoline; I opened it, and saw that it covered sheets and that it had enclosures, so I thought that before reading it I'll have my breakfast. And then, as I ate my boiled egg and drank my rather thick tea – but the toast was on its accustomed royal scale – I suddenly remembered the dubiousness of my position, and all that I had decided the night before. Nessa's – yes, one could only call it sulkiness – that oppressed silence all the evening after our late return – how could I doubt its meaning? – 'For heaven's sake – *can't* you leave me with Duncan for a moment? Is it *never* to be?' How her dumb animality – like some creature aux abois, as I've often thought – came out more unmistakably than I'd ever known! And yet, perhaps it *was* a mistake! How can one tell, I reflected, what that woman's thinking, with her extraordinary simplicities? But I was as certain as ever that I must do something to settle it one way or the other, that I should have to suggest my going, which meant of course Norton's too, I'd no doubt, and then – I could judge from how she took it what I was to do next. I did not like the thought of going away, though why I didn't I could not be sure. Certainly it might have been a much happier visit; somehow, I had been lonely – and why? There was Norton to talk to about the war and mathematics – wasn't that enough to satisfy me? – And they were all very kind; but had they been kind enough? Was it their married state that oppressed me? But then – were *they* married? – Perhaps it was their *un*married state. Perhaps if I could have lain with Bunny[4] – and then I smiled to think of my romantic visions before coming – of a recrudescence of that affair, under Duncan's nose – and of his dimness on my arrival, and of how very very little I wanted to lie

---

[2] H. T. J. Norton was the dedicatee of *Eminent Victorians*.
[3] Vanessa Bell.
[4] David Garnett.

with him now! – Only, all the same, the thought of going away depressed me. Perhaps it was simply because of the easy-goingness of the place and the quantities of food, or was it because . . . and then the vision of that young postman with the fair hair and lovely country complexion who had smiled at me and said 'Good evening, sir', as he passed on his bicycle, flashed upon me, and that other unexpected meeting – but I felt that *that* train of thought was too exciting to be hurried over, and decided, as I'd finished my breakfast, to get through Ott's letter before anything else.

I enjoyed reading it; for it was one of her tremendously expansive and affectionate letters, which invariably carry me off my feet. And it showed me *(apparently)* that she was not annoyed with me (though why one should care whether she was annoyed or not ...) and that she was ready to have me back again at Garsington, which was a relief, because, if I *had* to go away, it was as well to have somewhere to go to. As for the enclosure, it was an appalling coloured photograph of a young man by Titian, all vague and turd-tinted, and incredibly sentimental, which I was to give to Duncan with her love.

It took a long time getting all the writing clear, but I did it at last; and then, feeling considerably more cheerful, I fished my manuscripts out of the big envelope which I'd put the night before on the lower shelf of the table and began brooding over my poem on Kisses, but I added nothing, and my digestion beginning to work, I fell back drowsily on the pillow, and for a moment there was L. before my eyes. But only for a moment; it was the post-youth who fascinated me now. My scheme of meeting him in the long lane past the village recurred to me, and then I began embroidering romantic and only *just* possible adventures which might follow – the bedroom in the inn at Norwich, and all the rest; but there was the necessity of talking to him first; and I went once more through the calculations of time and place, and saw that my plan really might, if I had the nerve, come off. The down on his cheek, the delicious down on his cheek! It was true that his nose had looked stupid, but perhaps not *too* stupid. Oh! there was no doubt that he was nice. Why, why, had Norton been with me at that second meeting? And he had not even looked in his direction! He had not even been aware that a bicycle had passed!

It was about eleven by the time I was dressed, and when I came down I found Norton and Duncan in the drawing-room. I had hardly finished reading them Ott's letter when Vanessa came in. I gave it to her to read to herself, and of course she could hardly spell out a word of it, and thought a good deal of it dull. I was slightly annoyed, and went off to the dreadful E.C.,[5] where I could only just scrape together enough earth out of the tin coal-scuttle to cover my addition to the mountain, which, even before my addition, had been far too high.

The sun was shining, and there was my chair in the little arbour at the corner of the lawn. And Blanche came with my midday cocoa, and after that I studied the Bishop of Oxford's book on the Sermon on the Mount. It was a foolish book, but I found in it a charming little poem by an old lady in Torquay to Florrie Ewbank about the coal-strike and the neighbours and 'Sweep' who turned out to be a new dog – 'such a companion'. It was as good as anything in Samuel Butler. Then I saw that the time had come to face Vanessa. I went upstairs, and knocked at the door of her studio-room, which I'd never been in before, and went in, and there she was in front of me in the white room, on a dilapidated basket chair, and in one of her most collapsed and dreamy attitudes.

Was she plain or beautiful? I could not decide. I talked vaguely – about the room, about Ottoline – and she was very nice. I suddenly wondered why I had knocked at the door; was it idiotic? How well I know her! – And how little – how very little! Even her face, which seemed now almost chocolate-coloured, was strangely unfamiliar. If I could only have flung myself into her arms! – But I knew so well what would happen – her smile – her half-bewilderment, half infinitely sensible acceptance – and her odd relapse. As it was, I walked about uncomfortably, looking at moments vaguely out of the window; and I was decidedly uneasy when I said at last 'I think I shall have to drift off'. Of course she simply answered 'Shall you really?' I said, 'Yes – I think so – I think tomorrow.' She said 'Will you go to Garsington?' And I saw then, in the same moment, both that I couldn't bear the thought of going, and that I should have to go. I thought that perhaps she would have liked me to stay if that hadn't involved Norton's also staying; but I felt unable to disentangle that – and I got no atom of encouragement. When I had

[5] Earth Closet.

got out of the room, I entirely failed to shut the door, after repeated efforts; there was something wrong with the lock. She called out, still in her chair, that she would shut it. Before going, I had wildly glanced at a picture half-painted on an easel, representing a group of people, with what was apparently a saint in a halo in mid-air. It looked very niggly, and the colours were extremely garish – altogether it alarmed me. In the drawing-room I found the Daily News and the Daily Mirror, and went out with them into the garden again.

Norton had vanished; his chair in the sun was empty. There were only the children playing by the pond. I was terrified of their coming and pulling me to pieces, but for some reason or other they didn't, and I could read my newspapers in peace. I read the Daily News, but there was nothing to interest me. As for the Daily Mirror, what *could* there be to interest me in that? A face perhaps… but for weeks past I had never found a single one that wasn't disgusting; and I thought of that time at the Lacket, when every day I had found some living creature in it – usually killed. And then I *did* come on a face – a charming one – of a young boxer – 'Jimmy Wilde, the famous flyweight', whom I'd never heard of before. I longed to go and see him boxing: I have never seen a boxing-match. What would happen? I wondered. Would the blood pour down over his eyes? But the match he was to box was to be that very night, so that was impossible – though for a second I actually envisaged going up to London on some excuse that afternoon. But then – the post-boy? No! It was all ridiculous: the boxing-match would come and go without me; and after that what chance would I have of ever seeing Jimmy Wilde again? At that moment I looked up, and saw, slowly pounding along the farm-road on the other side of the house, a waggon and horses, driven by a youth. It was too far off to be sure, but he seemed handsome, I was feeling désœuvré and distracted, and so I thought I'll go and see what he was like. But then I thought after all I wouldn't, and remained sitting there – undecided, vague and miserable. I was in my slippers, I reflected: and how could I go through the dirt? The cart and horses and young man had vanished; but they might still be in the farm-yard: should I go after all? I still waited. I began to think that I should have to tell Norton that I was going next day, and that he would certainly then say that he was going too, so that we should have to travel together to London; oh! was there no way out of that? Or should I rather like it, really? He was so amusing, and so agreeable, and I liked talking to him; but how could one have adventures when he was there? Suddenly, for no apparent reason, I got up, went in, went up to my room, put on my boots, and came down again, and walked by the back way into the farm-yard.

There was no sign of a waggon; but I noticed, what I'd never noticed before, that the farm-road did not end in the farm-yard, but continued past some indefinite pig-styes, through a field, and then turned round a corner out of sight. So after all the waggon – and the waggonner – might be further on – not very far away – engaged in some promiscuous occupation. I began to walk through the farmyard, when Bunny appeared, at the door of a barn.

He was in his shirt, with the sleeves rolled up, engaged also, apparently, in some extremely promiscuous occupation. What *was* he always doing in those odd purlieus? Something with the rabbits I suppose.

I talked with him – vaguely; and felt once more the pleasure of being able to do that. And the happier I felt, the more my heart sank at the thought of going away. It sank down and down, and I kept chattering with him about the hens, and wanted to take hold of his large brown bare arm. *That* I knew was beautiful; and then my heart sank so very low that I conceived the possibility of *his* asking me to stay on, if I could suggest adroitly enough that I should like to. But who can be adroit with his heart in his boots? My attempt was really feeble; and when I blurted out, apropos of nothing, that I was going tomorrow, he said, in his charming way 'Oh, I *am* sorry', and I saw that I was dished again.

Then, after a little more talking – about the new Dostoievsky – I went on along the path, and he disappeared into the recesses of the barn. I passed the indeterminate pig-styes, went through a gate, turned the corner, and found myself in a field. No waggon was anywhere in view, but, as I crossed the field, I forgot all about it – I could think of nothing but the mere pleasure and beauty of the summer day. I came into a second field, and then, to one side of me, the country dipped down at a little distance, rising again in a lovely little landscape – lovely and yet perfectly ordinary – of fields and trees and hedges and blue sky. And the field I was in was full of splendid grasses, and there were wild flowers scattered all about, and wild roses in the hedge at my left hand. I walked entranced; that feeling of a sudden explanation came upon me – a sudden easy mysterious explanation of all the long difficult mysterious embroilments of the world. 'Est-ce que j'ai trouvé le grand Peut-être?' I thought. 'Am I luckier even than Rabelais? – How miraculously lucky I am!' And I sat down, absolutely comfortable, with a little bank of earth under the hedge for my back to lean against, and the charming English prospect before my eyes. I thought of my friends, and my extraordinary happiness. I thought of Death, of Keats and the Ode to the Nightingale, of 'easeful Death' – 'half in love with easeful Death' – and I was convinced, as I'd been convinced in the train coming down from London that if Death would only come to one in a mood of serene happiness, he would be very welcome. I thought of suddenly dying, painlessly, where I lay. I wondered whether that was morbid; and then I imagined them finding my dead body – so singularly thin – and what their thoughts would be. All the time the sun warmed me deliciously, and the landscape beamed in front of me, and visions of Jimmy Wilde, half naked, with bruised ears, floated in my imagination – or dressed, in a fascinating tweed suit, rather too big for him, staying with me for a week-end at my cottage at Garsington, coming out through the door onto the lawn ... And L? ... The dazzling happiness, coming, in flood after flood, over my soul, was so intense that it was like a religious conversion. And through it all there was an odd waft of melancholy – a kind of vibration of regret. A strange importance seemed to invest and involve into a unity the scene, the moment, and my state of feeling. But at last I knew it was time to go back to the house. As I walked back, I felt as if I had made an advance – as if I had got somewhere new. But it seemed far shorter going back than going, and very soon I was through the back premises, and, coming onto the lawn through the gap in the bushes, found them all quite close to me sitting in the verandah, having lunch. I was late – they had almost finished their meat – and it occurred to me that all the time I had been there I had never been late for lunch before. Nessa seemed slightly surprised, and asked me whether I'd been for a long walk. My plate was filled with food, and as I ate I began to ask Duncan about the National Sporting Club – whether he had ever been there, and what boxing was like. The wretch saw at once what I was up to and said 'You've been looking at the Daily Mirror'; I didn't attempt to deny it, and went on with my questions; but his answers were unsatisfactory. He said that I would certainly enjoy the National Sporting Club very much, because one had to go there in evening dress, and that I might get Lord Henry Bentinck to take me; but he admitted that he'd never been there himself; and Nessa said that he didn't understand me at all. Bunny advised me to go to some boxing haunt in the East End that he knew of, where he said the blood flowed by the bucket-full. Norton pursed himself up, and said that all this was very disgusting, and said that I was like Nero at a gladiatorial show. I rather testily replied that he was an 'anachoret', and Nessa again took my side. Then the conversation somehow got on to George, and my relations with him, and Duncan's relations with him; and Duncan was very amusing, confessing that he still sometimes thought of him sentimentally, and that at one time he would have been willing to give him a hundred a year, to have him as his mistress. We asked him where he would have got a hundred a year from, to give to George. He said he would have borrowed it. We asked 'Who from?' And Norton and I at once saw that of course it would have been from Maynard, and everybody laughed. After that Ottoline loomed up in her accustomed style, and there was a long and rather fierce argument as to whether she had any artistic capacity, and whether she was 'creative'; I said that she was, and that Garsington proved it; but all the others were against me. Norton declared that Garsington was the work of a bower-bird, and that to talk of its showing 'creativeness' was absurd. I answered in a voice more contemptuous than my feeling but gradually I felt my feeling growing as contemptuous as my voice. Then Nessa began on the 'artistic' tack, and for a moment I almost became better; all that violent discussion of my second evening shimmered in the background, and I got as far as saying that I didn't think I agreed with her notion of art. But it passed off, and the children appeared, and we all got up from the table. I found myself standing next to Duncan on the lawn, and he was holding the Daily Mirror open at the picture of Jimmy Wilde. I said 'Don't you think he's beautiful?' And he said 'Yes'; but added almost immediately, 'I expect it's only because he hasn't got a collar on. If his neck was covered he'd probably look like anyone else.' I didn't believe it, and I was slightly annoyed.

Then I went upstairs, heavy with all that eating, and lay down on my bed, where I began again thinking out my plan of campaign with the postboy, until I fell asleep; and I slept solidly for over an hour. I was woken up by the piercing screams of the children, as they played on the little piece of grass outside my window. The noise gradually penetrated my sleep, and reached a climax with Quentin bursting into sobs. I heard Julian's[6] cockney voice, full of guilt and self-justification, calling out to Flossie ('Flossay') that Quentin was very naughty and would *not* play with him. After a confused interval, Nessa's voice emerged – low and plaintive – 'I've *told* you, Julian, that you must *not* ... You're much stronger than Quentin, and he can't defend himself... I've *told* you ...' And then utter silence on the part of Julian. Irritation came upon me at the woman's weakness. – Or *was* it weakness? Wasn't it perhaps simply common sense? Did she see that no amount of punishment would ever prevent Julian from being cruel? That it would only make him dislike her to no purpose? Perhaps; but still I was angry with her for her lack of indignation; and my hatred of Julian was intense.

However, silence was re-established, and I picked up the copy of Temple Bar on the bed-table, to see if there was anything in it that I hadn't already read. I struck at once upon an article by some woman or other on political parties in Bohemia. It was all entirely new to me, and most interesting; I had never before seen the names of Rieger or Gregr; I knew nothing whatever of the history of those movements. The article was not very profound, but it was not badly done either. I was amazed and appalled by my ignorance – that at the age of 36 it should only be by a chance article in a back number of a second-rate magazine, written by an unknown woman, that I should have become acquainted with facts of that magnitude, with names as important in Austrian history as those of O'Connell and Parnell in ours. And I, and my likes, are supposed to be well educated persons! I then skimmed an article on Thurlow, which was slightly interesting too; by that time it was four o'clock, and I got up and went downstairs for my afternoon stroll.

On the lawn I saw Norton reading mathematics so I took the opportunity of telling him that I had decided to go away next day;

[6] Julian Bell, the elder son of Clive and Vanessa Bell, was then eight years old, Quentin, their younger, was six.

and he immediately announced that he would go with me. I assented, and drifted off, leaving him with his mathematics.

I drifted down the dreary road that goes in the opposite direction to the village. My mind, which (with exception of the interval of sleep) had been in a state of constant activity since 8 o'clock in the morning, now relapsed into dreaminess. The expectation of tea was one of the few things definitely present to it, as I walked along between the hedges on the empty road. – That, and the feeling that it was only *after* tea that anything exciting could happen – that *then* something exciting would happen – that *then* there would be the crisis of the meeting with the bicycle, and the conversation, and all the possibilities involved – so that *until* then I had nothing to do but to meander about and fill up the interval as best I could. I fancy I thought a little about Sarah Bernhardt, and, after I'd turned back, the puzzle of my relations with women flickered before me. Carrington[7] occurred to me, and then, for some odd reason, Maria.[8] Why on earth had I been so chaste during those Latin lessons? I saw how easily I could have been otherwise – how I might have put my hand on her bare neck, and even up her legs, with considerable enjoyment; and probably she would have been on the whole rather pleased. I became certain that the solution was that I was restrained by my knowledge that she would certainly inform 'Auntie'[9] of every detail of what had happened, at the earliest possible opportunity. It would be practically copulating with Ott looking through the keyhole – which I was by no means prepared to do. There are limits in these matters, I reflected; strange that it should be so, but there are. I turned in at the gate, passed the angle of the house, and saw to my delight that tea was ready and Vanessa actually pouring it out.

Norton appeared immediately, and Duncan and Bunny a little later. There was not very much conversation; what there was chiefly circled round the question of the train that Norton and I should go by. He wanted to go after lunch, and I wanted to go after tea. As he had no motive to produce and I had – viz. that dinner in a

[7] Strachey had met the painter Dora Carrington the previous autumn, and she had fallen in love with him.
[8] Maria Nys, who later became the first wife of Aldous Huxley.
[9] Lady Ottoline Morrell.

train was so amusing – it was eventually settled that I should have my way. I ate my frugal spongefingers contentedly, listening to their gibes. Duncan at last got up and went into the drawing-room, where he began to play his Bach composition. I followed him, with what I hoped was an air of detachment, pretended to look for a book, went out through the drawing-room door into the passage, and so through the front door out of the house.

My fear had been that Norton would want to walk out with me, but I seemed to have escaped him successfully. He would hardly follow me now. The time, too, was exactly right, so far as I could judge. I had nothing to do now but to walk forward, and I was bound to meet . . . the bicycle, either before I got to the pillar-box at the crossroads, or, if necessary, *at* it. I walked down the road towards the village, wondering how it would turn out. I felt to see that I had my letter to Ottoline in my pocket, and rehearsed the meeting – my stopping him, my asking him if he would mind taking the letter, and then, somehow, my offering him a cigarette. It was fairly clear, although I foresaw that the actual stopping of the bicycle might be difficult – especially if he was coming down hill – so far it was fairly clear; but after the opening – *after* the preliminary conversation and the cigarette – then everything was a blank, to be filled in at the moment according to his amiability, and as my presence of mind would suggest. But both his amiability and my presence of mind were highly dubious entities. I had the wildest, and bleakest, visions – of amusement and charm and successes culminating in Norwich, and of crushing failure – sheer stupidity, or undisguised annoyance – or perhaps of missing him altogether by some unforeseen mischance. It was a preposterous errand! I laughed, and imagined myself reading about myself in a novel by Tolstoy – reading quickly, and turning over the pages as fast as I could, in my excitement to know what would happen in the end. What *would* happen? I took the short-cut by the field with the poppies, emerged onto the high road, turned to the left, away from the village, and then off to the right, up the long narrow lane, at the end of which was the pillar-box. It was half-past five; the collection at the pillar-box was due at five minutes to six; the lane was probably about two miles long; therefore, if he was punctual, it seemed certain that I should meet him in it, as there was no other way from the pillar-box to the village, and he had to be in the village at half-past six. I had remembered the lane as being fairly level, but now it seemed to go up and down in the most alarming manner. If I were to come upon him as he was on a downward dip – should I have the nerve – or even the strength of voice – to stop him? And wouldn't he be furious if I did? Perhaps he would be mollified if he saw that my letter was to a Ladyship. Or perhaps . . . my mind lost itself in speculations. I imagined his nose, his cheek, and his complexion with a tantalizing mixture of indistinctness and intensity. His cap, too, and his yellow hair, lighter than his skin – and that odd armlet . . . and why, to be sure, *wasn't* he in the army? Surely he wasn't under age? . . . A woman in a drab mackintosh appeared on the road in front of me, going in the same direction. I passed her easily, and sped on. It seemed almost probable that I should reach the pillar-box before he did, in which case I should have to linger about; and then – if there were other people there? – old gaffers posting letters to their sons at the front? I might be done for in that case. I had passed the turning down which Norton and I had gone after meeting him the time before, so that, supposing the time to have been the same on that occasion, he might appear at any moment now. But he didn't appear: the lane went on and on indefinitely, its only merit being that it kept more or less straight, so that one could see people approaching from a good distance, and prepare accordingly. But no one did approach. Meanwhile the sky had been growing darker and darker, and I expected it to rain at any moment; that would be an additional complication. Then I saw that the pillar-box could not be far off; it was almost in sight, in a group of trees in front of me, I had no doubt; I recognized the place from some cottages on the right hand, so I *should* have to wait there, after all. Suddenly I heard a whistle – and an immediate reminiscence flashed upon me: it was of 'Signor Grasso', the postman on the Loch-an-Eilan road, when he came on his bicycle with the letters in the morning. My mind shot back for an instant to Milton Cottage – how many years ago? – with Pippa and Pernel in the garden, and Sharp Cottage, too, and its dreariness, and James of course – it all came and went in a moment; was it possible that *he* too – ? That he was whistling to warn those cottages that he was coming? Oh no! Such things weren't done out of the Highlands . . . and then his bicycle appeared, slowly advancing: it *was* he, there could be no doubt. But he did not stop at the cottage, he came on, and we should meet almost at once. He looked rather bigger than I had remembered him, and he had something in his mouth − a cigarette? Then *that* plan was shattered. But I saw at once that it was the whistle, and as I took the letter out of my pocket he actually began slowing down, almost as if he was expecting me to give it him. 'This is a very favourable beginning', I thought. And on the very heels of that, came the perception that something was all wrong, hopelessly wrong, that he wasn't − that he couldn't be − that it was somebody else. Yes, it was another postman, with black hair, and a red Presbyterian face, and a most unattractive briskness about him altogether, stopping with an écœurant politeness to take my letter, as I handed it to him, saying 'Would you mind taking this?' with the most natural air in the world. 'So *that's* all over,' I said to myself, as he vanished, and I turned automatically on my tracks, for obviously there was now nothing to be done but to trudge back home. I nearly burst out laughing aloud at the farcicality of my proceedings, but was restrained by the re-appearance of the woman in the mackintosh, whom I now saw, as I passed her, looked like a lower-class Vernon Lee. I began to wonder what had happened − why he had failed me − whether it was only a temporary change, or whether . . . Perhaps he'd joined the army, perhaps that armlet meant that he was going to be called up, and very likely, as today was Monday . . . anyhow it was just like my luck. There was a servant-maid waiting at the corner of the branch road − waiting rather mysteriously; she was pretty, and sad. Could she have been waiting for . . . ? I passed on, and by this time the clouds had disappeared from the sky and the sun was out again. I thought of the youth at Lockeridge who had been obliterated in the same silent way: but, after all, I considered, some remain. There are so many possibilities in this world, and I shouldn't have been much surprised if something extraordinary had happened almost at once. But nothing happened, except that, quite suddenly and apparently irrelevantly, a phrase from Handel sounded in my mind − a phrase that I don't believe I'd thought of for years. − 'Rejoice! Rejoice! Rejoi-oi-oi-oi-oice greatly!' And then the thought occurred to me of writing this microscopic description of a day. I was delighted with the idea, and went on elaborating it for a long time, until at last I drifted into the plan of a satirical poem on Winston in the style of the chorusses in Samson Agonistes, which should begin

'Strange are the ways of men;
And the ways of God are still more curious;

and I was still murmuring these lines when I reached the house; and
as I went upstairs to my room I saw that they would have to end the
poem too.

In my room, I fell with extraordinary energy on my Arabian
story, which I had a wild notion that I might finish before dinner. It
was obvious, really, that I couldn't, yet I wrote on at top speed for
more than an hour, covering the pages in a most unusual manner. I
heard them calling to me to come to dinner, but still wrote. They
called again, and then I realized that it was useless going on – the
wretched thing wasn't nearly finished; so I went down into the
kitchen and had dinner with them – rather silent, while they
discussed the superfetation of rabbits, and whether wildflowers
might be legitimately classified as yellow, blue and red.

I went out of the room before anyone else, and walked through
the drawing-room out onto the lawn. It was still quite light,
though it must have been past nine o'clock. I paced once or twice
up and down the lawn, when Bunny appeared and immediately
joined me. I had a sharp and most queer feeling that it was
somehow done by arrangement – though of course we had
arranged nothing of the sort. We went at once through the pergola
into the strip of kitchen garden, and began walking up and down
the path. I felt nervous, almost neurasthenic – what used to be called
'unstrung'. He was so calm and gentle, and his body was so large,
with his shirt (with nothing under it) open all the way down – that I
longed to throw myself onto him as if he were a feather-bed, to tell
him everything – everything, and to sob myself asleep. And yet, at
the same time, the more I longed to expand, the more I hated the
thought of it. It would be disgusting and ridiculous – it was out of
the question. And I became astringent, and would talk of nothing
but the vegetables as we walked up and down. The vegetables, and
still the vegetables – it almost seemed at last that there was nothing
else that one could possibly talk about; and, as the subject was not
very interesting, why not give it up and go in? I was in terror that
this would happen, and yet my congealment was such that when, at
the end of one of our turns, we got to the pergola, I made as if to go
through it, back on to the lawn. At that, he came out in that lovely

firm way that he sometimes so unexpectedly has, and turned right off through an asparagus bed into that other more remote part of the garden, where the grass is so thick and lush, and everything is tangled and overgrown with weeds and roses – a place that trembles on the edge of sentimentality, but is saved by being so small and unkempt and tumbledown. We went and sat on a dirty wooden seat at the farthest end of it, and I thought that if it had been a clean stone seat, and if he had been dressed in white knee-breeches and a blue coat with brass buttons, and if I had been a young lady in a high waist – or should it have been the other way round? – the scene would have done very well for an Academy picture by Marcus Stone.

And so we did talk at last – about other things than vegetables – about Barbara,[10] and that fandango of the letter; and he made me realize what a charming creature she was. And he chaffed me about my 'affair with Carrington',[11] and I explained in great detail that it couldn't be called that; and as we talked I grew comfortable, and in fact happy; and then, when the conversation touched upon the changeability of moods, I said that I had been in a wretched mood all day, that I had felt everything with an unnatural acuteness, as if I had had no skin. It wasn't at all an accurate statement, and his sympathy – 'Oh Lytton, how dreadful!' – made me feel myself a silly beast, and I quickly covered my tracks by bringing up the subject of his life at Wissett, and his prospects, and his general state. He talked for a long time about these things – about his settled happiness and the problems of his future – and I felt very sympathetic, and wished I had several thousand a year. He was

[10] Barbara Hiles, an ex-Slade student and friend of Carrington's, who married Nicholas Bagenal.

[11] 'What I remember must have been the next day – the day he apparently left', David Garnett told Michael Holroyd. 'We went for a walk along the edge of a cornfield and he told me that he was in love, or more than a little in love with Carrington and made me promise not to tell Vanessa or Duncan or anyone. He was afraid of Ottoline finding out – and I think of Virginia also. I kept my promise . . . I suppose it was the reassurance I had given him which led him to confide in me and he was also perhaps more ready to confide a heterosexual attachment to me than a daydream about the postman which would have strained my powers of sympathy!' See 'Lytton Strachey and Carrington' in *Great Friends* by David Garnett.

amusing, too, very amusing, and I saw how shy and distrustful of himself he was in company. It grew darker and colder, but we stayed on. At last it seemed quite natural to ask him whether he thought they really liked me. 'Who, Lytton?' – 'Duncan and Vanessa – no, not really; but sometimes they seem very severe. Perhaps I'm too uppish.' 'Oh Lytton, how absurd you are. They call you "the old gentleman". I heard them saying that they hoped the old gentleman was happy.' – The darling! How beautifully he had smoothed me down! So that everything was now calm and good – so that that was the ordinary state of the world – and all those doubts and itches – how futile and preposterous! I laughed, and said 'Do *you* call me "the old gentleman?"' He answered, flirting, 'The Prince of Darkness is a gentleman'. Without any difficulty I stretched out my hand and put it into his breast, which was glowing a warm pink in the twilight. I said 'An *old* gentleman?' and he answered 'No; that's just the difference'. 'Have I more experience than the Devil?' I murmured as we laughed. We came nearer to one another, and, with a divine vigour, embraced. I was amused to notice, just before it happened, that he looked very nervously in the direction of the house. We kissed a great deal, and I was happy. Physically, as well as mentally, he had assuaged me. That was what was so wonderful about him – he gave neither too little nor too much. I felt neither the disillusionment of having gone too far, nor any of the impatience of desire. I knew that we loved each other, and I was unaware that my cock had moved.

It was too cold to stay out any longer, and we came in to find the room in almost pitch darkness, with three figures over the fire. He went out with Duncan; left alone with Norton and Nessa, I instantly realized that we must have been out rather a long time. Norton said something which I took for an indecent joke, and I answered with unnecessary self-consciousness; then, of course, he said that he had meant nothing at all. There was a long pause, during which I imagined Duncan furious in the kitchen, and Bunny pacifying him. But when they appeared at last with the lamp, Duncan seemed perfectly cheerful, and the evening at once became very gay. We ranged over Ka[12] and her complicated

---

[12] Katherine Cox, the robust Fabian with whom Rupert Brooke had been in love, and who afterwards married Will Arnold-Forster.

history, we discussed our private weaknesses, and ended in a fantastic [blank in MS] of idiotic rhymes.

> Ka is my Ma,
> But who is my Pa?

was Norton's first inspiration, which set us all off in a string. How adorable was Nessa, as she sat, rocking with laughter at the bawdiness of the jokes! We got up from our chairs somehow, at about one o'clock. Duncan and Bunny disappeared as usual, to lock up. Nessa went off, and Norton briskly mounted his attic-ladder. I tore off my clothes in my bedroom, with only one desire – to sleep. In bed, I thought of Bunny, and then, as I was dozing off, something strange happened. I suddenly found myself with Duncan under the bushes in the drizzle on that first afternoon on Hampstead Heath. The vividness of it was so great that I woke up with a start. Then that too melted in oblivion; and it was L. who was with me when I finally fell asleep.

# Asquith

❧❦❧

A few remarks on Mr Asquith, whom I happen to have met, and who is bound to become 'historical'. (Clio nowadays, poor dear lady, finds she can no longer be as exclusive as she used to be.)

My first private vision of him was when Ottoline one evening produced, for Henry [Lamb's] and my benefit, his letters to her, preserved in a box. They were written during her pre-marriage Grosvenor Place period, when there had been some sort of flirtation. 'He used to come and see me in the evening—right up at the very top of the house.' The letters were written in very capable flowing handwriting, and were remarkably dull. They were mostly short, their incidental observations being of the most commonplace kind, with occasional mild (very mild) sentimentalities, and once at least some religious reflections indicating a belief in God, and even in Christianity. One letter, which promised to be more interesting, was at the last moment (owing to Philip [Morrell]) withheld. I gathered that he had made love to her – perhaps kissed, or tried to kiss her – that she had objected, and he had written to apologize. (Since then, we have grown less squeamish.)

The 'intimacy', such as it was, came to an end with her marriage, which had annoyed him. Typically, she had never mentioned Philip to him, and he had gone on, no doubt, with his mild sentimentalities until she had suddenly told him she was engaged. He drew off; but in the year or so before the war there was a decided recrudescence. Violet [Asquith] used to come to tea, and then it was rumoured that the old man himself was to be asked to one of the Thursday parties. In the summer of 1914 – it was at the height of the Ulster crisis, when he had just melodramatically taken over the War Office – I went there one Thursday, rather late, and found the room crowded. Ottoline immediately seized me, and hurried me into the inner room where Asquith was standing, talking to Gilbert Cannan. She brushed Cannan on one side with extraordinary vigour, and introduced me, then, on our both slightly hesitating, planted us down side by side on the sofa, and left us. (The sofa! How clearly I see it, almost feel it, at this moment – cushion by cushion! *Mais où sont les neiges d'antan?*) He was extremely gracious, partly with the professional graciousness of a man whose business in life it was to create a good impression, but partly also, I thought, with a genuine good-humour. He asked me what I was writing, and when I told him of my biographies talked a little about various public persons – Lord Randolph Churchill among others – and at last settled on Parnell, who, he said, was in his opinion the most remarkable man he'd known. Unfortunately it did not occur to me to suggest that Gladstone was surely more so, and after his telling how he'd met Parnell in the Temple one morning when the divorce proceedings had just become public, and how Parnell had shown that he had no notion of the hubbub that would be created, the conversation pausing for a moment, with a slight embarrassment, he got up, and with cordiality shook hands with me, and walked off into the other room.

The whole thing had lasted about ten minutes, and the impression left on me was just what the letters to Ottoline had led me to expect. He was singularly uninspired. If I hadn't known who he was, I should have guessed him to be one of those Oxford dons who have a smattering of the world – one of those clever, cautious, mediocre intelligences who make one thank Heaven one was at Cambridge. Two particulars only suggested a difference. His manner was a little nervous – it was really almost as if he was the whole time conscious, with a slight uneasiness, that he was the Prime Minister. And then, though his appearance on the whole was decidedly donnish – small and sleek and not too well-made in the details – his hands were different. Small and plump they were too; but there was a masterfulness in them and a mobility which made them remarkable. Later on, I saw him taking leave of Ottoline, with an extraordinary effusiveness. It occurred to me for a moment that he was a snob – that he was positively overcome by her being a Duke's sister. But surely that was impossible.

Two years later I had another view of him. One hot Sunday afternoon at Garsington – it was a week or two after the Irish rebellion – he motored over from the Wharf with Nathan, Lady Robert Cecil, and some deplorable Lady Meux. I thought him changed – at any rate he struck me very differently. He seemed much larger – and redder – a big sanguine, jovial man. Clearly he had had a good lunch, with several glasses of wine; and it would be impossible to imagine anyone who was more obviously enjoying life. There was a look of a Roman Emperor about him (one could imagine a wreath on his head), or a Renaissance Pope ('Well, let me enjoy the world, now that I am Vicar of Christ!'). One curiosity attracted my attention. His tongue – a little, pointed, cunning tongue – was perpetually darting out and licking his lips. Standing beside him on the lawn, in the brilliant sunshine, with the house behind us and the landscape below us, I reflected that since I had last seen him a change had come over the world, as well. It was disgusting; and yet, such was the extraordinary satisfaction of the man that, in spite of everything, one could not help feeling a kind of sympathetic geniality of one's own.

After he had gone, Ottoline hurried me away into the kitchen garden to describe the extreme vivacity of his attack upon her, during their tête-à-tête in her little room. 'Describe' is hardly the word, for all the details were left to be inferred; and I couldn't be at all certain to what point matters had proceeded; though there could be no doubt that, whatever he may or may not have permitted himself, her attitude was no longer the attitude of Grosvenor Place. She was just saying something to the effect of 'What a ninny I was in those days', when Philip inevitably appeared.

Later on that same summer, I happened to have another glimpse of him. I was in the Haymarket, latish one Friday or Saturday afternoon. The streets were very empty (I think it must have been August), and I was vaguely strolling when (without exaggeration) I became aware of a curious sensation of *bien-aise* in the air. Looking round I saw a motor coming up the hill; it was open and in it was Asquith, alone, with a look of radiant happiness upon his face – happiness which was indeed literally radiant, for I had actually felt it when my back was turned. He passed on without seeing me – he really looked too happy to see anything. I think there was a portmanteau on the car, and I suppose that he was going off somewhere for the weekend. Then, a year later, I saw him again at Garsington – this time with Margot [Asquith] – and a very diminished deflated object he appeared. He had been deprived of his Premiership in the interval. I have not seen him since.

The fundamental material of Mr Asquith I take to have been a middle-class, North-Country solidity – eminently respectable, almost nonconformist, moderate, cautious, humdrum, and with a not unintelligent eye on the main chance. Then came the influence of Balliol and Jowett, which infused the timid Oxford culture and the timid Oxford worldliness into the original undistinguished mass. After that the Bar, with its training in agility of case-putting and its habit of pomposity. So far the development was ordinary enough; but the final influence brought with it some odd contradictions. The Margot set – rich, smart, showy, and self-indulgent – got hold of Mr Asquith. The middle-class legal Don became a *viveur*, who carried a lot of liquor and was lecherous with the ladies. The result was certainly curious. Who would guess from this book of his which has just come out (*Occasional Addresses*) with its high-minded rotundities and cultivated respectabilities, that the writer of it would take a lady's hand, as she sat behind him on the sofa, and make her feel his erected instrument under his trousers? (this I had very directly from [Dorothy]Brett, to whose sister it happened at Garsington, and who told me as much of it as her maiden modesty allowed (egged on by Ottoline) and all of it to Carrington). His public career suggests a parallel with Walpole. But one gathers that under all Sir Robert's low-minded opportunism there was a certain grandeur, and that his actual capacity was supreme. In Asquith's case the inveterate lack of ideals and imagination seems really unredeemed; when one has peeled off the brown paper wrapping of phrases and compromises, one finds – just nothing at all. And as for his capacity, it was perhaps not much more than the skill of a parliamentary politician. He never could deal with a serious difficulty. He mismanaged Ireland; and, though it would be hardly fair to blame too severely his incompetence in the conduct of the war, his inability to cope with the internal situation was really inexcusable. Nothing is more damning than his having told Maynard [Keynes] (who told me of it at the time) that 'the Conscriptionists were fools', and that 'he was giving them enough rope to hang themselves by', three weeks before he was himself forced by them to bring in a bill for Conscription. If it was true (as Maynard assured me it was on what I gathered was the best authority) that in December, 1916, after he had been turned out with ignominy and treachery by Lloyd George and Bonar Law, he was willing and in fact anxious to act under them as Lord Chancellor, his wits must have sunk even lower than his sense of decency. I think eventually he must have grown positively fuddled – with too much food and drink, too much power, too much rotund speechifying, and too many of those jovial adventures of the *lugubre individu*, as Henry (quoting from the French newspapers) used to say, when describing the attempts of lascivious tramps at the corners of woods, or of . . . but this is becoming too personal.

May 2-6, 1918

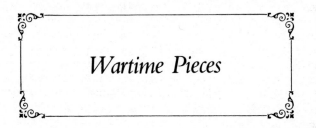

*Wartime Pieces*

# Militarism and Theology

❦

Ultimately the world is governed by moderate men. Extremists and fanatics and desperadoes may make a noise or a disturbance, they may even at times appear to control the course of events; but in reality they are always secondary figures – either symptoms or instruments; whatever happens, the great mass of ordinary, stolid, humdrum, respectable persons remains the dominating force in human affairs. For this reason, among others, the book,[1] lately written by Lieutenant-General Baron von Freytag-Loringhoven, and now translated into English, is a distressing book to read. For the Baron, besides being, as we are told, the Deputy-Chief of the General Staff in Germany, is obviously a moderate man. His book is not the work of some hectic fire-eater, but of a judicious, sensible, conservative gentleman; and that is why it strikes a damp upon the heart. Ostensibly a series of 'deductions' from the history of the war, it is, in fact, something much more portentous – an *exposé*, a cool, complacent, and eminently moderate *exposé* of the whole militarist point of view. The 'deductions' which the baron draws from the events of the last three years are concerned entirely with the machinery of armies, with the details of strategy, with the measures best calculated to bring to perfection the operations of military power. These are the lessons which the war has taught him – lessons about trench-fighting and shock tactics, and the value of barbed-wire entanglements, and the undesirability of democratic ideas. That any other kind of lesson could possibly be learnt from it has clearly never occurred to him. Militarism is an axiom taken for granted by every word in his book – and taken for granted so completely that it is hardly even discussed; it is simply

[1] *Deductions from the World War*. By Lieutenant-General Baron von Freytag-Loringhoven. Constable.

45

everywhere, and always implied. And this, surely, is a terrible phenomenon. Militarism yelled by a Reventlow, or a . . . but one need not particularize . . . is a sufficiently ghastly doctrine; but militarism blandly expounded by a Baron von Freytag-Loringhoven, with moderation, with little gentle touches of pedantry even, in a balanced unemotional style – that is a far more profoundly menacing spectacle. For it is a revelation of the state of mind of multitudes of ordinary men.

The book suggests a curious analogy. The unquestioning conviction with which its premises are held, its whole attitude of single-hearted devotion to a great underlying system of belief, reminds one of nothing so much as of a theological treatise. It has the kind of simplicity which one associates with religious faith – with the uncontroversial faith of the Middle Ages, when Catholicism was a fact as solid as the earth and as ubiquitous as the atmosphere. One can fancy the Baron as a Grand Inquisitor of those days, a pious and a moderate man, compiling his manual on the propagation of the faith, with chapters on the detection of witchcraft and the suppression of heresy. One can imagine his conscientious discussions of the most effective methods of obtaining confessions from recalcitrant persons – his nice comparisons of the rival merits of the thumbscrew and the rack. Instead of saying, for instance, as he now says, *apropos* of air raids – 'In the course of these raids some unfortified places without military significance have had to suffer. The bombardment of these places is in itself objectionable, but the limits of what is permissible are in this matter in many ways elastic' – one can picture him pointing out, with the same perfect reasonableness, the practical difficulties which sometimes stand in the way of an ideal administration of torture – how the executioner, with the best will in the world, may be compelled to break the wrists when he only means to dislocate the shoulders, that this is 'in itself objectionable', but that in such cases 'the limits of what is permissible are in many ways elastic' for the greater glory, not of Germany, but of God.

That remarkable branch of Theology, known as 'apologetic', also has its counterpart in the Baron's book. He devotes a few perfunctory pages to a militarist apologetic, in which, precisely in the manner of the theologian, he knocks over a few dummy opponents and advances triumphantly to a foregone conclusion. It is not that the validity of militarism is for a moment in doubt; it is simply that without these little dialectical flourishes something might still be wanting to the perfect realization of its beauty and its truth. There is a certain formality in such high matters, which must be gone through with a fitting solemnity. It would never do to make no mention of the well-known fact that eternal peace is a sentimentalist's dream, and of the equally familiar truths that peace is really not a desirable end, and that, at the same time, the justification of militarism is that it ensures peace (date of writing, A.D. 1917). Above all it is necessary to state that 'war has its basis in human nature, and as long as human nature remains unaltered war will', etc., etc. – it would be quite improper to leave that out. What, indeed, could be more self-evident? War has its basis in human nature: it must be so, for the Baron, looking back through history, observes that 'war has existed for thousands of years'; and besides— a still more cogent argument – the Baron himself, a moderate man, a representative specimen of human nature taken in the bulk, feels intimately convinced of the necessity of war through all eternity. Perhaps! But since the Baron has appealed to history, to history let us go. Bearing in mind our theological parallel, let us imagine the Baron in the last decade of the seventeenth century, surveying the world with the eye of a moderate and a deeply religious man. What would he have seen? Undoubtedly that religion was the dominating factor in human affairs; that religious questions had moulded the whole polity of Europe for the last 1400 years; that at that moment theological animosity was as strong as ever it had been – so strong that Louis XIV, by revoking the Edict of Nantes, had just committed an act of extraordinary barbarity, alienated half Europe, and dealt a fatal blow to the prosperity of France, merely in order that his religious zeal might find satisfaction. Surely the Baron would have remarked that intolerance had its basis in human nature, that religious wars were a part of the constitution of the universe, and would have felt, too, with the enormous majority of his contemporaries, quite certain that such a state of things was not only inevitable but, somehow or other, right. If he had been a Catholic he would have justified the *dragonnades,* as Bossuet did in fact justify them – Bossuet, the moderate man *par excellence* of that period, whose writings, owing to the accident of a gorgeous prose style, still survive to reveal to readers of today the singular

47

limitations of average passions and average thoughts. For within a generation of the time when the excellent bishop was proving in faultless periods the transcendent import of religion in history and politics, and the necessity of religious persecution and religious war, the religious motive had quietly slipped away altogether from the affairs of nations, and the age of toleration had begun. Civilization, taking a sudden turn round a corner, had put the theological frenzies of so many centuries behind it for ever.

How this happened – how it was that the moderate man whose views were expressed by Bossuet, became transformed into the moderate man whose views were expressed by Montesquieu and Hume – is no doubt a 'puzzling question'; but, whatever the causes of the change may have been, two things about it are certain – it was radical and it took place very quickly. There was a greater gulf between Montesquieu and Bossuet than between Bossuet and Bernard of Clairvaux; and Montesquieu might have been Bossuet's son. And perhaps in this consideration we may find some comfort when we next open Baron von Freytag-Loringhoven's depressing book. In spite of all the Baron may say, human nature does change, and it changes sometimes with remarkable rapidity. To moderate men like him, it may well be that militarism and the implications of militarism – the struggles and ambitions of opposing States, the desire for national power, the terror of national ruin, the armed organization of humanity – that all this seems inevitable with the inevitability of a part of the world's very structure; and yet it may well be, too, that they are wrong, that it is not so, that it is the 'fabric of a vision' which will melt suddenly and be seen no more. And in that case what will become of the Baron's book? Will it be read in after ages as a curious example of the aberrations of the moderate man? Alas! probably not; for its style, we fancy, is hardly as good as Bossuet's.

1918

# A Diplomatist: Li Hung-Chang

One of the favourite dodges of the satirist is the creation of an imaginary world, superficially different from our own, and yet turning out, on further acquaintance, to contain all the familiar vices and follies of humanity. Swift's Lilliput and Brobdingnag are contrived on this principle. The vanity of courtiers, the mischiefs of politicians, the physical degradations of men and women – these things strike upon our minds with a new intensity when they are shown to us as parts of some queer universe, preposterously minute or enormous. We gain a new vision of war and lust when we see the one waged by statesmen six inches high, and the other agitating young ladies of sixty feet. Mr Bland's book on Li Hung-Chang,[1] with its account of the society and institutions of China, produces – whether consciously or no it is a little difficult to say – very much the same effect. China is still so distant, its language is so incomprehensible, its customs are so singular, its whole civilization has such an air of topsy-turvydom about it, that our Western intelligence can survey it with a remote disinterestedness hardly less complete than if it were a part of Laputa or the moon. We do so, with Mr Bland's guidance; and we very soon perceive that China is, after all, only another Europe, with a touch of caricature and exaggeration here and there to give the satire point. Mr Bland himself, indeed, seems at times to be almost a second Gulliver, such is the apparent ingenuousness with which he marvels at the strange absurdities of Chinese life. This, however, may be merely a Swiftian subtlety on his part to heighten the effect. For instance, he tells us with great gravity that one of the chief misfortunes from which China suffers is that she is ruled by officials; that whatever changes of government, whatever revolutions may take place, the

---

[1] *Li Hung-Chang.* By J. O. P. Bland. Constable.

officials remain undisturbed in power; and that these officials form a close bureaucratic caste, cut off from the world at large, puffed up with petty vanity, and singularly ignorant of the actual facts of life. He then goes on to relate, with amazement, that the official caste is recruited by means of competitive examinations of a literary kind, and that it is possible – and indeed frequent – to obtain the highest places in these examinations merely through a knowledge of the classics. The foundation of Li Hung-Chang's administrative career, for example, was based on his having been able, in reply to one of his examiners, to repeat a celebrated classic not only forwards, but backwards as well. Then Mr Bland expatiates on the surprising and distressing atmosphere of 'make-believe' in China; he points out how it infects and vitiates the whole system of government, how it is even visible in works of history – even in the Press: 'They make their dynastic annals,' he says, 'conform to the official conception of the world-of-things-as-they-should-be, with little or no relation to the world-of-things-as-they-are, and the native Press, served chiefly by writers imbued with the same predilection for solemn make-believe in the discussion of public affairs, affords but little material for checking or amplifying the official annals.' It inevitably follows, as Mr Bland observes, that (in China) it is exceedingly difficult to discover the truth about any public event. Another singular characteristic of the Chinese is their hatred of foreigners. This passion they carry to extraordinary lengths; they are unwilling to believe that anything good ever came from a foreign country; they put high duties upon foreign importations; at moments of excitement the more violent among them clamour to 'make an end, once and for all, of all the obnoxious foreigners, whose presence creates grave difficulties and dangers for the Empire'. Strange to say, too, it is particularly the caste of officials which is infected by what Mr Bland calls 'this purblind ignorance and pride of race'.

Li Hung-Chang, however – the hero of Mr Bland's well-informed and spirited book – was different. Though a knowledge of the classics was the basis of his fortunes, it was not his only knowledge; though an official – and in many ways a typical official – he yet possessed a perspicacity which was never taken in by official 'make-believe'; above all, he understood something of the nature and the powers of foreigners. Mr Bland calls him a one-eyed man among the blind, and by 'the blind' we are to understand the rest of China. But, in truth, the description applies equally well to every leader in thought or action in every community under the sun. In Europe, no less than in China, the vast majority of men are blind – blind through ignorance and superstition and folly and senseless passions; and the statesmen and the thinkers are one-eyed leaders, who see neither very far nor very many objects, but who see what they do see quite clearly. Li Hung-Chang was a leader because he saw quite clearly the nature of China's position in international affairs. But his one-eyedness is amusingly illustrated by the manner in which this perception was originally forced upon his consciousness. It came through the chance of his being thrown together with General Gordon. It was Gordon who gave him his first vision of Europe. Nothing could be more ironical. The half-inspired, half-crazy Englishman, with his romance and his fatalism, his brandy-bottle and his Bible, the irresponsible knight-errant whom his countrymen first laughed at and neglected, then killed and canonized – a figure straying through the perplexed industrialism of the nineteenth century like some lost 'natural' from an earlier Age – this was the efficient cause of Li Hung-Chang's illumination, of his comprehension of the significance of Europe, of the whole trend of his long, cynical, successful, worldly-wise career.

It was particularly in diplomacy that that career achieved its most characteristic triumphs. Of all public servants, the diplomatist and the general alone must, if they are to succeed, have a grasp of actual facts. Politicians, lawyers, administrators, financiers even, can pass their lives in a mist of fictions and go down to posterity as great men. But the general who fails to perceive the facts that surround him will inevitably pay the penalty in defeat. The facts with which the diplomatist has to deal are less specialized and immediate, more subtle, indeterminate and diverse than those which confront the general; they are facts the perception of which requires an all-round intelligence; and thus, while it is possible for a great soldier to be a stupid man, a diplomatist who is stupid must be a failure. Li Hung-Chang's perspicacity was precisely of the universal kind; his cold gaze went through everything it met with an equal penetration. He could measure to a nicety all the complicated elements in the diplomatic game – the strength of his opponents, their intentions, their desires, their tenacity, their amenability to pressure, their susceptibility to bluff – and then the elaborate interactions of international forces, and the dubious movements of public opinion, and the curious influences of personal factors. More than this, he possessed a capacity, rare indeed save among the greatest masters of his craft – he could recognize the inevitable. And when that came, he understood the difficult art of bowing to it, as Mr Bland pithily remarks, 'with mental reservations'.

His limitations were no less remarkable than his powers. He was never in the slightest danger of believing in a principle, or of allowing his astuteness to degenerate into profundity. His imagination was purely practical, and his whole conception of life was of a perfectly conventional kind. In this he was only carrying out the high diplomatic tradition; he was following in the footsteps of Queen Elizabeth and Richelieu, Metternich and Bismarck. It seems as if the human mind was incapable of changing its focus: it must either apprehend what is near it or what is far off; it cannot combine the two. Of all the great realists of history, the master spirits in the matter-of-fact business of managing mankind, it is difficult to think of more than one or two at most who, in addition, were moved by philosophical ideals towards noble aims.

Another consideration is suggested by Mr Bland's book. There is something peculiarly fascinating about the diplomatic art. It is delightful to watch a skilled performer like Li Hung-Chang, baffling and befogging the English into humiliation, bluffing all Europe, by means of an imitation navy, into a genuine fear of a 'Yellow Peril', and, finally, when all his sins seem to have found him out, when Japan has 'seen' him, and his stakes are forfeit, 'tirant son épingle du jeu' with such supreme felicity. Certainly, it is a humane and elegant art, essentially intellectual, concerned, too, with momentous issues, and mingling, in a highly agreeable manner, the satisfactions of self-interest and altruism. Yet one cannot help perceiving indications that its days may be numbered. It belongs to a situation of affairs in the world, which there is no reason to suppose will be permanent, and of which the essential condition is the existence of a few strong States, of approximately equal power, interacting in competitive rivalry. This period began with the Renaissance; and it is at least possible that a time may come when it will have ended, and when the diplomatist will appear as romantic and extinct a creature as the medieval baron or the Italian *condottiere.* Perhaps – who knows? – the subtle Oriental with the piercing eye may turn out to have been among the very last of the charming race.

1918

# Voltaire and Frederick the Great

❧

At the present time,[1] when it is so difficult to think of anything but of what is and what will be, it may yet be worth while to cast occasionally a glance backward at what was. Such glances may at least prove to have the humble merit of being entertaining: they may even be instructive as well. Certainly it would be a mistake to forget that Frederick the Great once lived in Germany. Nor is it altogether useless to remember that a curious old gentleman, extremely thin, extremely active, and heavily bewigged, once decided that, on the whole, it would be as well for him *not* to live in France. For, just as modern Germany dates from the accession of Frederick to the throne of Prussia, so modern France dates from the establishment of Voltaire on the banks of the Lake of Geneva. The intersection of those two momentous lives forms one of the most curious and one of the most celebrated incidents in history. To English readers it is probably best known through the few brilliant paragraphs devoted to it by Macaulay; though Carlyle's masterly and far more elaborate narrative is familiar to every lover of *The History of Friedrich II*. Since Carlyle wrote, however, fifty years have passed. New points of view have arisen, and a certain amount of new material – including the valuable edition of the correspondence between Voltaire and Frederick published from the original documents in the Archives at Berlin – has become available. It seems, therefore, in spite of the familiarity of the main outlines of the story, that another rapid review of it will not be out of place.

Voltaire was forty-two years of age, and already one of the most famous men of the day, when, in August 1736, he received a letter from the Crown Prince of Prussia. This letter was the first in a

[1] October 1915.

correspondence which was to last, with a few remarkable intervals, for a space of over forty years. It was written by a young man of twenty-four, of whose personal qualities very little was known, and whose importance seemed to lie simply in the fact that he was heir-apparent to one of the secondary European monarchies. Voltaire, however, was not the man to turn up his nose at royalty, in whatever form it might present itself; and it was moreover clear that the young prince had picked up at least a smattering of French culture, that he was genuinely anxious to become acquainted with the tendencies of modern thought, and, above all, that his admiration for the author of the *Henriade* and *Zaïre* was unbounded.

La douceur et le support [wrote Frederick] que vous marquez pour tous ceux qui se vouent aux arts et aux sciences, me font espérer que vous ne m'exclurez pas du nombre de ceux que vous trouvez dignes de vos instructions. Je nomme ainsi votre commerce de lettres, qui ne peut être que profitable à tout être pensant. J'ose même avancer, sans déroger au mérite d'autrui, que dans l'univers entier il n'y aurait pas d'exception à faire de ceux dont vous ne pourriez être le maître.

The great man was accordingly delighted; he replied with all that graceful affability of which he was a master, declared that his correspondent was 'un prince philosophe qui rendra les hommes heureux', and showed that he meant business by plunging at once into a discussion of the metaphysical doctrines of 'le sieur Wolf', whom Frederick had commended as 'le plus célèbre philosophe de nos jours'. For the next four years the correspondence continued on the lines thus laid down. It was a correspondence between a master and a pupil: Frederick, his passions divided between German philosophy and French poetry, poured out with equal copiousness disquisitions upon Free Will and *la raison suffisante*, odes *sur la Flatterie*, and epistles *sur l'Humanité*, while Voltaire kept the ball rolling with no less enormous philosophical replies, together with minute criticisms of His Royal Highness's mistakes in French metre and French orthography. Thus, though the interest of these early letters must have been intense to the young Prince, they have far too little personal flavour to be anything but extremely tedious to the reader of today. Only very occasionally is it possible to detect, amid the long and careful periods, some faint signs of feeling or of

55

character. Voltaire's *empressement* seems to take on, once or twice, the colours of something like a real enthusiasm; and one notices that, after two years, Frederick's letters begin no longer with 'Monsieur' but with 'Mon cher ami', which glides at last insensibly into 'Mon cher Voltaire'; though the careful poet continues with his 'Monseigneur' throughout. Then, on one occasion, Frederick makes a little avowal, which reads oddly in the light of future events.

Souffrez [he says] que je vous fasse mon caractère, afin que vous ne vous y mépreniez plus . . . J'ai peu de mérite et peu de savoir; mais j'ai beaucoup de bonne volonté, et un fonds inépuisable d'estime et d'amitié pour les personnes d'une vertu distinguée, et avec cela je suis capable de toute la constance que la vraie amitié exige. J'ai assez de jugement pour vous rendre toute la justice que vous méritez; mais je n'en ai pas assez pour m'empêcher de faire de mauvais vers.

But this is exceptional; as a rule, elaborate compliments take the place of personal confessions; and, while Voltaire is never tired of comparing Frederick to Apollo, Alcibiades, and the youthful Marcus Aurelius, of proclaiming the rebirth of 'les talents de Virgile et les vertus d'Auguste', or of declaring that 'Socrate ne m'est rien, c'est Frédéric que j'aime', the Crown Prince is on his side ready with an equal flow of protestations, which sometimes rise to singular heights. 'Ne croyez pas,' he says, 'que je pousse mon scepticisime à outrance . . . Je crois, par exemple, qu'il n'y a qu'un Dieu et qu'un Voltaire dans le monde; je crois encore que ce Dieu avait besoin dans ce siècle d'un Voltaire pour le rendre aimable.' Decidedly the Prince's compliments were too emphatic, and the poet's too ingenious; as Voltaire himself said afterwards, 'les épithètes ne nous coûtaient rien'; yet neither was without a little residue of sincerity. Frederick's admiration bordered upon the sentimental; and Voltaire had begun to allow himself to hope that some day, in a provincial German court, there might be found a crowned head devoting his life to philosophy, good sense, and the love of letters. Both were to receive a curious awakening.

In 1740 Frederick became King of Prussia, and a new epoch in the relations between the two men began. The next ten years were, on both sides, years of growing disillusionment. Voltaire very soon discovered that his phrase about 'un prince philosophe qui rendra

les hommes heureux' was indeed a phrase and nothing more. His
*prince philosophe* started out on a career of conquest, plunged all
Europe into war, and turned Prussia into a great military power.
Frederick, it appeared, was at once a far more important and a far
more dangerous phenomenon than Voltaire had suspected. And,
on the other hand, the matured mind of the King was not slow to
perceive that the enthusiasm of the Prince needed a good deal of
qualification. This change of view, was, indeed, remarkably rapid.
Nothing is more striking than the alteration of the tone in
Frederick's correspondence during the few months which followed
his accession: the voice of the raw and inexperienced youth is heard
no more, and its place is taken – at once and for ever – by the self-
contained caustic utterance of an embittered man of the world. In
this transformation it was only natural that the wondrous figure of
Voltaire should lose some of its glitter – especially since Frederick
now began to have the opportunity of inspecting that figure in the
flesh with his own sharp eyes. The friends met three or four times,
and it is noticeable that after each meeting there is a distinct coolness
on the part of Frederick. He writes with a sudden brusqueness to
accuse Voltaire of showing about his manuscripts, which, he says,
had only been sent him on the condition of *un secret inviolable*. He
writes to Jordan complaining of Voltaire's avarice in very stringent
terms. 'Ton avare boira la lie de son insatiable désir de s'enrichir . . .
Son apparition de six jours me coûtera par journée cinq cent
cinquante écus. C'est bien payer un fou; jamais bouffon de grand
seigneur n'eut de pareils gages.' He declares that 'la cervelle du
poète est aussi légère que le style de ses ouvrages', and remarks
sarcastically that he is indeed a man *extraordinaire en tout*.

Yet, while his opinion of Voltaire's character was rapidly
growing more and more severe, his admiration of his talents
remained undiminished. For, though he had dropped metaphysics
when he came to the throne, Frederick could never drop his passion
for French poetry; he recognized in Voltaire the unapproachable
master of that absorbing art; and for years he had made up his mind
that, some day or other, he would *posséder* – for so he put it – the
author of the *Henriade*, would keep him at Berlin as the brightest
ornament of his court, and, above all, would have him always
ready at hand to put the final polish on his own verses. In the
autumn of 1743 it seemed for a moment that his wish would be

gratified. Voltaire spent a visit of several weeks in Berlin; he was dazzled by the graciousness of his reception and the splendour of his surroundings; and he began to listen to the honeyed overtures of the Prussian Majesty. The great obstacle to Frederick's desire was Voltaire's relationship with Madame du Châtelet. He had lived with her for more than ten years; he was attached to her by all the ties of friendship and gratitude; he had constantly declared that he would never leave her – no, not for all the seductions of princes. She would, it is true, have been willing to accompany Voltaire to Berlin; but such a solution would by no means have suited Frederick. He was not fond of ladies – even of ladies like Madame du Châtelet – learned enough to translate Newton and to discuss by the hour the niceties of the Leibnitzian philosophy; and he had determined to *posséder* Voltaire either completely or not at all. Voltaire, in spite of repeated temptations, had remained faithful; but now, for the first time, poor Madame du Châtelet began to be seriously alarmed. His letters from Berlin grew fewer and fewer, and more and more ambiguous; she knew nothing of his plans; 'il est ivre absolument' she burst out in her distress to d'Argental, one of his oldest friends. By every post she dreaded to learn at last that he had deserted her for ever. But suddenly Voltaire returned. The spell of Berlin had been broken, and he was at her feet once more.

What had happened was highly characteristic both of the Poet and of the King. Each had tried to play a trick on the other, and each had found the other out. The French Government had been anxious to obtain an insight into the diplomatic intentions of Frederick, in an unofficial way; Voltaire had offered his services, and it had been agreed that he should write to Frederick declaring that he was obliged to leave France for a time owing to the hostility of a member of the Government, the Bishop of Mirepoix, and asking for Frederick's hospitality. Frederick had not been taken in: though he had not disentangled the whole plot, he had perceived clearly enough that Voltaire's visit was in reality that of an agent of the French Government; he also thought he saw an opportunity of securing the desire of his heart. Voltaire, to give verisimilitude to his story, had, in his letter to Frederick, loaded the Bishop of Mirepoix with ridicule and abuse; and Frederick now secretly sent this letter to Mirepoix himself. His calculation was that Mirepoix would be so outraged that he would make it impossible for Voltaire ever to return to France; and in that case – well, Voltaire would have no other course open to him but to stay where he was, in Berlin, and Madame du Châtelet would have to make the best of it. Of course, Frederick's plan failed, and Voltaire was duly informed by Mirepoix of what had happened. He was naturally very angry. He had been almost induced to stay in Berlin of his own accord, and now he found that his host had been attempting, by means of treachery and intrigue, to force him to stay there whether he liked it or not. It was a long time before he forgave Frederick. But the King was most anxious to patch up the quarrel; he still could not abandon the hope of ultimately securing Voltaire; and besides, he was now possessed by another and a more immediate desire – to be allowed a glimpse of that famous and scandalous work which Voltaire kept locked in the innermost drawer of his cabinet and revealed to none but the most favoured of his intimates – *La Pucelle*.

Accordingly the royal letters became more frequent and more flattering than ever; the royal hand cajoled and implored. 'Ne me faites point injustice sur mon caractère; d'ailleurs il vous est permis de badiner sur mon sujet comme il vous plaira.' '*La Pucelle! La Pucelle! La Pucelle!* et encore *La Pucelle!*' he exclaims. 'Pour l'amour de Dieu, ou plus encore pour l'amour de vous-même, envoyez-la-moi.' And at last Voltaire was softened. He sent off a few fragments of his *Pucelle* – just enough to whet Frederick's appetite – and he declared himself reconciled. 'Je vous ai aimé tendrement,' he wrote in March 1749; 'j'ai été fâché contre vous, je vous ai pardonné, et actuellement je vous aime à la folie.' Within a year of this date his situation had undergone a complete change. Madame du Châtelet was dead; and his position at Versailles, in spite of the friendship of Madame de Pompadour, had become almost as impossible as he had pretended it to have been in 1743. Frederick eagerly repeated his invitation; and this time Voltaire did not refuse. He was careful to make a very good bargain; obliged Frederick to pay for his journey; and arrived at Berlin in July 1750. He was given rooms in the royal palaces both at Berlin and Potsdam; he was made a Court Chamberlain, and received the Order of Merit, together with a pension of £800 a year. These arrangements caused considerable amusement in Paris; and for some days hawkers, carrying prints of Voltaire dressed in furs, and crying 'Voltaire le prussien! Six sols le fameux prussien!' were to be seen walking up and down the Quays.

The curious drama that followed, with its farcical περιπέτεια and its tragi-comic *dénouement*, can hardly be understood without a brief consideration of the feelings and intentions of the two chief actors in it. The position of Frederick is comparatively plain. He had now completely thrown aside the last lingering remnants of any esteem which he may once have entertained for the character of Voltaire. He frankly thought him a scoundrel. In September 1749, less than a year before Voltaire's arrival, and at the very period of Frederick's most urgent invitations, we find him using the following language in a letter to Algarotti: 'Voltaire vient de faire un tour qui est indigne.' (He had been showing to all his friends a garbled copy of one of Frederick's letters.)

Il mériterait d'être fleurdelisé au Parnasse. C'est bien dommage qu'une âme aussi lâche soit unie à un aussi beau génie. Il a les gentillesses et les malices d'un singe. Je vous conterai ce que c'est, lorsque je vous reverrai; cependant je ne ferai semblant de rien, car j'en ai besoin pour l'étude de l'élocution française. On peut apprendre de bonnes choses d'un scélérat. Je veux savoir son français; que m'importe sa morale? Cet homme a trouvé le moyen de réunir tous les contraires. On admire son esprit, en même temps qu'on méprise son caractère.

There is no ambiguity about this. Voltaire was a scoundrel; but he was a scoundrel of genius. He would make the best possible teacher of *l'élocution française*; therefore it was necessary that he should come and live in Berlin. But as for anything more – as for any real interchange of sympathies, any genuine feeling of friendliness, of respect, or even of regard – all that was utterly out of the question. The avowal is cynical, no doubt; but it is at any rate straightforward, and above all it is peculiarly devoid of any trace of self-deception. In the face of these trenchant sentences, the view of Frederick's attitude which is suggested so assiduously by Carlyle – that he was the victim of an elevated misapprehension, that he was always hoping for the best, and that, when the explosion came he was very much surprised and profoundly disappointed – becomes obviously untenable. If any man ever acted with his eyes wide open, it was Frederick when he invited Voltaire to Berlin.

Yet, though that much is clear, the letter to Algarotti betrays, in more than one direction, a very singular state of mind. A warm devotion to *l'élocution française* is easy enough to understand; but

Frederick's devotion was much more than warm; it was so absorbing and so intense that it left him no rest until by hook or by crook, by supplication, or by trickery, or by paying down hard cash, he had obtained the close and constant proximity of – what? – of a man whom he himself described as a 'singe' and a 'scélérat', a man of base soul and despicable character. And Frederick appears to see nothing surprising in this. He takes it quite as a matter of course that he should be, not merely willing, but delighted to run all the risks involved by Voltaire's undoubted roguery, so long as he can be sure of benefiting from Voltaire's no less undoubted mastery of French versification. This is certainly strange; but the explanation of it lies in the extraordinary vogue – a vogue, indeed, so extraordinary that it is very difficult for the modern reader to realize it – enjoyed throughout Europe by French culture and literature during the middle years of the eighteenth century. Frederick was merely an extreme instance of a universal fact. Like all Germans of any education, he habitually wrote and spoke in French; like every lady and gentleman from Naples to Edinburgh, his life was regulated by the social conventions of France; like every amateur of letters from Madrid to St. Petersburg, his whole conception of literary taste, his whole standard of literary values, was French. To him, as to the vast majority of his contemporaries, the very essence of civilization was concentrated in French literature, and especially in French poetry; and French poetry meant to him, as to his contemporaries, that particular kind of French poetry which had come into fashion at the court of Louis XIV. For this curious creed was as narrow as it was all-pervading. The *Grand Siècle* was the Church Infallible; and it was heresy to doubt the Gospel of Boileau.

Frederick's library, still preserved at Potsdam, shows us what literature meant in those days to a cultivated man: it is composed entirely of the French Classics, of the works of Voltaire, and of the masterpieces of antiquity translated into eighteenth-century French. But Frederick was not content with mere appreciation; he too would create; he would write alexandrines on the model of Racine, and madrigals after the manner of Chaulieu; he would press in person into the sacred sanctuary, and burn incense with his own hands upon the inmost shrine. It was true that he was a foreigner; it was true that his knowledge of the French language was incomplete and incorrect; but his sense of his own ability urged him forward, and his indefatigable pertinacity kept him at his strange task throughout the whole of his life. He filled volumes, and the contents of those volumes afford probably the most complete illustration in literature of the very trite proverb – *Poeta nascitur, non fit*. The spectacle of that heavy German Muse, with her feet crammed into pointed slippers, executing, with incredible conscientiousness, now the stately measure of a Versailles minuet, and now the spritely steps of a Parisian jig, would be either ludicrous or pathetic – one hardly knows which – were it not so certainly neither the one nor the other, but simply dreary with an unutterable dreariness, from which the eyes of men avert themselves in shuddering dismay. Frederick himself felt that there was something wrong – something, but not really very much. All that was wanted was a little expert advice; and obviously Voltaire was the man to supply it – Voltaire, the one true heir of the Great Age, the dramatist who had revived the glories of Racine (did not Frederick's tears flow almost as copiously over *Mahomet* as over *Britannicus?*), the epic poet who had eclipsed Homer and Virgil (had not Frederick every right to judge, since he had read the 'Iliad' in French prose and the 'Æneid' in French verse?), the lyric master whose odes and whose epistles occasionally even surpassed (Frederick confessed it with amazement) those of the Marquis de la Fare. Voltaire, there could be no doubt, would do just what was needed; he would know how to squeeze in a little further the waist of the German Calliope, to apply with his deft fingers precisely the right dab of rouge to her cheeks, to instil into her movements the last *nuances* of correct deportment. And, if he did that, of what consequence were the blemishes of his personal character? 'On peut apprendre de bonnes choses d'un scélérat.'

And, besides, though Voltaire might be a rogue, Frederick felt quite convinced that he could keep him in order. A crack or two of the master's whip – a coldness in the royal demeanour, a hint at a stoppage of the pension – and the monkey would put an end to his tricks soon enough. It never seems to have occurred to Frederick that the possession of genius might imply a quality of spirit which was not that of an ordinary man. This was his great, his fundamental error. It was the ingenuous error of a cynic. He knew that he was under no delusion as to Voltaire's faults, and so he supposed that he could be under no delusion as to his merits. He innocently imagined that the capacity for great writing was something that could be as easily separated from the owner of it as a hat or a glove. 'C'est bien dommage qu'une âme aussi lâche soit unie à un aussi beau génie.' *C'est bien dommage!* – as if there was nothing more extraordinary in such a combination than that of a pretty woman and an ugly dress. And so Frederick held his whip a little tighter, and reminded himself once more that, in spite of that *beau génie*, it was a monkey that he had to deal with. But he was wrong: it was not a monkey; it was a devil, which is a very different thing.

A devil – or perhaps an angel? One cannot be quite sure. For, amid the complexities of that extraordinary spirit, where good and evil were so mysteriously interwoven, where the elements of darkness and the elements of light lay crowded together in such ever-deepening ambiguity, fold within fold, the clearer the vision the greater the bewilderment, the more impartial the judgment the profounder the doubt. But one thing at least is certain: that spirit, whether it was admirable or whether it was odious, was moved by a terrific force. Frederick had failed to realize this; and indeed, though Voltaire was fifty-six when he went to Berlin, and though his whole life had been spent in a blaze of publicity, there was still not one of his contemporaries who understood the true nature of his genius; it was perhaps hidden even from himself. He had reached the threshold of old age, and his life's work was still before him; it was not as a writer of tragedies and epics that he was to take his place in the world. Was he, in the depths of his consciousness, aware that this was so? Did some obscure instinct urge him forward, at this late hour, to break with the ties of a lifetime, and rush forth into the unknown?

What his precise motives were in embarking upon the Berlin adventure it is very difficult to say. It is true that he was disgusted with Paris – he was ill-received at Court, and he was pestered by endless literary quarrels and jealousies; it would be very pleasant to show his countrymen that he had other strings to his bow, that, if they did not appreciate him, Frederick the Great did. It is true, too, that he admired Frederick's intellect, and that he was flattered by his favour. 'Il avait de l'esprit,' he said afterwards, 'des grâces, et, de plus, il était roi; ce qui fait toujours une grande séduction, attendu la faiblesse humaine.' His vanity could not resist the prestige of a royal intimacy; and no doubt he relished to the full even the increased consequence which came to him with his Chamberlain's key and his order – to say nothing of the addition of £800 to his income. Yet, on the other hand, he was very well aware that he was exchanging freedom for servitude, and that he was entering into a bargain with a man who would make quite sure that he was getting his money's worth; and he knew in his heart that he had something better to do than to play, however successfully, the part of a courtier. Nor was he personally attached to Frederick; he was personally attached to no one on earth. Certainly he had never been a man of feeling, and now that he was old and hardened by the uses of the world he had grown to be completely what in essence he always was – a fighter, without tenderness, without scruples, and without remorse. No, he went to Berlin for his own purposes – however dubious those purposes may have been.

And it is curious to observe that in his correspondence with his niece, Madame Denis, whom he had left behind him at the head of his Paris establishment and in whom he confided – in so far as he can be said to have confided in anyone – he repeatedly states that there is nothing permanent about his visit to Berlin. At first he declares that he is only making a stay of a few weeks with Frederick, that he is going on to Italy to visit 'sa Sainteté' and to inspect 'la ville souterraine', that he will be back in Paris in the autumn. The autumn comes, and the roads are too muddy to travel by; he must wait till the winter, when they will be frozen hard. Winter comes, and it is too cold to move; but he will certainly return in the spring. Spring comes, and he is on the point of finishing his *Siècle de Louis XIV*; he really must wait just a few weeks more. The book is published; but then how can he appear in Paris until he is quite sure of its success? And so he lingers on, delaying and prevaricating, until a whole year has passed, and still he lingers on, still he is on the point of going, and still he does not go. Meanwhile, to all appearances, he was definitely fixed, a salaried official, at Frederick's court; and he was writing to all his other friends, to assure them that he had never been so happy, that he could see no reason why he should ever come away. What were his true intentions? Could he himself have said? Had he perhaps, in some secret corner of his brain, into which even he hardly dared to look, a premonition of the future? At times, in this Berlin adventure, he seems to resemble some great buzzing fly, shooting suddenly into a room through an open window and dashing frantically from side to side; when all at once, as suddenly, he swoops away and out through another window which opens in quite a different direction, towards wide and flowery fields; so that perhaps the reckless creature knew where he was going after all.

In any case, it is evident to the impartial observer that Voltaire's visit could only have ended as it did – in an explosion. The elements of the situation were too combustible for any other conclusion. When two confirmed egotists decide, for purely selfish reasons, to set up house together, everyone knows what will happen. For some time their sense of mutual advantage may induce them to tolerate each other, but sooner or later human nature will assert itself, and the *ménage* will break up. And, with Voltaire and Frederick, the difficulties inherent in all such cases were intensified by the fact that the relationship between them was, in effect, that of servant and master; that Voltaire, under a very thin disguise, was a paid menial, while Frederick, condescend as he might, was an autocrat whose will was law. Thus the two famous and perhaps mythical sentences, invariably repeated by historians of the incident, about orange-skins and dirty linen, do in fact sum up the gist of the matter. 'When one has sucked the orange, one throws away the skin,' somebody told Voltaire that the King had said, on being asked how much longer he would put up with the poet's vagaries. And Frederick, on his side, was informed that Voltaire, when a batch of the royal verses were brought to him for correction, had burst out with 'Does the man expect me to go on washing his dirty linen for ever?' Each knew well enough the weak spot in his position, and each was acutely and uncomfortably conscious that the other knew it too. Thus, but a very few weeks after Voltaire's arrival, little clouds of discord become visible on the horizon; electrical discharges of irritability begin to take place, growing more and more frequent and violent as time goes on; and one can overhear the pot and the kettle, in strictest privacy, calling each other black. 'The monster,' whispers Voltaire to Madame Denis, 'he opens all our letters in the post' – Voltaire, whose light-handedness with other people's correspondence was only too notorious. 'The monkey,' mutters Frederick, 'he shows my private letters to his friends' – Frederick, who had thought nothing of betraying Voltaire's letters to the Bishop of Mirepoix. 'How happy I should be here,' exclaims the callous old poet, 'but for one thing – his Majesty is utterly heartless!' And meanwhile Frederick, who had never let a farthing escape from his close fist without some very good reason, was busy concocting an epigram upon the avarice of Voltaire.

It was, indeed, Voltaire's passion for money which brought on the first really serious storm. Three months after his arrival in Berlin, the temptation to increase his already considerable fortune by a stroke of illegal stock-jobbing proved too strong for him; he became involved in a series of shady financial transactions with a Jew; he quarrelled with the Jew; there was an acrimonious lawsuit, with charges and counter-charges of the most discreditable kind; and, though the Jew lost his case on a technical point, the poet certainly did not leave the court without a stain upon his character. Among other misdemeanours, it is almost certain – the evidence is not quite conclusive – that he committed forgery in order to support a false oath. Frederick was furious, and for a moment was on the brink of dismissing Voltaire from Berlin. He would have been wise if he had done so. But he could not part with his *beau génie* so soon. He cracked his whip, and, setting the monkey to stand in the corner, contented himself with a shrug of the shoulders and the exclamation 'C'est l'affaire d'un fripon qui a voulu tromper un filou.' A few weeks later the royal favour shone forth once more, and Voltaire, who had been hiding himself in a suburban villa, came out and basked again in those refulgent beams.

And the beams were decidedly refulgent – so much so, in fact, that they almost satisfied even the vanity of Voltaire. Almost, but not quite. For, though his glory was great, though he was the centre of all men's admiration, courted by nobles, flattered by princesses – there is a letter from one of them, a sister of Frederick's, still extant, wherein the trembling votaress ventures to praise the great man's works, which, she says, 'vous rendent si célèbre et immortel' – though he had ample leisure for his private activities, though he enjoyed every day the brilliant conversation of the King, though he could often forget for weeks together that he was the paid servant of a jealous despot – yet, in spite of all, there was a crumpled rose-leaf amid the silken sheets, and he lay awake o' nights. He was not the only Frenchman at Frederick's court. That monarch had surrounded himself with a small group of persons – foreigners for the most part – whose business it was to instruct him when he wished to improve his mind, to flatter him when he was out of temper, and to entertain him when he was bored. There was hardly one of them that was not thoroughly second-rate. Algarotti was an elegant dabbler in scientific matters – he had written a book to explain Newton to the ladies; d'Argens was an amiable and erudite writer of a dull free-thinking turn; Chasot was a retired military man with too many debts, and Darget was a good-natured secretary with too many love affairs; La Mettrie was a doctor who had been exiled from France for atheism and bad manners; and Pöllnitz was a decaying baron who, under stress of circumstances, had unfortunately been obliged to change his religion six times.

These were the boon companions among whom Frederick chose to spend his leisure hours. Whenever he had nothing better to do, he would exchange rhymed epigrams with Algarotti, or discuss the Jewish religion with d'Argens, or write long improper poems about Darget, in the style of *La Pucelle*. Or else he would summon La Mettrie, who would forthwith prove the irrefutability of materialism in a series of wild paradoxes, shout with laughter, suddenly shudder and cross himself on upsetting the salt, and eventually pursue his majesty with his buffooneries into a place where even royal persons are wont to be left alone. At other times Frederick would amuse himself by first cutting down the pension of Pöllnitz, who was at the moment a Lutheran, and then writing long and serious letters to him suggesting that if he would only become a Catholic again he might be made a Silesian Abbot. Strangely enough, Frederick was not popular, and one or other of the inmates of his little menagerie was constantly escaping and running away. Darget and Chasot both succeeded in getting through the wires; they obtained leave to visit Paris, and stayed there. Poor d'Argens often tried to follow their example; more than once he set off for France, secretly vowing never to return; but he had no money, Frederick was blandishing, and the wretch was always lured back to captivity. As for La Mettrie, he made his escape in a different manner – by dying after supper one evening of a surfeit of pheasant pie. 'Jésus! Marie!' he gasped, as he felt the pains of death upon him. 'Ah!' said a priest who had been sent for, 'vous voilà enfin retourné à ces noms consolateurs.' La Mettrie, with an oath, expired; and Frederick, on hearing of this unorthodox conclusion, remarked, 'J'en suis bien aise, pour le repos de son âme.'

Among this circle of down-at-heel eccentrics there was a single figure whose distinction and respectability stood out in striking contrast from the rest – that of Maupertuis, who had been, since 1745, the President of the Academy of Sciences at Berlin. Maupertuis has had an unfortunate fate: he was first annihilated by the ridicule of Voltaire, and then recreated by the humour of Carlyle; but he was an ambitious man, very anxious to be famous, and his desire has been gratified in overflowing measure. During his life he was chiefly known for his voyage to Lapland, and his observations there, by which he was able to substantiate the Newtonian doctrine of the flatness of the earth at the poles. He possessed considerable scientific attainments, he was honest, he was energetic; he appeared to be just the man to revive the waning glories of Prussian science; and when Frederick succeeded in inducing him to come to Berlin as President of his Academy the choice seemed amply justified. Maupertuis had, moreover, some pretensions to wit; and in his earlier days his biting and elegant sarcasms had more than once overwhelmed his scientific adversaries. Such accomplishments suited Frederick admirably. Maupertuis, he declared, was an *homme d'esprit*, and the happy President became a constant guest at the royal supper-parties. It was the happy – the too happy – President who was the rose-leaf in the bed of Voltaire. The two men had known each other slightly for many years, and had always expressed the highest admiration for each other; but their mutual amiability was now to be put to a severe test. The sagacious Buffon observed the danger from afar: 'ces deux hommes,' he wrote to a friend, 'ne sont pas faits pour demeurer ensemble dans la même chambre.' And indeed to the vain and sensitive poet, uncertain of Frederick's cordiality, suspicious of hidden enemies, intensely jealous of possible rivals, the spectacle of Maupertuis at supper, radiant, at his ease, obviously protected, obviously superior to the shady mediocrities who sat around – that sight was gall and wormwood; and he looked closer, with a new malignity; and then those piercing eyes began to make discoveries, and that relentless brain began to do its work.

Maupertuis had very little judgment; so far from attempting to conciliate Voltaire, he was rash enough to provoke hostilities. It was very natural that he should have lost his temper. He had been for five years the dominating figure in the royal circle, and now suddenly he was deprived of his pre-eminence and thrown completely into the shade. Who could attend to Maupertuis while Voltaire was talking? – Voltaire, who as obviously outshone Maupertuis as Maupertuis outshone La Mettrie and Darget and the rest. In his exasperation the President went to the length of openly giving his protection to a disreputable literary man, La Beaumelle, who was a declared enemy of Voltaire. This meant war, and war was not long in coming.

Some years previously Maupertuis had, as he believed, discovered an important mathematical law – the 'principle of least action'. The law was, in fact, important, and has had a fruitful history in the development of mechanical theory; but, as Mr Jourdain has shown in a recent monograph, Maupertuis enunciated it incorrectly without realizing its true import, and a far more accurate and scientific statement of it was given, within a few months, by Euler. Maupertuis, however, was very proud of his discovery, which, he considered, embodied one of the principal reasons for believing in the existence of God; and he was therefore exceedingly angry when, shortly after Voltaire's arrival in Berlin, a Swiss mathematician, Koenig, published a polite memoir attacking both its accuracy and its originality, and quoted in support of his contention an unpublished letter by Leibnitz, in which the law was more exactly expressed. Instead of arguing upon the merits of the case, Maupertuis declared that the letter of Leibnitz was a forgery, and that therefore Koenig's remarks deserved no further consideration. When Koenig expostulated, Maupertuis decided upon a more drastic step. He summoned a meeting of the Berlin Academy of Sciences, of which Koenig was a member, laid the case before it, and moved that it should solemnly pronounce Koenig a forger, and the letter of Leibnitz supposititious and false. The members of the Academy were frightened; their pensions depended upon the President's good will; and even the illustrious Euler was not ashamed to take part in this absurd and disgraceful condemnation.

Voltaire saw at once that his opportunity had come. Maupertuis had put himself utterly and irretrievably in the wrong. He was wrong in attributing to his discovery a value which it did not possess; he was wrong in denying the authenticity of the Leibnitz letter; above all he was wrong in treating a purely scientific question as the proper subject for the disciplinary jurisdiction of an Academy. If Voltaire struck now, he would have his enemy on the hip. There was only one consideration to give him pause, and that was a grave one: to attack Maupertuis upon this matter was, in effect, to attack the King. Not only was Frederick certainly privy to Maupertuis' action, but he was extremely sensitive of the reputation of his Academy and of its President, and he would certainly consider any interference on the part of Voltaire, who himself drew his wages from the royal purse, as a flagrant act of disloyalty. But Voltaire decided to take the risk. He had now been more than two years in Berlin, and the atmosphere of a Court was beginning to weigh upon his spirit; he was restless, he was reckless, he was spoiling for a fight; he would take on Maupertuis singly or Maupertuis and Frederick combined – he did not much care which, and in any case he flattered himself that he would settle the hash of the President.

As a preparatory measure, he withdrew all his spare cash from Berlin, and invested it with the Duke of Würtemberg. 'Je mets tout doucement ordre à mes affaires,' he told Madame Denis. Then, on September 18, 1752, there appeared in the papers a short article entitled 'Réponse d'un Académicien de Berlin à un Académicien de Paris'. It was a statement, deadly in its bald simplicity, its studied coldness, its concentrated force, of Koenig's case against Maupertuis. The President must have turned pale as he read it; but the King turned crimson. The terrible indictment could, of course, only have been written by one man, and that man was receiving a royal pension of £800 a year and carrying about a Chamberlain's gold key in his pocket. Frederick flew to his writing-table, and composed an indignant pamphlet which he caused to be published with the Prussian arms on the title-page. It was a feeble work, full of exaggerated praises of Maupertuis, and of clumsy invectives against Voltaire: the President's reputation was gravely compared to that of Homer; the author of the 'Réponse d'un Académicien de Berlin' was declared to be a 'faiseur de libelles sans génie', an 'imposteur effronté', a 'malheureux écrivain'; while the 'Réponse' itself was a 'grossièreté plate', whose publication was an 'action malicieuse, lâche, infâme', a 'brigandage affreux'. The presence of the royal insignia only intensified the futility of the outburst. 'L'aigle, le sceptre, et la couronne,' wrote Voltaire to Madame Denis, 'sont bien étonnés de se trouver là.' But one thing was now certain: the King had joined the fray. Voltaire's blood was up, and he was not sorry. A kind of exaltation seized him; from this moment his course was clear – he would do as much damage as he could, and then leave Prussia for ever. And it so happened that just then an unexpected opportunity occurred for one of those furious onslaughts so dear to his heart, with that weapon which he knew so well how to wield. 'Je n'ai point de sceptre,' he ominously shot out to Madame Denis, 'mais j'ai une plume.'

Meanwhile the life of the Court – which passed for the most part at Potsdam, in the little palace of Sans Souci which Frederick had built for himself – proceeded on its accustomed course. It was a singular life, half military, half monastic, rigid, retired, from which all the ordinary pleasures of society were strictly excluded. 'What do you do here?' one of the royal princes was once asked. 'We conjugate the verb *s'ennuyer*,' was the reply. But, wherever he might be, that was a verb unknown to Voltaire. Shut up all day in the strange little room, still preserved for the eyes of the curious, with its windows opening on the formal garden, and its yellow walls thickly embossed with the brightly coloured shapes of fruits, flowers, birds, and apes, the indefatigable old man worked away at his histories, his tragedies, his *Pucelle*, and his enormous correspondence. He was, of course, ill – very ill; he was probably, in fact, upon the brink of death; but he had grown accustomed to that situation; and the worse he grew the more furiously he worked. He was a victim, he declared, of erysipelas, dysentery, and scurvy; he was constantly attacked by fever, and all his teeth had fallen out. But he continued to work. On one occasion a friend visited him, and found him in bed. 'J'ai quatre maladies mortelles,' he wailed. 'Pourtant,' remarked the friend, 'vous avez l'œil fort bon.' Voltaire leapt up from the pillows: 'Ne savez–vous pas,' he shouted, 'que les scorbutiques meurent l'œil enflammé?' When the evening came it was time to dress, and, in all the pomp of flowing wig and diamond order, to proceed to the little music-room, where his Majesty, after the business of the day, was preparing to relax himself upon the flute. The orchestra was gathered together; the audience was seated; the concerto began. And then the sounds of beauty flowed and trembled, and seemed, for a little space, to triumph over the pains of living and the hard hearts of men; and the royal master poured out his skill in some long and elaborate cadenza, and the adagio came, the marvellous adagio, and the conqueror of Rossbach drew tears from the author of *Candide*. But a moment later it was supper-time; and the night ended in the oval dining-room, amid laughter and champagne, the ejaculations of La Mettrie, the epigrams of Maupertuis, the sarcasms of Frederick, and the devastating corus-cations of Voltaire.

Yet, in spite of all the jests and roses, everyone could hear the rumbling of the volcano under the ground. Everyone could hear, but nobody would listen; the little flames leapt up through the surface, but still the gay life went on; and then the irruption came. Voltaire's enemy had written a book. In the intervals of his more serious labours, the President had put together a series of 'Letters', in which a number of miscellaneous scientific subjects were treated in a mildly speculative and popular style. The volume was rather dull, and very unimportant; but it happened to appear at this particular moment, and Voltaire pounced upon it with the swift swoop of a hawk on a mouse. The famous *Diatribe du Docteur Akakia* is still fresh with a fiendish gaiety after a hundred and fifty years; but to realize to the full the skill and malice which went to the making of it, one must at least have glanced at the flat insipid production which called it forth, and noted with what a diabolical art the latent absurdities in poor Maupertuis' *rêveries* have been detected, dragged forth into the light of day, and nailed to the pillory of an immortal ridicule. The *Diatribe*, however, is not all mere laughter; there is a real criticism in it, too. For instance, it was not simply a farcical exaggeration to say that Maupertuis had set out to prove the existence of God by 'A plus B divided by Z'; in substance, the charge was both important and well founded. 'Lorsque la métaphysique entre dans la géometrie,' Voltaire wrote in a private letter some months afterwards, 'c'est Arimane qui entre dans le royaume d'Oromasde, et qui y apporte des ténèbres'; and Maupertuis had in fact vitiated his treatment of the 'principle of least action' by his metaphysical pre-occupations. Indeed, all through Voltaire's pamphlet, there is an implied appeal to true scientific principles, an underlying assertion of the paramount importance of the experimental method, a consistent attack upon *a priori* reasoning, loose statement, and vague conjecture. But of course, mixed with all this, and covering it all, there is a bubbling, sparkling fountain of effervescent raillery – cruel, personal, insatiable – the raillery of a demon with a grudge. The manuscript was shown to Frederick, who laughed till the tears ran down his cheeks. But, between his gasps, he forbade Voltaire to publish it on pain of his most terrible displeasure. Naturally Voltaire was profuse with promises, and a few days later, under a royal licence obtained for another work, the little book appeared in print. Frederick still managed to keep his wrath within bounds: he collected all the copies of the edition and had them privately destroyed; he gave a furious wigging to Voltaire; and he flattered himself that he had heard the last of the business.

Ne vous embarrassez de rien, mon cher Maupertuis [he wrote to the President in his singular orthography]; l'affaire des libelles est finie. J'ai parlé si vrai à l'hôme, je lui ai lavé si bien la tête que je ne crois pas qu'il y retourne, et je connais son âme lache, incapable de sentiments d'honneur. Je l'ai intimidé du côté de la boursse, ce qui a fait tout l'effet que j'attendais. Je lui ai déclaré enfin nettement que ma maison devait être un sanctuaire et non une retraite de brigands ou de célérats qui distillent des poissons.

Apparently it did not occur to Frederick that this declaration had come a little late in the day. Meanwhile Maupertuis, overcome by illness and by rage, had taken to his bed. 'Un peu trop d'amour-propre,' Frederick wrote to Darget, 'l'a rendu trop sensible aux manœuvres d'un singe qu'il devait mépriser après qu'on l'avait fouetté.' But now the monkey *had* been whipped, and doubtless all would be well. It seems strange that Frederick should still, after more than two years observation, have had no notion of the material he was dealing with. He might as well have supposed that he could stop a mountain torrent in spate with a wave of his hand, as have imagined that he could impose obedience upon Voltaire in such a crisis by means of a lecture and a threat 'du côté de la boursse'. Before the month was out all Germany was swarming with *Akakias*; thousands of copies were being printed in Holland; and editions were going off in Paris like hot cakes. It is difficult to withhold one's admiration from the audacious old spirit who thus, on the mere strength of his mother-wits, dared to defy the enraged master of a powerful state. 'Votre effronterie m'étonne,' fulminated Frederick in a furious note, when he suddenly discovered that all Europe was ringing with the absurdity of the man whom he had chosen to be the President of his favourite Academy, whose cause he had publicly espoused, and whom he had privately assured of his royal protection. 'Ah! Mon Dieu, Sire,' scribbled Voltaire on the same sheet of paper, 'dans l'état où je suis!' (He was, of course, once more dying.) 'Quoi! vous me jugeriez sans entendre! Je demande justice et la mort.' Frederick replied by having copies of *Akakia* burnt by the common hangman in the streets of Berlin. Voltaire thereupon returned his Order, his gold key, and his pension. It might have been supposed that the final rupture had now really come at last. But three months elapsed before Frederick could bring himself to realize that all was over, and to agree to the departure of his extraordinary guest. Carlyle's suggestion that this last delay arose from the unwillingness of Voltaire to go, rather than from Frederick's desire to keep him, is plainly controverted by the facts. The King not only insisted on Voltaire's accepting once again the honours which he had surrendered, but actually went so far as to write him a letter of forgiveness and reconciliation. But the poet would not relent; there was a last week of suppers at Potsdam – 'soupers de Damoclès' Voltaire called them; and then, on March 26, 1753, the two men parted for ever.

The storm seemed to be over; but the tail of it was still hanging in the wind. Voltaire, on his way to the waters of Plombières, stopped at Leipzig, where he could not resist, in spite of his repeated promises to the contrary, the temptation to bring out a new and enlarged edition of *Akakia*. Upon this Maupertuis utterly lost his head: he wrote to Voltaire, threatening him with personal chastisement. Voltaire issued yet another edition of *Akakia*, appended a somewhat unauthorized version of the President's letter, and added that if the dangerous and cruel man really persisted in his threat he would be received with a vigorous discharge from those instruments of intimate utility which figure so freely in the comedies of Molière. This stroke was the *coup de grâce* of Maupertuis. Shattered in body and mind, he dragged himself from Berlin to die at last in Basle under the ministration of a couple of Capuchins and a Protestant valet reading aloud the Genevan Bible. In the meantime Frederick had decided on a violent measure. He had suddenly remembered that Voltaire had carried off with him one of the very few privately printed copies of those poetical works upon which he had spent so much devoted labour; it occurred to him that they contained several passages of a highly damaging kind; and he could feel no certainty that those passages would not be given to the world by the malicious Frenchman. Such, at any rate, were his own excuses for the step which he now took; but it seems possible that he was at least partly swayed by feelings of resentment and revenge which had been rendered uncontrollable by the last onslaught upon Maupertuis. Whatever may have been his motives, it is certain that he ordered the Prussian Resident in Frankfort, which was Voltaire's next stopping-place, to hold the poet in arrest until he delivered over the royal volume. A multitude of strange blunders and ludicrous incidents followed, upon which much controversial and patriotic ink has been spilt by a succession of French and German biographers. To an English reader it is clear that in this little comedy of errors none of the parties concerned can escape from blame – that Voltaire was hysterical, undignified, and untruthful, that the Prussian Resident was stupid and domineering, that Frederick was careless in his orders and cynical as to their results. Nor, it is to be hoped, need any Englishman be reminded that the consequences of a system of government in which the arbitrary will of an individual takes the place of the rule of law are apt to be disgraceful and absurd.

After five weeks' detention at Frankfort, Voltaire was free – free in every sense of the word – free from the service of Kings and the clutches of Residents, free in his own mind, free to shape his own destiny. He hesitated for several months, and then settled down by the Lake of Geneva. There the fires, which had lain smouldering so long in the profundities of his spirit, flared up, and flamed over Europe, towering and inextinguishable. In a few years letters began to flow once more to and from Berlin. At first the old grievances still rankled; but in time even the wrongs of Maupertuis and the misadventures of Frankfort were almost forgotten. Twenty years passed, and the King of Prussia was submitting his verses as anxiously as ever to Voltaire, whose compliments and cajoleries were pouring out in their accustomed stream. But their relationship was no longer that of master and pupil, courtier and King; it was that of two independent and equal powers. Even Frederick the Great was forced to see at last in the Patriarch of Ferney something more than a monkey with a genius for French versification. He actually came to respect the author of *Akakia*, and to cherish his memory. 'Je lui fais tous les matins ma prière,' he told d'Alembert, when Voltaire had been two years in the grave; 'je lui dis, Divin Voltaire, *ora pro nobis*.'

1915

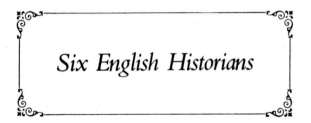

*Six English Historians*

# Hume

In what resides the most characteristic virtue of humanity? In good works? Possibly. In the creation of beautiful objects? Perhaps. But some would look in a different direction, and find it in detachment. To all such David Hume must be a great saint in the calendar; for no mortal being was ever more completely divested of the trammels of the personal and the particular, none ever practised with a more consummate success the divine art of impartiality. And certainly to have no axe to grind is something very noble and very rare. It may be said to be the antithesis of the bestial. A series of creatures might be constructed, arranged according to their diminishing interest in the immediate environment, which would begin with the amœba and end with the mathematician. In pure mathematics the maximum of detachment appears to be reached: the mind moves in an infinitely complicated pattern, which is absolutely free from temporal considerations. Yet this very freedom – the essential condition of the mathematician's activity – perhaps gives him an unfair advantage. He can only be wrong – he cannot cheat. But the metaphysician can. The problems with which he deals are of overwhelming importance to himself and the rest of humanity; and it is his business to treat them with an exactitude as unbiased as if they were some puzzle in the theory of numbers. That is his business – and his glory. In the mind of a Hume one can watch at one's ease this superhuman balance of contrasting opposites – the questions of so profound a moment, the answers of so supreme a calm. And the same beautiful quality may be traced in the current of his life, in which the wisdom of philosophy so triumphantly interpenetrated the vicissitudes of the mortal lot.

His history falls into three stages – youth, maturity, repose. The first was the most important. Had Hume died at the age of twenty-six his real work in the world would have been done, and his fame irrevocably established. Born in 1711, the younger son of a small Scottish landowner, he was very early dominated by that passion for literary pursuits which never left him for the rest of his life. When he was twenty-two one of those crises occurred – both physical and mental – which not uncommonly attack young men of genius when their adolescence is over, and determine the lines of their destiny. Hume was suddenly overcome by restlessness, ill-health, anxiety and hesitation. He left home, went to London, and then to Bristol, where, with the idea of making an independent fortune, he became a clerk in a merchant's office. 'But,' as he wrote long afterwards in his autobiography, 'in a few months I found that scene totally unsuitable to me.' No wonder; and then it was that, by a bold stroke of instinctive wisdom, he took the strange step which was the starting-point of his career. He went to France, where he remained for three years – first at Rheims, then at La Flèche, in Anjou – entirely alone, with only just money enough to support an extremely frugal existence, and with only the vaguest prospects before him. During those years he composed his *Treatise of Human Nature*, the masterpiece which contains all that is most important in his thought. The book opened a new era in philosophy. The last vestiges of theological prepossessions – which were still faintly visible in Descartes and Locke – were discarded; and reason, in all her strength and all her purity, came into her own. It is in the sense that Hume gives one of being committed absolutely to reason – of following wherever reason leads, with a complete, and even reckless confidence – that the great charm of his writing consists. But it is not only that: one is not alone; one is in the company of a supremely competent guide. With astonishing vigour, with hea-venly lucidity, Hume leads one through the confusion and the darkness of speculation. One has got into an aeroplane, which has glided imperceptibly from the ground; with thrilling ease one mounts and mounts; and, supported by the mighty power of intellect, one looks out, to see the world below one, as one has never seen it before. In the Treatise there is something that does not appear again in Hume's work – a feeling of excitement – the excitement of discovery. At moments he even hesitates, and stands back, amazed at his own temerity. 'The *intense* view of these manifold contradictions and imperfections in human reason has so wrought upon me, and heated my brain, that I am ready to reject all belief and reasoning, and can look upon no opinion even as more probable or likely than another. Where am I, or what? From what causes do I derive my existence, and to what condition shall I return? Whose favour shall I court, and whose anger must I dread? What beings surround me? and on whom have I any influence, or who have influence on me? I am confounded with all these questions, and begin to fancy myself in the most deplorable condition imaginable, environed with the deepest darkness, and utterly deprived of the use of every member and faculty.' And then his courage returns once more, and he speeds along on his exploration.

The Treatise, published in 1738, was a complete failure. For many years more Hume remained in poverty and insignificance. He eked out a living by precarious secretaryships, writing meanwhile a series of essays on philosophical, political and æsthetic subjects, which appeared from time to time in small volumes, and gradually brought him a certain reputation. It was not till he was over forty, when he was made librarian to the Faculty of Advocates in Edinburgh, that his position became secure. The appointment gave him not only a small competence, but the command of a large library; and he determined to write the history of England – a task which occupied him for the next ten years.

The History was a great success; many editions were printed; and in his own day it was chiefly as a historian that Hume was known to the general public. After his death his work continued for many years the standard history of England, until, with a new age, new fields of knowledge were opened up and a new style of historical writing became fashionable. The book is highly typical of the eighteenth century. It was an attempt – one of the very earliest – to apply intelligence to the events of the past. Hitherto, with very few exceptions (Bacon's *Henry the Seventh* was one of them) history had been in the hands of memoir writers like Commines and Clarendon, or moralists like Bossuet. Montesquieu, in his *Considérations sur les Romains*, had been the first to break the new ground; but his book, brilliant and weighty as it was, must be classed rather as a philosophical survey than a historical narration. Voltaire, almost exactly contemporary with Hume, was indeed a master of narrative, but was usually too much occupied with discrediting Christianity to be a satisfactory historian. Hume had no such *arrière pensée*; he only wished to tell the truth as he saw it, with clarity and elegance. And he succeeded. In his volumes – especially those on the Tudors and Stuarts – one may still find entertainment and even instruction. Hume was an extremely intelligent man, and anything that he had to say on English history could not fail to be worth attending to. But, unfortunately, mere intelligence is not itself quite enough to make a great historian. It was not simply that Hume's knowledge of his subjects was insufficient – that an enormous number of facts, which have come into view since he wrote, have made so many of his statements untrue and so many of his comments unmeaning; all that is serious, but is not more serious than the circumstance that his cast of mind was in reality ill-fitted for the task he had undertaken. The virtues of a metaphysician are the vices of a historian. A generalized, colourless, unimaginative view of things is admirable when one is considering the law of causality, but one needs something else if one has to describe Queen Elizabeth.

This fundamental weakness is materialized in the style of the History. Nothing could be more enchanting than Hume's style when he is discussing philosophical subjects. The grace and clarity of exquisite writing are enhanced by a touch of colloquialism – the tone of a polished conversation. A personality – a most engaging personality – just appears. The cat-like touches of ironic malice – hints of something very sharp behind the velvet – add to the effect. 'Nothing,' Hume concludes, after demolishing every argument in favour of the immortality of the soul, 'could set in a fuller light the infinite obligations which mankind have to divine revelation, since we find that no other medium could ascertain this great and important truth.' The sentence is characteristic of Hume's writing at its best, where the pungency of the sense varies in direct proportion with the mildness of the expression. But such effects are banished from the History. A certain formality, which Hume doubtless supposed was required by the dignity of the subject, is interposed between the reader and the author; an almost completely latinized vocabulary makes vividness impossible; and a habit of *oratio obliqua* has a deadening effect. We shall never know exactly what Henry the Second said – in some uncouth dialect of French or English – in his final exasperation against Thomas of Canterbury; but it was certainly something about 'a set of fools and cowards', and 'vengeance', and 'an upstart clerk'. Hume, however, preferred to describe the scene as follows: 'The King himself being vehemently agitated, burst forth with an exclamation against his servants, whose want of zeal, he said, had so long left him exposed to the enterprises of that ungrateful and imperious prelate.' Such phrasing, in conjunction with the Middle Ages, is comic. The more modern centuries seem to provide a more appropriate field for urbanity, aloofness and common sense. The measured cynicism of Hume's comments on Cromwell, for instance, still makes good reading – particularly as a corrective to the *O, altitudo!* sentimentalities of Carlyle.

Soon after his completion of the History Hume went to Paris as the secretary to the English Ambassador. He was now a celebrity, and French society fell upon him with delirious delight. He was flattered by princes, worshipped by fine ladies, and treated as an oracle by the *philosophes*. To such an extent did he become the fashion that it was at last positively *de rigueur* to have met him, and a lady who, it was discovered, had not even seen the great philosopher, was banished from Court. His appearance, so strangely out of keeping with mental agility, added to the fascination. 'His face,' wrote one of his friends, 'was broad and flat, his mouth wide, and without any other expression than that of imbecility. His eyes vacant and spiritless, and the corpulence of his whole person was far better fitted to communicate the idea of a turtle-eating alderman than of a refined philosopher.' All this was indeed delightful to the French. They loved to watch the awkward affability of the uncouth figure, to listen in rapt attention to the extraordinary French accent, and when, one evening, at a party, the adorable man appeared in a charade as a sultan between two lovely ladies and could only say, as he struck his chest, over and over again 'Eh bien, mesdemoiselles, eh bien, vous voilà donc!' their ecstasy reached its height. It seemed indeed almost impossible to believe in this combination of the outer and inner man. Even his own mother never got below the surface. 'Our Davie,' she is reported to have said, 'is a fine good-natured cratur, but uncommon wake-minded.' In no sense whatever was this true. Hume was not only brilliant as an abstract thinker and a writer; he was no less competent in the practical affairs of life. In the absence of the Ambassador he was left in Paris for some months as *chargé d'affaires*, and his despatches still exist to show that he understood diplomacy as well as ratiocination.

Entirely unmoved by the raptures of Paris, Hume returned to Edinburgh, at last a prosperous and wealthy man. For seven years he lived in his native capital, growing comfortably old amid leisure, books, and devoted friends. It is to this final period of his life that those pleasant legends belong which reveal the genial charm, the happy temperament, of the philosopher. There is the story of the tallow–chandler's wife, who arrived to deliver a monitory message from on High, but was diverted from her purpose by a tactful order for an enormous number of candles. There is the well-known tale of the weighty philosopher getting stuck in the boggy ground at the base of the Castle rock, and calling on a passing old woman to help him out. She doubted whether any help should be given to the author of the Essay on Miracles. 'But, my good woman, does not your religion as a Christian teach you to do good, even to your enemies?' 'That may be,' was the reply, 'but ye shallna get out of that till ye become a Christian yersell: and repeat the Lord's Prayer and the Belief' – a feat that was accomplished with astonishing alacrity. And there is the vision of the mountainous metaphysician seated, amid a laughing party of young ladies, on a chair that was too weak for him, and suddenly subsiding to the ground.

In 1776, when Hume was sixty-five, an internal complaint, to which he had long been subject, completely undermined his health, and recovery became impossible. For many months he knew he was dying, but his mode of life remained unaltered, and, while he gradually grew weaker, his cheerfulness continued unabated. With ease, with gaiety, with the simplicity of perfect taste, he gently welcomed the inevitable. This wonderful equanimity lasted till the very end. There was no ostentation of stoicism, much less any Addisonian dotting of death-bed i's. Not long before he died he amused himself by writing his autobiography – a model of pointed brevity. In one of his last conversations – it was with Adam Smith – he composed an imaginary conversation between himself and Charon, after the manner of Lucian: ' "Have a little patience, good Charon, I have been endeavouring to open the eyes of the Public. If I live a few years longer, I may have the satisfaction of seeing the downfall of some of the prevailing systems of superstition." But Charon would then lose all temper and decency. "You loitering rogue, that will not happen these many hundred years. Do you fancy I will grant you a lease for so long a term? Get into the boat this instant, you lazy, loitering rogue." ' Within a few days of his death he wrote a brief letter to his old friend, the Comtesse de Boufflers; it was the final expression of a supreme detachment. 'My disorder,' he said, 'is a diarrhœa, or disorder in my bowels, which has been gradually undermining me these two years; but, within these six months, has been visibly hastening me to my end. I see death approach gradually, without anxiety or regret. I salute you, with great affection and regard, for the last time.'

1928

# Gibbon

❦

Happiness is the word that immediately rises to the mind at the thought of Edward Gibbon: and happiness in its widest connotation – including good fortune as well as enjoyment. Good fortune, indeed, followed him from the cradle to the grave in the most tactful way possible; occasionally it appeared to fail him; but its absence always turned out to be a blessing in disguise. Out of a family of seven he alone had the luck to survive – but only with difficulty; and the maladies of his childhood opened his mind to the pleasures of study and literature. His mother died; but her place was taken by a devoted aunt, whose care brought him through the dangerous years of adolescence to a vigorous manhood. His misadventures at Oxford saved him from becoming a don. His exile to Lausanne, by giving him a command of the French language, initiated him into European culture, and at the same time enabled him to lay the foundations of his scholarship. His father married again; but his stepmother remained childless and became one of his dearest friends. He fell in love; the match was forbidden; and he escaped the dubious joys of domestic life with the future Madame Necker. While he was allowed to travel on the Continent, it seemed doubtful for some time whether his father would have the resources or the generosity to send him over the Alps into Italy. His fate hung in the balance; but at last his father produced the necessary five hundred pounds and, in the autumn of 1764, Rome saw her historian. His father died at exactly the right moment, and left him exactly the right amount of money. At the age of thirty-three Gibbon found himself his own master, with a fortune just sufficient to support him as an English gentleman of leisure and fashion. For ten years he lived in London, a member of Parliament, a placeman, and a diner-out, and during those ten years he produced the first three volumes of his History. After that he lost his place, failed to obtain another, and, finding his income unequal to his expenses, returned to Lausanne, where he took up his residence in the house of a friend, overlooking the Lake of Geneva. It was the final step in his career, and no less fortunate than all the others. In Lausanne he was rich once more, he was famous, he enjoyed a delightful combination of retirement and society. Before another ten years were out he had completed his History; and in ease, dignity, and absolute satisfaction his work in this world was accomplished.

One sees in such a life an epitome of the blessings of the eighteenth century – the wonderful μηδὲν ἄγαν of that most balmy time – the rich fruit ripening slowly on the sun-warmed wall, and coming inevitably to its delicious perfection. It is difficult to imagine, at any other period in history, such a combination of varied qualities, so beautifully balanced – the profound scholar who was also a brilliant man of the world – the votary of cosmopolitan culture, who never for a moment ceased to be a supremely English 'character'. The ten years of Gibbon's life in London afford an astonishing spectacle of interacting energies. By what strange power did he succeed in producing a masterpiece of enormous erudition and perfect form, while he was leading the gay life of a man about town, spending his evenings at White's or Boodle's or the Club, attending Parliament, oscillating between his house in Bentinck Street, his country cottage at Hampton Court, and his little establishment at Brighton, spending his summers in Bath or Paris, and even, at odd moments, doing a little work at the Board of Trade, to show that his place was not entirely a sinecure? Such a triumph could only have been achieved by the sweet reasonableness of the eighteenth century. 'Monsieur Gibbon n'est point mon homme,' said Rousseau. Decidedly! The prophet of the coming age of sentiment and romance could have nothing in common with such a nature. It was not that the historian was a mere frigid observer of the golden mean – far from it. He was full of fire and feeling. His youth had been at moments riotous – night after night he had reeled hallooing down St. James's Street. Old age did not diminish the natural warmth of his affections; the beautiful letter – a model of its kind – written on the death of his aunt, in his fiftieth year, is a proof of it. But the fire and the feeling were controlled and co-ordinated. Boswell was a Rousseau-ite, one of the first of the

Romantics, an inveterate sentimentalist, and nothing could be more complete than the contrast between his career and Gibbon's. He, too, achieved a glorious triumph; but it was by dint of the sheer force of native genius asserting itself over the extravagance and disorder of an agitated life – a life which, after a desperate struggle, seemed to end at last in darkness and shipwreck. With Gibbon there was never any struggle: everything came naturally to him – learning and dissipation, industry and indolence, affection and scepticism – in the correct proportions; and he enjoyed himself up to the very end.

To complete the picture one must notice another antithesis: the wit, the genius, the massive intellect, were housed in a physical mould that was ridiculous. A little figue, extraordinarily rotund, met the eye, surmounted by a top-heavy head, with a button nose, planted amid a vast expanse of cheek and ear, and chin upon chin rolling downward. Nor was this appearance only; the odd shape reflected something in the inner man. Mr Gibbon, it was noticed, was always slightly over-dressed; his favourite wear was flowered velvet. He was a little vain, a little pompous; at the first moment one almost laughed; then one forgot everything under the fascination of that even flow of admirably intelligent, exquisitely turned, and most amusing sentences. Among all his other merits this obviously ludicrous egotism took its place. The astonishing creature was able to make a virtue even of absurdity. Without that touch of nature he would have run the risk of being too much of a good thing; as it was there was no such danger; he was preposterous and a human being.

It is not difficult to envisage the character and figure; what seems strange, and remote, and hard to grasp is the connection between this individual and the decline and fall of the Roman Empire. The paradox, indeed, is so complete as to be almost romantic. At a given moment – October 15, 1764 – at a given place – the Capitoline Hill, outside the church of Aracoeli – the impact occurred between the serried centuries of Rome and Edward Gibbon. His life, his work, his fame, his place in the history of civilization, followed from that circumstance. The point of his achievement lay precisely in the extreme improbability of it. The utter incongruity of those combining elements produced the masterpiece – the gigantic ruin of Europe through a thousand years, mirrored in the mind of an eighteenth-century English gentleman.

How was the miracle accomplished? Needless to say, Gibbon was a great artist – one of those rare spirits, with whom a vital and penetrating imagination and a supreme capacity for general conceptions express themselves instinctively in an appropriate form. That the question has ever been not only asked but seriously debated, whether History was an art, is certainly one of the curiosities of human ineptitude. What else can it possibly be? It is obvious that History is not a science: it is obvious that History is not the accumulation of facts, but the relation of them. Only the pedantry of incomplete academic persons could have given birth to such a monstrous supposition. Facts relating to the past, when they are collected without art, are compilations; and compilations, no doubt, may be useful; but they are no more History than butter, eggs, salt and herbs are an omelette. That Gibbon was a great artist, therefore, is implied in the statement that he was a great historian; but what is interesting is the particular nature of his artistry. His whole genius was pre-eminently classical; order, lucidity, balance, precision – the great classical qualities – dominate his work; and his History is chiefly remarkable as one of the supreme monuments of Classic Art in European literature.

'L'ordre est ce qu'il y a de plus rare dans les opérations de l'esprit.' Gibbon's work is a magnificent illustration of the splendid dictum of Fénelon. He brought order out of the enormous chaos of his subject – a truly stupendous achievement! With characteristic good fortune, indeed, the material with which he had to cope was still just not too voluminous to be digested by a single extremely competent mind. In the following century even a Gibbon would have collapsed under the accumulated mass of knowledge at his disposal. As it was, by dint of a superb constructive vision, a serene self-confidence, a very acute judgment, and an astonishing facility in the manipulation of material, he was able to dominate the known facts. To dominate, nothing more; anything else would have been foreign to his purpose. He was a classicist; and his object was not comprehension but illumination. He drove a straight, firm road through the vast unexplored forest of Roman history; his readers could follow with easy pleasure along the wonderful way; they might glance, as far as their eyes could reach, into the entangled recesses on either side of them; but they were not invited to stop, or wander, or camp out, or make friends with the natives; they must be content to look and to pass on.

It is clear that Gibbon's central problem was the one of exclusion: how much, and what, was he to leave out? This was largely a question of scale – always one of the major difficulties in literary composition – and it appears from several passages in the Autobiographies that Gibbon paid particular attention to it. Incidentally, it may be observed that the six Autobiographies were not so much excursions in egotism – though no doubt it is true that Gibbon was not without a certain fondness for what he himself called 'the most disgusting of the pronouns' – as exercises on the theme of scale. Every variety of compression and expansion is visible among those remarkable pages; but apparently, since the manuscripts were left in an unfinished state, Gibbon still felt, after the sixth attempt, that he had not discovered the right solution. Even with the scale of the History he was not altogether satisfied; the chapters on Christianity, he thought, might, with further labour, have been considerably reduced. But, even more fundamental than the element of scale, there was something else that, in reality, conditioned the whole treatment of his material, the whole scope and nature of his History; and that was the style in which it was written. The style once fixed, everything else followed. Gibbon was well aware of this. He wrote his first chapter three times over, his second and third twice; then at last he was satisfied, and after that he wrote on without a hitch. In particular the problem of exclusion was solved. Gibbon's style is probably the most exclusive in literature. By its very nature it bars out a great multitude of human energies. It makes sympathy impossible, it takes no cognizance of passion, it turns its back upon religion with a withering smile. But that was just what was wanted. Classic beauty came instead. By the penetrating influence of style – automatically, inevitably – lucidity, balance and precision were everywhere introduced; and the miracle of order was established over the chaos of a thousand years.

Of course, the Romantics raised a protest. 'Gibbon's style,' said Coleridge, 'is detestable; but,' he added, 'it is not the worst thing about him.' Critics of the later nineteenth century were less consistent. They admired Gibbon for everything except his style, imagining that his History would have been much improved if it had been written in some other way; they did not see that, if it had been written in any other way, it would have ceased to exist; just as St. Paul's would cease to exist if it were rebuilt in Gothic. Obsessed by the colour and movement of romantic prose, they were blind to the subtlety, the clarity, the continuous strength of Gibbon's writing. Gibbon could turn a bold phrase with the best of them – 'the fat slumbers of the Church', for instance – if he wanted to: but he very rarely wanted to; such effects would have disturbed the easy, close-knit, homogeneous surface of his work. His use of words is, in fact, extremely delicate. When, describing St. Simeon Stylites on his pillar, he speaks of 'this last and lofty station', he succeeds, with the least possible emphasis, merely by the combination of those two alliterative epithets with that particular substantive, in making the whole affair ridiculous. One can almost see his shoulders shrug. The nineteenth century found him pompous; they did not relish the irony beneath the pomp. He produces some of his most delightful effects by rhythm alone. In the *Vindication* – a work which deserves to be better known, for it shows us Gibbon, as one sees him nowhere else, really letting himself go – there is an admirable example of this. 'I still think,' he says, in reply to a criticism by Dr Randolph, 'I still think that an hundred Bishops, with Athanasius at their head, were as competent judges of the discipline of the fourth century, as even the Lady Margaret's Professor of Divinity in the University of Oxford.' Gibbon's irony, no doubt, is the salt of his work; but, like all irony, it is the product of style. It was not for nothing that he read through every year the *Lettres Provinciales* of Pascal. From this point of view it is interesting to compare him with Voltaire. The irony of the great Frenchman was a flashing sword – extreme, virulent, deadly – a terrific instrument of propaganda. Gibbon uses the weapon with far more delicacy; he carves his enemy 'as a dish fit for the Gods'; his mocking is aloof, almost indifferent, and perhaps, in the long run, for that very reason, even more effective.

At every period of his life Gibbon is a pleasant thing to contemplate, but perhaps most pleasant of all in the closing weeks of it, during his last visit to England. He had hurried home from Lausanne to join his friend Lord Sheffield, whose wife had died suddenly, and who, he felt, was in need of his company. The journey was no small proof of his affectionate nature; old age was approaching; he was corpulent, gouty, and accustomed to every comfort; and the war of the French Revolution was raging in the districts through which he had to pass. But he did not hesitate, and after skirting the belligerent armies in his chaise, arrived safely in England. After visiting Lord Sheffield he proceeded to Bath, to stay with his stepmother. The amazing little figure, now almost spherical, bowled along the Bath Road in the highest state of exhilaration. 'I am always,' he told his friend, 'so much delighted and improved with this union of ease and motion, that, were not the expense enormous, I would travel every year some hundred miles, more especially in England.' Mrs Gibbon, a very old lady, but still full of vitality, worshipped her stepson, and the two spent ten days together, talking, almost always *tête-à-tête*, for ten hours a day. Then the historian went off to Althorpe, where he spent a happy morning with Lord Spencer, looking at early editions of Cicero. And so back to London. In London a little trouble arose. A protuberance in the lower part of his person, which, owing to years of characteristic *insouciance*, had grown to extraordinary proportions, required attention; an operation was necessary; but it went off well, and there seemed to be no danger. Once more Mr Gibbon dined out. Once more he was seen, in his accustomed attitude, with advanced forefinger, addressing the company, and rapping his snuff box at the close of each particularly pointed phrase. But illness came on again – nothing very serious. The great man lay in bed discussing how much longer he would live – he was fifty-six – ten years, twelve years, or perhaps twenty. He ate some chicken and drank three glasses of madeira. Life seemed almost as charming as usual. Next morning, getting out of bed for a necessary moment, 'Je suis plus adroit,' he said with his odd smile to his French valet. Back in bed again, he muttered something more, a little incoherently, lay back among the pillows, dozed, half-woke, dozed again, and became unconscious – for ever.

1928

# Macaulay

In Apollo's house there are many mansions; there is even one (unexpectedly enough) for the Philistine. So complex and various are the elements of literature that no writer can be damned on a mere enumeration of faults. He may always possess merits which make up for everything; if he loses on the swings, he may win on the roundabouts. Macaulay – whatever the refined and the sublime may say to the contrary – is an example of this. A coarse texture of mind – a metallic style – an itch for the obvious and the emphatic – a middle-class, Victorian complacency – it is all too true; Philistine is, in fact, the only word to fit the case; and yet, by dint of sheer power of writing, the Philistine has reached Parnassus. It is a curious occurrence, and deserves a closer examination.

What are the qualities that make a historian? Obviously these three – a capacity for absorbing facts, a capacity for stating them, and a point of view. The two latter are connected, but not necessarily inseparable. The late Professor Samuel Gardiner, for instance, could absorb facts, and he could state them; but he had no point of view; and the result is that his book on the most exciting period of English history resembles nothing so much as a very large heap of sawdust. But a point of view, it must be remembered, by no means implies sympathy. One might almost say that it implies the reverse. At any rate it is curious to observe how many instances there are of great historians who have been at daggers drawn with their subjects. Gibbon, a highly civilized scoffer, spent twenty years of his life writing about barbarism and superstition. Michelet was a romantic and a republican; but his work on medieval France and the Revolution is far inferior to his magnificent delineation of the classic and despotic centuries. Macaulay's great-nephew, Professor Trevelyan, has, it is true, written a delightful account of the Italian Risorgimento, of which he is an enthusiastic devotee. But, even here, the rule seems to apply; one cannot but feel that Professor Trevelyan's epic would have been still more delightful if it had contained a little of the salt of criticism – if, in fact, he had not swallowed Garibaldi whole.

As for Macaulay's point of view, everyone knows it was the Whig one. In reality this is simplifying too much; but, however we may describe it, there can be no doubt that Macaulay's vision was singularly alien to the England of the latter years of the seventeenth century. Like Gibbon, like Michelet, like the later Carlyle, he did not – to put it succinctly – understand what he was talking about. Charles II, James II – that whole strange age in which religion, debauchery, intellect, faction, wit and brutality seethed and bubbled together in such an extraordinary *olla podrida* – escaped him. He could see parts of it; but he could not see into the depths; and so much the better: he had his point of view. The definiteness, the fixity, of his position is what is remarkable. He seems to have been created *en bloc*. His manner never changed; as soon as he could write at all – at the age of eight – he wrote in the style of his History. The three main factors in his mental growth – the Clapham sect, Cambridge, Holland House – were not so much influences as suitable environments for the development of a predetermined personality. Whatever had happened to him, he would always have been a middle-class intellectual with Whig views. It is possible, however, that he may actually have gained something from Holland House. The modern habit of gently laughing at Whigs and Whiggery is based on a misconception. A certain *a priori* stuffiness which seems to hang about that atmosphere is in reality a Victorian innovation. The true pre-Reform Bill Whig was a tremendous aristocrat – the heir to a great tradition of intellectual independence and spiritual pride. When the Hollands' son travelled as a youth in Italy he calmly noted in his diary that someone he had met had a face 'almost as stupid as the Duke of Wellington's'; the young Fox was a chip of the old block. Such surroundings must have been good for Macaulay. It was not only that they supported his self-confidence – he had enough of that already – but that they brought him into touch with the severity, the grandeur, and the amenity of an old civilization. Without them he might have been provincial or academic; but he was not so; on every page of his work one sees the manifest signs of the culture and the traffic of the great world.

Thus Macaulay's Whiggism was a composite affair – it was partly eighteenth-century and partly Victorian. But the completeness with which it dominated him gave him his certainty of attitude and his clarity of vision. It enabled him to stand up against the confusion and frenzy of the seventeenth century and say, very loudly and very distinctly, what he thought of it. So far so good. The misfortune is that what he thought was not of a finer quality. The point of view is distinct enough, but it is without distinction; and Macaulay in consequence remains an excellent but not a supreme historian. His Whiggism was in itself a very serious drawback – not because it was a cause of bias, but because it was a symptom of crudity. The bias was of the wrong kind; it was the outcome of party politics, and the sad truth is that, in the long run, party politics become a bore. They did not, indeed, succeed in making Macaulay a bore; that was impossible; but, though he is never dull, one constantly feels that he might have been much more interesting. Too often he misses the really exciting, the really fascinating, point. And how can one fail to miss a great deal if one persists in considering the world from one side or other of the House of Commons?

A certain crudity, a certain coarseness of fibre – the marks of a party politician – are particularly obvious in those character sketches of great persons which form so important a part of Macaulay's History. Within their limits they are admirably done; but their limits are too narrow. They lack colour; they are steel engravings – unsatisfactory compromises between a portrait in oils and a realistic snapshot. One has only to compare them with Clarendon's splendid presentments to realize their inadequacy. With what a gorgeous sinuosity, with what a grandiose delicacy, the older master elaborates, through his enormous sentences, the lineaments of a soul! Beside them the skimpy lines and cheap contrasts of Macaulay's black and white are all too obvious.

But the Whig politician was not only crude; he was also, to a strange degree, ingenuous and complacent. A preposterous optimism fills his pages. The Revolution of 1688 having succeeded, all was well; Utopia was bound to follow; and it actually had followed – in the reign of Victoria. Thus he contrasts with delight, almost with awe, the state of Torbay at the time of William's landing and its condition in 1850. In 1688 'the huts of ploughmen and fishermen were thinly scattered over what is now the site of crowded marts and of luxurious pavilions'. A description of the modern Torquay becomes irresistible. 'The inhabitants are about ten thousand in number. The newly-built churches and chapels, the baths and libraries, the hotels and public gardens, the infirmary and the museum, the white streets, rising terrace above terrace, the gay villas peeping from the midst of shrubberies and flower beds, present a spectacle widely different from any that in the seventeenth century England could show.' They do indeed.

The style is the mirror of the mind, and Macaulay's style is that of a debater. The hard points are driven home like nails with unfailing dexterity; it is useless to hope for subtlety or refinement; one cannot hammer with delicacy. The repetitions, the antitheses, resemble revolving cog-wheels; and indeed the total result produces an effect which suggests the operations of a machine more than anything else – a comparison which, no doubt, would have delighted Macaulay. The descriptive passages are the most deplorable. In a set-piece, such as the account of Westminster Hall at the impeachment of Hastings, all the horrors of a remorseless rhetoric are made manifest. From the time of Cicero downwards, the great disadvantage of oratory has been that it never lets one off. One must hear everything, however well one knows it, and however obvious it is. For such writers a dose of Stendhal is to be recommended. Macaulay, however, would not have benefited by the prescription, for he was a hopeless case. The tonic pages of the *Chartreuse de Parme* would have had no effect on him whatever. When he wished to state that Schomberg was buried in Westminster Abbey, he *had* to say that 'the illustrious warrior' was laid in 'that venerable abbey, hallowed by the dust of many generations of princes, heroes and poets'. There is no escaping it; and the incidental drawback that Schomberg was not buried at Westminster at all, but in Dublin, is, in comparison with the platitude of the style, of very small importance.

The curiously metallic quality in Macaulay's writing – its hardness of outline, its slightly hollow ring – is so characteristic that it is difficult not to see in it the indication of some profound psychological state. The stout, square man with the prodigious memory and the inexhaustible capacity for conversation, was apparently a normal human being, except in one direction: he never married, and there seems no reason to suppose that he was ever in love. An entertaining essay might perhaps be written on the sexlessness of historians; but it would be entertaining and nothing more: we do not know enough either about the historians or sex. Yet, in Macaulay's case, one cannot resist the conclusion that the absence from his make-up of intense physical emotion brought a barrenness upon his style. His sentences have no warmth and no curves; the embracing fluidity of love is lacking. And it is noticeable how far more effective he is in his treatment of those whom he dislikes than of those whom he admires. His Marlborough is a fine villain. His James II is a caricature, with a queer vitality of its own – the vitality of a marionette. But his William of Orange is a failure – a lifeless image of waxwork perfection. Macaulay's inability to make his hero live – his refusal to make any attempt to illuminate the mysteries of that most obscure and singular character – epitomizes all that is weakest in his work.

Probably the futility of his aesthetic judgments was another effect of the same cause. Whenever he writes of pure poetry – in the essay on Byron, for instance – he is plainly at sea; his lack of sensibility becomes painfully obvious. A true child of his age, he had a profound distrust, amounting at times to an actual hatred, of art. That Queen Mary should have ruined her father, turned him out of his kingdon, and seized his throne for herself – all that was no blemish at all on her character: was she not acting upon strictly Whig principles? But one fault she did have. She was responsible for 'a frivolous and inelegant fashion'. She was the first person in England to form 'a vast collection of hideous images, and of vases on which houses, trees, bridges and mandarins were depicted in outrageous defiance of all the laws of perspective'. Queen Mary, in fact, liked china; and that could not be forgiven her.

The weaknesses are obvious, and the strength, suitably enough, is obvious too. History is primarily a narrative, and in power of narration no one has ever surpassed Macaulay. In that he is a genius. When it comes to telling a story, his faults disappear or change into virtues. Narrowness becomes clarity, and crudity turns into force. The rhetoric of the style, from being the ornament of platitude, becomes the servant of excitement. Every word is valuable: there is no hesitation, no confusion, and no waste. It is clear from his journal that Macaulay realized the dominating importance of this side of his work. He laboured at his purely narrative passages for weeks at a time, with the result that they are masterpieces. Nobody who has once read them can ever forget his account of the trial of the Bishops, the siege of Derry, and the battle of Killiecrankie. To write so is to write magnificently, and if one has to be a Philistine to bring off those particular effects one can only say, so much the better for the Philistine. But it is not only in certain passages that Macaulay triumphs. His whole History is conditioned by a supreme sense of the narrative form. It presses on, with masterly precipitation, from start to finish. Everything falls into place. Unsatisfying characters, superficial descriptions, jejune reflections, are seen to be no longer of importance in themselves – they are merely stages in the development of the narrative. They are part of the pattern – the enthralling, ever-shifting pattern of the perfect kaleidoscope. A work of art? Yes, there is no denying it: the Philistine was also an artist. And there he is – squat, square and perpetually talking – on Parnassus.

1928

# Carlyle

My grandfather, Edward Strachey, an Anglo-Indian of cultivation and intelligence, once accompanied Carlyle on an excursion to Paris in pre-railroad days. At their destination the postilion asked my grandfather for a tip; but the reply – it is Carlyle who tells the story – was a curt refusal, followed by the words – 'Vous avez drivé devilish slow.' The reckless insularity of this remark illustrates well enough the extraordinary change which had come over the English governing classes since the eighteenth century. Fifty years earlier a cultivated Englishman would have piqued himself upon answering the postilion in the idiom and the accent of Paris. But the Napoleonic wars, the industrial revolution, the romantic revival, the Victorian spirit, had brought about a relapse from the cosmopolitan suavity of eighteenth-century culture; the centrifugal forces, always latent in English life, had triumphed, and men's minds had shot off into the grooves of eccentricity and provincialism. It is curious to notice the flux and reflux of these tendencies in the history of our literature: the divine amenity of Chaucer followed by the no less divine idiosyncrasy of the Elizabethans; the exquisite vigour of the eighteenth century followed by the rampant vigour of the nineteenth; and today the return once more towards the Latin elements in our culture, the revulsion from the Germanic influences which obsessed our grandfathers, the preference for what is swift, what is well arranged, and what is not too good.

Carlyle was not an English gentleman, he was a Scotch peasant; and his insularity may be measured accordingly – by a simple sum in proportion. In his youth, no doubt, he had German preoccupations; but on the whole he is, with Dickens, probably the most complete example of a home growth which the British Islands have to offer to the world. The result is certainly remarkable. There is much to be said for the isolated productions of special soils; they are full of strength and character; their freedom from outside forces releases in them a spring of energy which leads, often enough, to astonishing consequences. In Carlyle's case the release was terrific. His vitality burst out into an enormous exuberance, filling volume after volume with essays, histories, memoirs and philosophizings, pouring itself abroad through an immense correspondence, and erupting for eighty years in a perpetual flood of red-hot conversation. The achievements of such a spirit take one's breath away; one gazes in awe at the serried row of heavy books on the shelf; one reads on and on until one's eyes are blinded by the endless glare of that aurora borealis, and one's ears deafened by the roar and rattle of that inexhaustible artillery. Then one recovers – very quickly. That is the drawback. The northern lights, after all, seen to give out no heat, and the great guns were only loaded with powder. So, at any rate, it appears to a perverse generation. It was all very well in the days when English gentlemen could say with perfect sang-froid 'Vous avez drivé devilish slow' to French postilions. Then the hurricane that was Carlyle came into contact with what was exactly appropriate to it – gnarled oaks – solitary conifers; and the effect was sublime; leaves whirled, branches crashed, and fathers of the forest were uprooted. But nowadays it hurls itself upon a congregation of tremulous reeds; they bend down low, to the very earth, as the gale passes; and then immediately they spring up again, and are seen to be precisely as they were before.

The truth is that it is almost as fatal to have too much genius as too little. What was really valuable in Carlyle was ruined by his colossal powers and his unending energy. It is easy to perceive that, amid all the rest of his qualities, he was an artist. He had a profound relish for words; he had a sense of style which developed, gradually and consistently, into interesting and original manifestations; he had an imaginative eye; he had a grim satiric humour. This was an admirable outfit for a historian and a memoir writer, and it is safe to prophesy that whatever is permanent in Carlyle's work will be found in that section of his writings. But, unfortunately, the excellence, though it is undoubtedly there, is a fitful and fragmentary one. There are vivid flashes – visions thrown up out of the darkness of the past by the bull's-eye lantern of a stylistic imagination – Coleridge at Highgate, Maupertuis in Berlin, the grotesque image of the 'sea-green Incorruptible'; there are passages of accomplished caricature, and climaxes of elaborately characteristic writing; and then the artist's hand falters, his eye wanders, his mind is distracted and led away. One has only to compare Carlyle with Tacitus to realize what a disadvantage it is to possess unlimited powers. The Roman master, undisturbed by other considerations, was able to devote himself entirely to the creation of a work of art. He triumphed: supremely conscious both of his capacities and his intentions, he built up a great design, which in all its parts was intense and beautiful. The Carlylean qualities – the satiric vision, the individual style – were his; but how differently he used them! He composed a tragedy, while Carlyle spent himself in melodrama; he made his strange sentences the expression of a profound personality, while Carlyle's were the vehicle of violence and eccentricity.

The stern child of Ecclefechan held artists in low repute, and no doubt would have been disgusted to learn that it was in that guise that he would win the esteem of posterity. He had higher views: surely he would be remembered as a prophet. And no doubt he had many of the qualifications for that profession – a loud voice, a bold face, and a bad temper. But unfortunately there was one essential characteristic that he lacked – he was not dishonoured in his own country. Instead of being put into a pit and covered with opprobrium, he made a comfortable income, was supplied by Mrs Carlyle with everything that he wanted, and was the favourite guest at Lady Ashburton's fashionable parties. Prophecies, in such circumstances, however voluminous and disagreeable they may be, are apt to have something wrong with them. And, in any case, who remembers prophets? Isaiah and Jeremiah, no doubt, have gained a certain reputation; but then Isaiah and Jeremiah have had the extraordinary good fortune to be translated into English by a committee of Elizabethan bishops.

To be a prophet is to be a moralist, and it was the moral preoccupation in Carlyle's mind that was particularly injurious to his artistic instincts. In Latin countries – the fact is significant – morals and manners are expressed by the same word; in England it is not so; to some Britons, indeed, the two notions appear to be positively antithetical. Perhaps this is a mistake. Perhaps if Carlyle's manners had been more polished his morals would have been less distressing. Morality, curiously enough, seems to belong to that class of things which are of the highest value, which perform a necessary function, which are, in fact, an essential part of the human mechanism, but which should only be referred to with the greatest circumspection. Carlyle had no notion that this was the case, and the result was disastrous. In his history, especially, it is impossible to escape from the devastating effects of his reckless moral sense.

Perhaps it is the platitude of such a state of mind that is its most exasperating quality. Surely, one thinks, poor Louis XV might be allowed to die without a sermon from Chelsea. But no! The opportunity must not be missed; the preacher draws a long breath, and expatiates with elaborate emphasis upon all that is most obvious about mortality, crowns, and the futility of self-indulgence. But an occasional platitude can be put up with; what is really intolerable is the all-pervadingness of the obsession. There are some German cooks who have a passion for caraway seeds: whatever dish they are preparing, from whipped cream to legs of mutton, they cannot keep them out. Very soon one begins to recognize the fatal flavour; one lies in horrified wait for it; it instantly appears; and at last the faintest suspicion of caraway almost produces nausea. The histories of Carlyle (and no less, it may be observed in passing, the novels of Thackeray) arouse those identical sensations – the immediate recognition of the first approaches of the well-known whiff – the inevitable saturation – the heart that sinks and sinks. And, just as one feels that the cook was a good cook, and that the dish would have been done to a turn if only the caraway canister could have been kept out of reach, so one perceives that Carlyle had a true gift for history which was undone by his moralizations. There is an imaginative greatness in his conception of Cromwell, for instance, a vigour and a passion in the presentment of it; but all is spoilt by an overmastering desire to turn the strange Protector into a moral hero after Carlyle's own heart, so that, after all, the lines are blurred, the composition is confused, the picture unconvincing.

But the most curious consequence of this predilection is to be seen in his Frederick the Great. In his later days Carlyle evolved a kind of super-morality by which all the most unpleasant qualities of human nature – egotism, insensitiveness, love of power – became the object of his religious adoration – a monstrous and inverted ethic, combining every possible disadvantage of virtue and of vice. He then, for some mysterious reason, pitched upon Frederick of Prussia as the great exemplar of this system, and devoted fourteen years of ceaseless labour to the elucidation of his history. Never was a misconception more complete. Frederick was in reality a knave of genius, a sceptical, eighteenth-century gambler with a strong will and a turn for organization; and this was the creature whom Carlyle converted into an Ideal Man, a God-like Hero, a chosen instrument of the Eternal Powers. What the Eternal Powers would have done if a stray bullet had gone through Frederick's skull in the battle of Molwitz, Carlyle does not stop to inquire. By an ironical chance there happened to be two attractive elements in Frederick's mental outfit; he had a genuine passion for French literature, and he possessed a certain scurrilous wit, which constantly expressed itself in extremely truculent fashion. Fate could not have selected two more unfortunate qualities with which to grace a hero of Carlyle's. Carlyle considered French literature trash; and the kind of joke that Frederick particularly relished filled him with profound aversion. A copy of Frederick's collected works still exists, with Carlyle's pencilled annotations in the margin. Some of the King's poetical compositions are far from proper; and it is amusing to observe the historian's exclamations of agitated regret whenever the Ideal Man alludes, as in some mocking epigram, to his own or his friends' favourite peccadilloes. One can imagine, if Frederick were to return to earth for a moment and look over one's shoulder, his grin of fiendish delight.

The cruel Hohenzollern would certainly have laughed; but to gentler beings the spectacle of so much effort gone so utterly awry seems rather a matter for lamentation. The comedy of Carlyle's case topples over into tragedy – a tragedy of waste and unhappiness. If only he could have enjoyed himself! But he never did. Is it possible, one wonders, to bring forth anything that is worth bringing forth, without some pleasure – whatever pains there may be as well – in the parturition? One remembers Gibbon, cleaving his way, with such a magisterial gaiety, through the Decline and Fall of the Roman Empire. He, too, no doubt, understood very little of his subject; but all was well with him and with his work. Why was it? The answer seems to be – he understood something that, for his purposes, was more important even than the Roman

Empire – himself. He knew his own nature, his powers, his limitations, his desires; he was the master of an inward harmony. From Carlyle such knowledge was hidden. Blindness is always tragic; but the blindness that brings mighty strength to baffled violence, towering aspirations to empty visions, and sublime self-confidence to bewilderment, remorse and misery, is terrible and pitiable indeed.

Unfortunately it was not only upon Carlyle himself that the doom descended. A woman of rare charm and brilliant powers was involved in his evil destiny. Regardless both of the demands of her temperament and the qualities of her spirit, he used her without scruple to subserve his own purposes, and made her as wretched as himself. She was his wife, and that was the end of the matter. She might have become a consummate writer or the ruler and inspirer of some fortunate social group; but all that was out of the question; was she not Mrs Carlyle? It was her business to suppress her own instincts, to devote her whole life to the arrangement of his domestic comforts, to listen for days at a time, as she lay racked with illness on the sofa, to his descriptions of the battles of Frederick the Great. The time came when she felt that she could bear it no longer, and that at all hazards she must free herself from those stifling bonds. It is impossible not to wish that she had indeed fled as she intended with the unknown man of her choice. The blow to Carlyle's egoism would have been so dramatic, and the upheaval in that well-conducted world so satisfactory to contemplate! But, at the last moment, she changed her mind. Curiously enough, when it came to the point, it turned out that Mrs Carlyle agreed with her husband. Even that bold spirit succumbed to the influences that surrounded it; she, too, was a mid-Victorian at heart. The woman's tragedy may be traced in those inimitable letters, whose intoxicating merriment flashes like lightning about the central figure, as it moves in sinister desolation against the background of a most peculiar age: an age of barbarism and prudery, of nobility and cheapness, of satisfaction and desperation; an age in which everything was discovered and nothing known; an age in which all the outlines were tremendous and all the details sordid; when gas-jets struggled feebly through the circumambient fog, when the hour of dinner might be at any moment between two and six, when the doses of rhubarb were periodic and gigantic, when pet dogs threw themselves out of upper storey windows, when cooks reeled drunk in areas, when one sat for hours with one's feet in dirty straw dragged along the streets by horses, when an antimacassar was on every chair, and the baths were minute tin circles, and the beds were full of bugs and disasters.

After it was all over and his wife was dead, Carlyle realized what had happened. But all that he could do was to take refuge from the truth in the vain vehemence of sentimental self-reproaches. He committed his confessions to Froude without sufficient instructions; and when he died he left behind him a legacy of doubt and scandal. But now, at length, some enjoyment appeared upon the scene. No one was happier than Froude, with an agitated conscience and a sense of duty that involved the divulgation of dreadful domesticities; while the Victorian public feasted upon the unexpected banquet to its heart's content.

1928

# Froude

❦

James Anthony Froude was one of the salient figures of mid-Victorian England. In that society of prepotent personages he more than held his own. He was not merely the author of the famous *History*; he was a man of letters who was also a man of the world, an accomplished gentleman, whose rich nature overflowed with abounding energy, a sportsman, a yachtsman, a brilliant and magnificent talker – and something more: one in whose presence it was impossible not to feel a hint of mystery, of strange melancholy, an uncomfortable suggestion of enigmatic power. His most impressive appearance completed the effect: the height, the long, pale face, the massive, vigorous features, the black hair and eyebrows, and the immense eyes, with their glowing darkness, whose colour – so a careful observer noted – was neither brown, nor blue, nor black, but red. What was the explanation of it all? What was the inner cause of this *brio* and this sadness, this passionate earnestness and this sardonic wit? One wonders, as his after-dinner listeners used to wonder, in the 'sixties, with a little shiver, while the port went round, and the ladies waited in the drawing-room.

Perhaps it is easier for us than for them to make, at any rate, a guess; for we know more of the facts, and we have our modern psychology to give us confidence. Perhaps the real explanation was old Mr Froude, who was a hunting parson of a severely conventional type, with a marked talent for water-colours. Mrs Froude had died early, leaving the boy to be brought up by this iron-bound clergyman and some brothers much older than himself. His childhood was wretched, his boyhood was frightful. He was sent, ill and overgrown, to college at Westminster, and there – it was, as the biographers dutifully point out, in the bad old days before the influence of Dr Arnold had turned the Public Schools into models of industry and civilized behaviour – he

106

suffered, for two years, indescribable torment. He was removed in disgrace, flogged by his father for imaginary delinquencies, and kept at home for two years more in the condition of an outcast. His eldest brother, Hurrell, who was one of the leaders in the new fashion of taking Christianity seriously, and mortified his own flesh by eating fish on Fridays, egged on the parental discipline with pious glee. At last, grown too old for castigation, the lad was allowed to go to Oxford. There, for the first time in his life, he began to enjoy himself, and became engaged to an attractive young lady. But he had run up bills with the Oxford tradesmen, had told his father they were less than they were, the facts had come out, and old Mr Froude, declaring that his son was little better than a common swindler, denounced him as such to the young lady's father, who thereupon broke off the engagement. It seems surprising that Anthony resisted the temptation of suicide – that he had the strength and the courage to outface his misfortunes, to make a career for himself and become a highly successful man. What is more surprising is that his attitude towards his father never ceased, from first to last, to be one of intense admiration. He might struggle, he might complain, he might react, but he always, with a strange overpowering instinctiveness, adored. Old Mr Froude had drawn a magic circle round his son, from which escape was impossible; and the creature whose life had been almost ruined by his father's moral cruelty, who – to all appearances – had thrown off the yoke, and grown into maturity with the powerful, audacious, sceptical spirit of a free man, remained, in fact, in secret servitude – a disciplinarian, a Protestant, even a church-goer, to the very end.

Possibly the charm might have been exorcised by an invocation to science, but Froude remained curiously aloof from the dominating influence of his age; and instead, when his father had vanished, submitted himself to Carlyle. The substitution was symptomatic: the new father expressed in explicit dogma the unconscious teaching of the old. To the present generation Carlyle presents a curious problem – it is so very difficult to believe that real red-hot lava ever flowed from that dry, neglected crater; but the present generation never heard Carlyle talk. For many years Froude heard little else; he became an evangelist; but when he produced his gospel it met, like some others, with a mixed reception. The Victorian public, unable to understand a form of hero-worship which laid bare the faults of the hero, was appalled, and refused to believe what was the simple fact – that Froude's adoration was of so complete a kind that it shrank with horror from the notion of omitting a single wart from the portrait. To us the warts are obvious: our only difficulty is to account for the adoration. However, since it led incidentally to the publication of Mrs Carlyle's letters as well as her husband's, we can only be thankful.

The main work of Froude's life, the *History of England from the Fall of Wolsey to the Defeat of the Spanish Armada*, began to appear in 1856, and was completed in 1870. It is undoubtedly a deeply interesting book, full of thought, of imagination and of excitement, the product of great industry and great power of writing: whether it ranks among the small first class of histories is less certain. Contemporary critics found much to complain of in it, but their strictures were, on the whole, beside the mark. Among them the most formidable was Professor Freeman, who dissected Froude with the utmost savagery month after month and year after year in the pages of the *Saturday Review*. Freeman was a man of considerable learning, and of an ill temper even more considerable; his minute knowledge of the Early English, his passionate devotion to the Anglo-Saxons, and his intimate conviction (supported by that of Dr Stubbs), that he (with the possible exception of Dr Stubbs) was the supreme historian, made a strange mixture in his mind, boiling and simmering together over the flames of a temperamental vexation. Unfortunately no particle of this heat ever reached his printed productions, which were remarkable for their soporific qualities and for containing no words but those of Anglo-Saxon descent. The spirit, not only of the school but of the Sunday school, was what animated those innumerable pages, adorning with a parochial earnestness the heavy burden of research. Naturally enough Froude's work, so coloured, so personal, so obviously written by somebody who was acquainted with the world as well as Oxford, acted like a red rag on the professor. He stormed, he stamped, his fiery and choleric beard shook with indignation. He declared that the book was a mass of inaccuracies and a dastardly attack upon the Church of England. The former accusation was the more important, and the professor devoted years to the proof of it. Unluckily for him, however, the years only revealed more and more clearly the indisputable value of Froude's work in the domain of pure erudition. He was not a careful transcriber, and he occasionally made a downright blunder; but such blemishes are of small moment compared with the immense addition he made to historical knowledge by his exploration and revelation of the manuscripts at Simancas. Froude was dignified; he kept silence for twenty years, and then replied to his tormentor in an article so crushing as to elicit something almost like an apology.

But he was more completely avenged in a very different and quite unexpected manner. Mr Horace Round, a 'burrower into wormholes' living in Brighton, suddenly emerged from the parchments among which he spent his life deliciously gnawing at the pedigrees of the proudest families of England, and in a series of articles fell upon Freeman with astonishing force. The attack was particularly serious because it was delivered at the strongest point in the professor's armour – his exactitude, his knowledge of his authorities, his undeviating attention to fact, and it was particularly galling because it was directed against the very crown and culmination of the professor's history – his account of the Battle of Hastings. With masterly skill Mr Round showed that, through a variety of errors, the whole nature of the battle had been misunderstood and misrepresented; more than that, he proved that the name of 'Senlac' with which Freeman had christened it, and which he had imposed upon the learned world, was utterly without foundation, and had been arrived at by a foolish mistake. Mr Round was an obscure technician, but he deserves the gratitude of Englishmen for having extirpated that odious word from their vocabulary. The effect of these articles on Freeman was alarming; his blood boiled, but he positively made no reply. For years the attacks continued, and for years the professor was dumb. Fulminating rejoinders rushed into his brain, only to be whisked away again – they were not quite fulminating enough. The most devastating article of all was written, was set up in proof, but was not yet published; it contained the *exposé* of 'Senlac', and rumours of its purport and approaching appearance were already flying about in museums and common-rooms. Freeman was aghast at this last impertinence; but still he nursed his wrath. Like King Lear, he would do such things – what they were yet he knew not – but they should be the terrors of the earth. At last, silent and purple, he gathered his female attendants about him, and left England for an infuriated holiday. There was an ominous pause; and then the fell news reached Brighton. The professor had gone pop in Spain. Mr Round, however, was remorseless, and published. It was left for his adversary's pupils and admirers to struggle with him as best they could, but they did so ineffectively; and he remained, like the Normans, in possession of the field.

A true criticism of Froude's *History* implies a wider view than Freeman's. The theme of the book was the triumph of the Reformation in England – a theme not only intensely dramatic in itself, but one which raised a multitude of problems of profound and perennial interest. Froude could manage the drama (though in his hands it sometimes degenerated into melodrama) well enough: it was his treatment of the philosophical issues that was defective. Carlyle – it seems hardly credible – actually believed that the Revolution was to be explained as a punishment meted out to France for her loose living in the eighteenth century; and Froude's ethical conceptions, though they were not quite so crude, belonged to the same infantile species as his master's. The Protestants were right and the Catholics were wrong. Henry VIII enabled the Protestants to win, therefore Henry VIII was an admirable person: such was the kind of proposition by which Froude's attitude towards that period of vast and complicated import was determined. His Carlylean theories demanded a hero, and Henry VIII came pat to hand; he refused to see – what is plain to any impartial observer – that the Defender of the Faith combined in a peculiar manner the unpleasant vices of meanness and brutality; no! he made the Reformation – he saved England – he was a demi-god. How the execution of Catherine Howard – a young girl who amused herself – helped forward Protestant England, we are not told. Froude's insensitiveness to cruelty becomes, indeed, at times, almost pathological. When King and Parliament between them have a man boiled alive in Smithfield Market, he is favourably impressed; it is only when Protestants are tortured that there is talk of martyrdom. The bias, no doubt, gives a spice to the work, but it is cheap spice – bought, one feels, at the Co-operative Stores. The Whiggery of Macaulay may be tiresome, but it has the flavour of an aristocracy about it, of a high intellectual tradition; while Froude's Protestantism is – there is really only one word for it – provincial.

A certain narrowness of thought and feeling: that may be forgiven, if it is expressed in a style of sufficient mastery. Froude was an able, a brilliant writer, copious and vivid, with a picturesque imagination and a fine command of narrative. His grand set-pieces – the execution of Somerset and Mary Queen of Scots, the end of Cranmer, the ruin of the Armada – go off magnificently, and cannot be forgotten; and, apart from these, the extraordinary succession of events assumes, as it flows through his pages, the thrilling lineaments of a great story, upon whose issue the most *blasé* reader is forced to hang entranced. Yet the supreme quality of style seems to be lacking. One is uneasily aware of a looseness in the texture, an absence of concentration in the presentment, a failure to fuse the *whole* material into organic life. Perhaps, after all, it is the intellect and the emotion that are at fault here too; perhaps when one is hoping for genius, it is only talent – only immense talent – that one finds. One thinks of the mysterious wisdom of Thucydides, of the terrific force of Tacitus, of the Gibbonian balance and lucidity and co-ordination – ah! to few, to very few, among historians is it granted to bring the κτῆμα ἐς ἀεί into the world. And yet . . . if only, one feels, this gifted, splendid man could have stepped back a little, could have withdrawn from the provinciality of Protestantism and the crudity of the Carlylean dogma, could have allowed himself, untrammelled, to play upon his subject with his native art and his native wit! Then, surely, he would have celebrated other virtues besides the unpleasant ones; he would have seen some drawbacks to power and patriotism, he would have preferred civilization to fanaticism, and Queen Elizabeth to John Knox. He might even have written immortal English. But alas! these are vain speculations; old Mr Froude would never have permitted anything of the sort.

1930

# Creighton

The Church of England is one of the most extraordinary of institutions. An incredible concoction of Queen Elizabeth's, it still flourishes, apparently, and for three hundred years had remained true to type. Or perhaps, in reality, Queen Elizabeth had not very much to do with it; perhaps she only gave, with her long, strong fingers, the final twist to a stem that had been growing for ages, deep-rooted in the national life. Certainly our cathedrals – so careful and so unæsthetic, so class-conscious and so competent – suggest that view of the case. English Gothic seems to show that England was Anglican long before the Reformation – as soon as she ceased to be Norman, in fact. Pure piety, it cannot be denied, has never been her Church's strong point. Anglicanism has never produced – never could produce – a St. Teresa. The characteristic great men of the institution – Whitgift, Hooker, Laud, Butler, Jowett – have always been remarkable for virtues of a more secular kind: those of scholarship or of administrative energy. Mandell Creighton was (perhaps) the last of the long line. Perhaps; for who can tell? It is difficult to believe that a man of Creighton's attainments will ever again be Bishop of London. That particular concatenation seems to have required a set of causes to bring it into existence – a state of society, a habit of mind – which have become obsolete. But the whirligigs of time are, indeed, unpredictable; and England, some day or other, may well be blessed with another Victorian Age.

In Creighton *both* the great qualities of Anglican tradition were present to a remarkable degree. It would be hard to say whether he were more distinguished as a scholar or a man of affairs; but – such is the rather unfair persistence of the written word – there can be little doubt that he will be remembered chiefly as the historian of the Papacy. Born when the world was becoming extremely scientific, he belonged to the post-Carlyle-and-Macaulay generation – the school of Oxford and Cambridge inquirers, who sought to reconstruct the past solidly and patiently, with nothing but facts to assist them – pure facts, untwisted by political or metaphysical bias and uncoloured by romance. In this attempt Creighton succeeded admirably. He was industrious, exact, clear-headed, and possessed of a command over words that was quite sufficient for his purposes. He succeeded more completely than Professor Samuel Gardiner, whose history of the Early Stuarts and the Civil Wars was a contemporary work. Gardiner did his best, but he was not an absolute master of the method. Strive as he would, he could not prevent himself, now and then, from being a little sympathetic to one or other of his personages; sometimes he positively alluded to a physical circumstance; in short, humanity would come creeping in. A mistake! For Professor Gardiner's feelings about mankind are not illuminating; and the result is a slight blur. Creighton was made of sterner stuff. In his work a perfectly grey light prevails everywhere; there is not a single lapse into psychological profundity; every trace of local colour, every suggestion of personal passion, has been studiously removed. In many ways all this is a great comfort. One is not worried by moral lectures or purple patches, and the field is kept clear for what Creighton really excelled in – the lucid exposition of complicated political transactions, and the intricate movements of thought with which they were accompanied. The biscuit is certainly exceedingly dry; but at any rate there are no weevils in it. As one reads, one gets to relish, with a sober satisfaction, this plumless fare. It begins to be very nearly a pleasure to follow the intrigues of the great Councils, or to tread the labyrinth of the theological theory of indulgences. It is a curious cross-section of history that Creighton offers to the view. He has cut the great tree so near to the ground that leaf and flower have vanished; but he has worked his saw with such steadiness and precision that every grain in the wood is visible, and one can look *down* at the mighty structure, revealed in all its complex solidity like a map to the mind's eye.

Charming, indeed, are the ironies of history; and not the least charming those that involve the historian. It was very natural that Creighton, a clever and studious clergyman of the Church of England, should choose as the subject of his investigations that group of events which, centring round the Italian popes, produced at last the Reformation. The ironical fact was that those events happened to take place in a world where no clever and studious clergyman of the Church of England had any business to be. 'Sobriety,' as he himself said, was his aim; but what could sobriety do when faced with such figures as Savonarola, Cæsar Borgia, Julius II, and Luther? It could only look somewhere else. It is pleasant to witness the high-minded husband and father, the clever talker at Cambridge dinner tables, the industrious diocesan administrator, picking his way with an air of calm detachment amid the recklessness, the brutality, the fanaticism, the cynicism, the lasciviousness, of those Renaissance spirits. 'In his private life,' Creighton says of Alexander VI, 'it is sufficiently clear that he was at little pains to repress a strongly sensual nature. . . . We may hesitate to believe the worst charges brought against him; but the evidence is too strong to enable us to admit that even after his accession to the papal office he discontinued the irregularities of his previous life.' There is high comedy in such a tone on such a topic. One can imagine the father of the Borgias, if he could have read that sentence, throwing up his hands in delighted amazement, and roaring out the obscene blasphemy of his favourite oath.

The truth was that, in spite of his wits and his Oxford training, the admirable north-country middle-class stock, from which Creighton came, dominated his nature. His paradoxes might astound academical circles, his free speech might agitate the lesser clergy, but at heart he was absolutely sound. Even a friendship with that dæmonic imp, Samuel Butler, left him uncorroded. He believed in the Real Presence. He was opposed to Home Rule. He read with grave attention the novels of Mrs Humphry Ward. The emancipation of a Victorian bishop could never be as that of other men. The string that tied him to the peg of tradition might be quite a long one; but it was always there. Creighton enjoyed his little runs with the gusto and vitality that were invariably his. The sharp aquiline face, with the grizzled beard, the bald forehead, and the gold spectacles, gleamed and glistened, the long, slim form, so dapper in its episcopal gaiters, preened itself delightedly, as an epigram – a devastating epigram – shot off and exploded, and the Fulham teacups tinkled as they had never tinkled before. Then, a moment later, the guests gone, the firm mouth closed in severe determination; work was resumed. The duties of the day were despatched swiftly; the vast and stormy diocese of London was controlled with extraordinary efficiency; while a punctual calmness reigned, for, however pressed and pestered, the Bishop was never known to fuss. Only once on a railway journey, when he believed that some valuable papers had gone astray, did his equanimity desert him. 'Where's my black bag?' was his repeated inquiry. His mischievous children treasured up this single lapse; and, ever afterwards, 'Where's my black bag?' was thrown across the table at the good-humoured prelate when his family was in a teasing mood.

When the fourth volume of the *History of the Papacy* appeared there was a curious little controversy, which illustrated Creighton's attitude to history and, indeed, to life. 'It seems to me,' he wrote in the preface, 'neither necessary to moralise at every turn in historical writing, nor becoming to adopt an attitude of lofty superiority over any one who ever played a prominent part in European affairs, nor charitable to lavish undiscriminating censure on any man.' The wrath of Lord Acton was roused. He wrote a violent letter of protest. The learning of the eminent Catholic was at least equal to Creighton's, but he made no complaint upon matters of erudition; it was his moral sense that was outraged. Creighton, it seemed to him, had passed over, with inexcusable indifference, the persecution and intolerance of the medieval Church. The popes of the thirteenth and fourteenth centuries, he wrote, '. . . instituted a system of persecution. . . . It is the most conspicuous fact in the history of the medieval Papacy. . . . But what amazes and disables me is that you speak of the Papacy not as exercising a just severity, but as not exercising any severity. You ignore, you even deny, at least implicitly, the existence of the torture chamber and the stake. . . . Now the Liberals think persecution a crime of a worse order than adultery, and the acts done by Ximenes considerably worse than the entertainment of Roman courtesans by Alexander VI. The responsibility exists whether the thing permitted be good or bad. If the thing be criminal, then the authority permitting it bears the guilt. . . . You say that people in authority are not to be snubbed or sneered at from our pinnacle of conscious rectitude. I really don't know whether you exempt them because of their rank, or of their success and power, or of their date. . . . Historic responsibility has to make up for the want of legal responsibility.

Power tends to corrupt, and absolute power corrupts absolutely. Great men are almost always bad.' These words, surely, are magnificent. One sees with surprise and exhilaration the rôles reversed – the uncompromising fervour of Catholicism calling down fire from Heaven upon its own abominable popes and the worldly Protestantism that excused them. Creighton's reply was as Anglican as might have been expected. He hedged. One day, he wrote, John Bright had said, 'If the people knew what sort of men statesmen were, they would rise and hang the whole lot of them.' Next day Gladstone had said 'Statesmanship is the noblest way to serve mankind.' 'I am sufficient of a Hegelian to be able to combine both judgments; but the results of my combination cannot be expressed in the terms of the logic of Aristotle. . . . Society is an organism,' etc. It is clear enough that his real difference with Lord Acton was not so much over the place of morals in history as over the nature of the historical acts upon which moral judgments are to be passed. The Bishop's imagination was not deeply stirred by the atrocities of the Inquisition; what interested him, what appealed to him, what he really understood, were the difficulties and the expedients of a man of affairs who found himself at the head of a great administration. He knew too well, with ritualists on one side and Kensitites on the other, the trials and troubles from which a clerical ruler had to extricate himself as best he could, not to sympathize (in his heart of hearts) with the clerical rulers of another age who had been clever enough to devise regulations for the elimination of heresy and schism, and strong enough to put those regulations into force.

He himself, however, was never a persecutor; his great practical intelligence prevented that. Firmly fixed in the English tradition of common sense, compromise and comprehension, he held on his way amid the shrieking of extremists with imperturbable moderation. One of his very last acts was to refuse to prosecute two recalcitrant clergymen who had persisted in burning incense in a forbidden manner. He knew that, in England at any rate, persecution did not work. Elsewhere, perhaps, it might be different; in Russia, for instance. . . . There was an exciting moment in Creighton's life when he was sent to Moscow to represent the Church of England at the Coronation of the Emperor Nicholas; and his comments on that occasion were significant. Clad in a gorgeous cope of red and gold, with mitre and crozier, the English prelate attracted every eye. He thoroughly relished the fact; he tasted, too, to the full, the splendour of the great ceremonies and the extraordinary display of autocratic power. That there might have been some degree of spiritual squalor mixed with those magnificent appearances never seemed to occur to him. He was fascinated by the apparatus of a mighty organization, and, with unerring instinct, made straight for the prime mover of it, the Chief Procurator of the Holy Synod, the sinister Pobiedonostzeff, with whom he struck up a warm friendship. He was presented to the Emperor and Empress, and found them charming. 'I was treated with great distinction, as I was called in first. The Empress looked very nice, dressed in white silk.' The aristocratic Acton would, no doubt, have viewed things in a different light. 'Absolute power corrupts absolutely' – so he had said; but Creighton had forgotten the remark. He was no Daniel. He saw no Writing on the Wall.

The Bishop died in his prime, at the height of his success and energy, and was buried in St. Paul's Cathedral. Not far from his tomb, which a Victorian sculptor did his best to beautify, stands the strange effigy of John Donne, preaching, in his shroud, an incredible sermon upon mortality. Lingering in that corner, one's mind flashes oddly to other scenes and other persons. One passes down the mouldering street of Ferrara, and reaches an obscure church. In the half-light, from an inner door, an elderly humble nun approaches, indicating with her patois a marble slab in the pavement – a Latin inscription – the grave of Lucrezia Borgia. Mystery and oblivion were never united more pathetically. But there is another flash, and one is on a railway platform under the grey sky of England. A tall figure hurries by, spectacled and bearded, with swift clerical legs, and a voice – a competent, commanding, yet slightly agitated voice – says sharply: 'Where's my black bag?'

1929

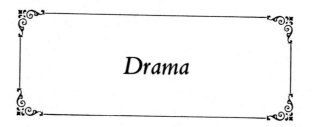

*Drama*

# Shakespeare's Final Period

The whole of the modern criticism of Shakespeare has been
fundamentally affected by one important fact. The chronological
order of the plays, for so long the object of the vaguest speculation,
of random guesses, or at best of isolated 'points', has been now
discovered and reduced to a coherent law. It is no longer possible to
suppose that *The Tempest* was written before *Romeo and Juliet*; that
*Henry VI* was produced in succession to *Henry V*; or that *Antony and
Cleopatra* followed close upon the heels of *Julius Caesar*. Such
theories were sent to limbo for ever, when a study of those plays of
whose date we have external evidence revealed the fact that, as
Shakespeare's life advanced, a corresponding development took
place in the metrical structure of his verse. The establishment of
metrical tests, by which the approximate position and date of any
play can be readily ascertained, at once followed; chaos gave way to
order; and, for the first time, critics became able to judge, not only
of the individual works, but of the whole succession of the works of
Shakespeare.

Upon this firm foundation modern writers have been only too
eager to build. It was apparent that the Plays, arranged in
chronological order, showed something more than a mere
development in the technique of verse – a development, that is to
say, in the general treatment of characters and subjects, and in the
sort of feelings which those characters and subjects were intended
to arouse; and from this it was easy to draw conclusions as to the
development of the mind of Shakespeare itself. Such conclusions
have, in fact, been constantly drawn. But it must be noted that they
all rest upon the tacit assumption, that the character of any given
drama is, in fact, a true index to the state of mind of the dramatist
composing it. The validity of this assumption has never been
proved; it has never been shown, for instance, why we should

suppose a writer of farces to be habitually merry; or whether we are really justified in concluding, from the fact that Shakespeare wrote nothing but tragedies for six years, that, during that period, more than at any other, he was deeply absorbed in the awful problems of human existence. It is not, however, the purpose of this essay to consider the question of what are the relations between the artist and his art; for it will assume the truth of the generally accepted view, that the character of the one can be inferred from that of the other. What it will attempt to discuss is whether, upon this hypothesis, the most important part of the ordinary doctrine of Shakespeare's mental development is justifiable.

What, then, is the ordinary doctrine? Dr Furnivall states it as follows:

Shakespeare's course is thus shown to have run from the amorousness and fun of youth, through the strong patriotism of early manhood, to the wrestlings with the dark problems that beset the man of middle age, to the gloom which weighed on Shakespeare (as on so many men) in later life, when, though outwardly successful, the world seemed all against him, and his mind dwelt with sympathy on scenes of faithlessness of friends, treachery of relations and subjects, ingratitude of children, scorn of his kind; till at last, in his Stratford home again, peace came to him, Miranda and Perdita in their lovely freshness and charm greeted him, and he was laid by his quiet Avon side.

And the same writer goes on to quote with approval Professor Dowden's

likening of Shakespeare to a ship, beaten and storm-tossed, but yet entering harbour with sails full-set, to anchor in peace.

Such, in fact, is the general opinion of modern writers upon Shakespeare; after a happy youth and a gloomy middle age he reached at last – it is the universal opinion – a state of quiet serenity in which he died. Professor Dowden's book on 'Shakespeare's Mind and Art' gives the most popular expression to this view, a view which is also held by Mr Ten Brink, by Sir I. Gollancz, and, to a great extent, by Dr Brandes. Professor Dowden, indeed, has gone so far as to label this final period with the appellation of 'On the Heights', in opposition to the preceding one, which, he says, was passed 'In the Depths'. Sir Sidney Lee, too, seems to find, in the Plays at least, if not in Shakespeare's mind, the orthodox succession of gaiety, of tragedy, and of the serenity of meditative romance.

Now it is clear that the most important part of this version of Shakespeare's mental history is the end of it. That he did eventually attain to a state of calm content, that he did, in fact, die happy – it is this that gives colour and interest to the whole theory. For some reason or another, the end of a man's life seems naturally to afford the light by which the rest of it should be read; last thoughts do appear in some strange way to be really best and truest; and this is particularly the case when they fit in nicely with the rest of the story, and are, perhaps, just what one likes to think oneself. If it be true that Shakespeare, to quote Professor Dowden, 'did at last attain to the serene self-possession which he had sought with such persistent effort'; that, in the words of Dr Furnivall, 'forgiven and forgiving, full of the highest wisdom and peace, at one with family and friends and foes, in harmony with Avon's flow and Stratford's level meads, Shakespeare closed his life on earth' – we have obtained a piece of knowledge which is both interesting and pleasant. But if it be not true, if, on the contrary, it can be shown that something very different was actually the case, then will it not follow that we must not only reverse our judgment as to this particular point, but also readjust our view of the whole drift and bearing of Shakespeare's 'inner life'?

The group of works which has given rise to this theory of ultimate serenity was probably entirely composed after Shakespeare's final retirement from London, and his establishment at New Place. It consists of three plays – *Cymbeline*, *The Winter's Tale*, and *The Tempest* – and three fragments – the Shakespearean parts of *Pericles*, *Henry VIII*, and *The Two Noble Kinsmen*. All these plays and portions of plays form a distinct group; they resemble each other in a multitude of ways, and they differ in a multitude of ways from nearly all Shakespeare's previous work.

One other complete play, however, and one other fragment, do resemble in some degree these works of the final period; for, immediately preceding them in date, they show clear traces of the beginnings of the new method, and they are themselves curiously different from the plays they immediately succeed – that great series of tragedies which began with *Hamlet* in 1601 and ended in 1608 with *Antony and Cleopatra*. In the latter year, indeed, Shakespeare's entire method underwent an astonishing change. For six years he had been persistently occupied with a kind of writing which he had himself not only invented but brought to the highest point of excellence – the tragedy of character. Every one of his masterpieces has for its theme the action of tragic situation upon character; and, without those stupendous creations in character, his greatest tragedies would obviously have lost the precise thing that has made them what they are. Yet, after *Antony and Cleopatra* Shakespeare deliberately turned his back upon the dramatic methods of all his past career. There seems no reason why he should not have continued, year after year, to produce *Othellos*, *Hamlets*, and *Macbeths*; instead, he turned over a new leaf, and wrote *Coriolanus*.

*Coriolanus* is certainly a remarkable, and perhaps an intolerable play: remarkable, because it shows the sudden first appearance of the Shakespeare of the final period; intolerable, because it is impossible to forget how much better it might have been. The subject is thick with situations; the conflicts of patriotism and pride, the effects of sudden disgrace following upon the very height of fortune, the struggles between family affection on the one hand and every interest of revenge and egotism on the other – these would have made a tragic and tremendous setting for some character worthy to rank with Shakespeare's best. But it pleased him to ignore completely all these opportunities; and, in the play he has given us, the situations, mutilated and degraded, serve merely as miserable props for the gorgeous clothing of his rhetoric. For rhetoric, enormously magnificent and extraordinarily elaborate, is the beginning and the middle and the end of *Coriolanus*. The hero is not a human being at all; he is the statue of a demi-god cast in bronze, which roars its perfect periods, to use a phrase of Sir Walter Raleigh's, through a melodious megaphone. The vigour of the presentment is, it is true, amazing; but it is a presentment of decoration, not of life. So far and so quickly had Shakespeare already wandered from the subtleties of *Cleopatra*. The transformation is indeed astonishing; one wonders, as one beholds it, what will happen next.

At about the same time, some of the scenes in *Timon of Athens* were in all probability composed: scenes which resemble *Coriolanus* in their lack of characterization and abundance of rhetoric, but differ from it in the peculiar grossness of their tone. For sheer virulence of foul-mouthed abuse, some of the speeches in *Timon* are probably unsurpassed in any literature; an outraged drayman would speak so, if draymen were in the habit of talking poetry. From this whirlwind of furious ejaculation, this splendid storm of nastiness, Shakespeare, we are confidently told, passed in a moment to tranquillity and joy, to blue skies, to young ladies, and to general forgiveness.

From 1604 to 1610 [says Professor Dowden] a show of tragic figures, like the kings who passed before Macbeth, filled the vision of Shakespeare; until at last the desperate image of Timon rose before him; when, as though unable to endure or to conceive a more lamentable ruin of man, he turned for relief to the pastoral loves of Prince Florizel and Perdita; and as soon as the tone of his mind was restored, gave expression to its ultimate mood of grave serenity in *The Tempest*, and so ended.

This is a pretty picture, but is it true? It may, indeed, be admitted at once that Prince Florizel and Perdita are charming creatures, that Prospero is 'grave', and that Hermione is more or less 'serene'; but why is it that, in our consideration of the later plays, the whole of our attention must always be fixed upon these particular characters? Modern critics, in their eagerness to appraise everything that is beautiful and good at its proper value, seem to have entirely forgotten that there is another side to the medal; and they have omitted to point out that these plays contain a series of portraits of peculiar infamy, whose wickedness finds expression in language of extraordinary force. Coming fresh from their pages to the pages of *Cymbeline*, *The Winter's Tale*, and *The Tempest*, one is astonished and perplexed. How is it possible to fit into their scheme of roses and maidens that 'Italian fiend' the 'yellow Iachimo', or Cloten, that 'thing too bad for bad report', or the 'crafty devil', his mother, or Leontes, or Caliban, or Trinculo? To omit these figures of discord and evil from our consideration, to banish them comfortably to the background of the stage, while Autolycus and Miranda dance before the footlights, is surely a fallacy in proportion; for the presentment of the one group of persons is every whit as distinct and vigorous as that of the other. Nowhere, indeed, is Shakespeare's violence of expression more constantly displayed than in the 'gentle utterances' of his last period; it is here that one finds Paulina, in a torrent of indignation as far from 'grave serenity' as it is from 'pastoral love', exclaiming to Leontes:

What studied torments, tyrant, hast for me?
What wheels? racks? fires? what flaying? boiling
In leads or oils? what old or newer torture
Must I receive, whose every word deserves
To taste of thy most worst? Thy tyranny,
Together working with thy jealousies,
Fancies too weak for boys, too green and idle
For girls of nine, O! think what they have done,
And then run mad indeed, stark mad; for all
Thy by-gone fooleries were but spices of it.
That thou betray'dst Polixenes, 'twas nothing;
That did but show thee, of a fool, inconstant
And damnable ingrateful; nor was't much
Thou would'st have poison'd good Camillo's honour,
To have him kill a king; poor trespasses,
More monstrous standing by; whereof I reckon
The casting forth to crows thy baby daughter
To be or none or little; though a devil
Would have shed water out of fire ere done't.
Nor is't directly laid to thee, the death
Of the young prince, whose honourable thoughts,
Thoughts high for one so tender, cleft the heart
That could conceive a gross and foolish sire
Blemished his gracious dam.

Nowhere are the poet's metaphors more nakedly material;
nowhere does he verge more often upon a sort of brutality of
phrase, a cruel coarseness. Iachimo tells us how:

The cloyed will,
That satiate yet unsatisfied desire, that tub
Both filled and running, ravening first the lamb,
Longs after for the garbage.

and talks of:

an eye
Base and unlustrous as the smoky light
That's fed with stinking tallow.

'The south fog rot him!' Cloten burst out to Imogen, cursing her
husband in an access of hideous rage.

What traces do such passages as these show of 'serene self-
possession', of 'the highest wisdom and peace', or of 'meditative

romance'? English critics, overcome by the idea of Shakespeare's ultimate tranquillity, have generally denied to him the authorship of the brothel scenes in *Pericles*; but these scenes are entirely of a piece with the grossnesses of *The Winter's Tale* and *Cymbeline*.

> Is there no way for men to be, but women
> Must be half-workers?

says Posthumus when he hears of Imogen's guilt.

> We are all bastards;
> And that most venerable man, which I
> Did call my father, was I know not where
> When I was stamped. Some coiner with his tools
> Made me a counterfeit; yet my mother seemed
> The Dian of that time; so doth my wife
> The nonpareil of this – O vengeance, vengeance!
> Me of my lawful pleasure she restrained
> And prayed me, oft, forbearance; did it with
> A pudency so rosy, the sweet view on't
> Might well have warmed old Saturn, that I thought her
> As chaste as unsunned snow – O, all the devils!
> This yellow Iachimo, in an hour, – was't not?
> Or less, – at first: perchance he spoke not; but,
> Like a full-acorned boar, a German one,
> Cried, oh! and mounted: found no opposition
> But what he looked for should oppose, and she
> Should from encounter guard.

And Leontes, in a similar situation, expresses himself in images no less to the point.

> There have been,
> Or I am much deceived, cuckolds ere now,
> And many a man there is, even at this present,
> Now, while I speak this, holds his wife by the arm,
> That little thinks she has been sluiced in's absence
> And his pond fished by his next neighbour, by
> Sir Smile, his neighbour: nay, there's comfort in't,
> Whiles other men have gates, and those gates opened,
> As mine, against their will. Should all despair
> That have revolted wives, the tenth of mankind
> Would hang themselves. Physic for't there's none;
> It is a bawdy planet, that will strike

Where 'tis predominant; and 'tis powerful, think it,
From east, west, north and south: be it concluded,
No barricado for a belly, know't;
It will let in and out the enemy
With bag and baggage: many thousand on's
Have the disease, and feel't not.

It is really a little difficult, in the face of such passages, to agree with Professor Dowden's dictum: 'In these latest plays the beautiful pathetic light is always present.'

But how has it happened that the judgment of so many critics has been so completely led astray? Charm and gravity, and even serenity, are to be found in many other plays of Shakespeare. Ophelia is charming, Brutus is grave, Cordelia is serene; are we then to suppose that *Hamlet*, and *Julius Caesar*, and *King Lear* give expression to the same mood of high tranquillity which is betrayed by *Cymbeline*, *The Tempest*, and *The Winter's Tale*? 'Certainly not,' reply the orthodox writers, 'for you must distinguish. The plays of the last period are not tragedies; they all end happily' – 'in scenes,' says Sir I. Gollancz, 'of forgiveness, reconciliation, and peace.' Virtue, in fact, is not only virtuous, it is triumphant; what would you more?

But to this it may be retorted, that, in the case of one of Shakespeare's plays, even the final vision of virtue and beauty triumphant over ugliness and vice fails to dispel a total effect of horror and of gloom. For, in *Measure for Measure* Isabella is no whit less pure and lovely than any Perdita or Miranda, and her success is as complete; yet who would venture to deny that the atmosphere of *Measure for Measure* was more nearly one of despair than of serenity? What is it, then, that makes the difference? Why should a happy ending seem in one case futile, and in another satisfactory? Why does it sometimes matter to us a great deal, and sometimes not at all, whether virtue is rewarded or not?

The reason, in this case, is not far to seek. *Measure for Measure* is, like nearly every play of Shakespeare's before *Coriolanus*, essentially realistic. The characters are real men and women; and what happens to them upon the stage has all the effect of what happens to real men and women in actual life. Their goodness appears to be real goodness, their wickedness real wickedness; and, if their sufferings are terrible enough, we regret the fact, even though in the end they triumph, just as we regret the real sufferings of our friends. But, in the plays of the final period, all this has changed; we are no longer in the real world, but in a world of enchantment, of mystery, of wonder, a world of shifting visions, a world of hopeless anachronisms, a world in which anything may happen next. The pretences of reality are indeed usually preserved, but only the pretences. Cymbeline is supposed to be the king of a real Britain, and the real Augustus is supposed to demand tribute of him; but these are the reasons which his queen, in solemn audience with the Roman ambassador, urges to induce her husband to declare for war:

> Remember, sir, my liege,
> The Kings your ancestors, together with
> The natural bravery of your isle, which stands
> As Neptune's park, ribbed and paled in
> With rocks unscaleable and roaring waters,
> With sands that will not bear your enemies' boats,
> But suck them up to the topmast. A kind of conquest
> Caesar made here; but made not here his brag
> Of 'Came, and saw, and overcame'; with shame –
> The first that ever touched him – he was carried
> From off our coast, twice beaten; and his shipping –
> Poor ignorant baubles! – on our terrible seas,
> Like egg-shells moved upon the surges, crack'd
> As easily 'gainst our rocks; for joy whereof
> The famed Cassibelan, who was once at point –
> O giglot fortune! – to master Caesar's sword,
> Made Lud's town with rejoicing fires bright
> And Britons strut with courage.

It comes with something of a shock to remember that this medley of poetry, bombast, and myth will eventually reach the ears of no other person than the Octavius of *Antony and Cleopatra*; and the contrast is the more remarkable when one recalls the brilliant scene of negotiation and diplomacy in the latter play, which passes between Octavius, Maecenas, and Agrippa on the one side, and Antony and Enobarbus on the other, and results in the reconciliation of the rivals and the marriage of Antony and Octavia.

Thus strangely remote is the world of Shakespeare's latest period; and it is peopled, this universe of his invention, with beings equally unreal, with creatures either more or less than human, with fortunate princes and wicked step-mothers, with goblins and spirits, with lost princesses and insufferable kings. And of course, in this sort of fairy land, it is an essential condition that everything shall end well; the prince and princess are bound to marry and live happily ever afterwards, or the whole story is unnecessary and absurd; and the villains and the goblins must naturally repent and be forgiven. But it is clear that such happy endings, such conventional closes to fantastic tales, cannot be taken as evidences of serene tranquillity on the part of their maker; they merely show that he knew, as well as anyone else, how such stories ought to end.

Yet there can be no doubt that it is this combination of charming heroines and happy endings which has blinded the eyes of modern critics to everything else. Iachimo, and Leontes, and even Caliban, are to be left out of account, as if, because in the end they repent or are forgiven, words need not be wasted on such reconciled and harmonious fiends. It is true they are grotesque; it is true that such personages never could have lived; but who, one would like to know, has ever met Miranda, or become acquainted with Prince Florizel of Bohemia? In this land of faery, is it right to neglect the goblins? In this world of dreams, are we justified in ignoring the nightmares? Is it fair to say that Shakespeare was in 'a gentle, lofty spirit, a peaceful, tranquil mood', when he was creating the Queen in *Cymbeline*, or writing the first two acts of *The Winter's Tale*?

Attention has never been sufficiently drawn to one other characteristic of these plays, though it is touched upon both by Professor Dowden and Dr Brandes – the singular carelessness with which great parts of them were obviously written. Could anything drag more wretchedly than the *dénouement* of *Cymbeline*? And with what perversity is the great pastoral scene in *The Winter's Tale* interspersed with long-winded intrigues, and disguises, and homilies! For these blemishes are unlike the blemishes which enrich rather than lessen the beauty of the earlier plays; they are not, like them, interesting or delightful in themselves; they are usually merely necessary to explain the action, and they are sometimes purely irrelevant. One is, it cannot be denied, often bored, and occasionally irritated, by Polixenes and Camillo and Sebastian and Gonzalo and Belarius; these personages have not even the life of ghosts; they are hardly more than speaking names, that give patient utterance to involution upon involution. What a contrast to the minor characters of Shakespeare's earlier works!

It is difficult to resist the conclusion that he was getting bored himself. Bored with people, bored with real life, bored with drama, bored, in fact, with everything except poetry and poetical dreams. He is no longer interested, one often feels, in what happens, or who says what, so long as he can find place for a faultless lyric, or a new, unimagined rhythmical effect, or a grand and mystic speech. In this mood he must have written his share in *The Two Noble Kinsmen*, leaving the plot and characters to Fletcher to deal with as he pleased, and reserving to himself only the opportunities for pompous verse. In this mood he must have broken off half-way through the tedious history of *Henry VIII*; and in this mood he must have completed, with all the resources of his rhetoric, the miserable archaic fragment of *Pericles*.

Is it not thus, then, that we should imagine him in the last years of his life? Half enchanted by visions of beauty and loveliness, and half bored to death; on the one side inspired by a soaring fancy to the singing of ethereal songs, and on the other urged by a general disgust to burst occasionally through his torpor into bitter and violent speech? If we are to learn anything of his mind from his last works, it is surely this.

And such is the conclusion which is particularly forced upon us by a consideration of the play which is in many ways most typical of Shakespeare's later work, and the one which critics most consistently point to as containing the very essence of his final benignity – *The Tempest*. There can be no doubt that the peculiar characteristics which distinguish *Cymbeline* and *The Winter's Tale* from the dramas of Shakespeare's prime, are present here in a still greater degree. In *The Tempest*, unreality has reached its apotheosis. Two of the principal characters are frankly not human beings at all; and the whole action passes, through a series of impossible occurrences, in a place which can only by courtesy be said to exist. The Enchanted Island, indeed, peopled, for a timeless moment, by this strange fantastic medley of persons and of things, has been cut adrift for ever from common sense, and floats buoyed up by a sea, not of waters, but of poetry. Never did Shakespeare's magnificence of diction reach more marvellous heights than in some of the speeches of Prospero, or his lyric art a purer beauty than in the songs of Ariel; nor is it only in these ethereal regions that the triumph of his language asserts itself. It finds as splendid a vent in the curses of Caliban:

> All the infection that the sun sucks up
> From bogs, fens, flats, on Prosper fall, and make him
> By inch-meal a disease!

and in the similes of Trinculo:

Yond' same black cloud, yond' huge one, looks like a foul bombard that would shed his liquor.

The *dénouement* itself, brought about by a preposterous piece of machinery, and lost in a whirl of rhetoric, is hardly more than a peg for fine writing.

> O, it is monstrous, monstrous!
> Methought the billows spoke and told of it;
> The winds did sing it to me; and the thunder,
> That deep and dreadful organ-pipe, pronounced
> The name of Prosper; it did bass my trespass.
> Therefore my son i' th' ooze is bedded, and
> I'll seek him deeper than e'er plummet sounded,
> And with him there lie mudded.

And this gorgeous phantasm of a repentance from the mouth of the pale phantom Alonzo is a fitting climax to the whole fantastic play.

A comparison naturally suggests itself, between what was perhaps the last of Shakespeare's completed works, and that early drama which first gave undoubted proof that his imagination had taken wings. The points of resemblance between *The Tempest* and *A Midsummer Night's Dream*, their common atmosphere of romance and magic, the beautiful absurdities of their intrigues, their studied contrasts of the grotesque with the delicate, the ethereal with the earthly, the charm of their lyrics, the *verve* of the vulgar comedy – these, of course, are obvious enough; but it is the points of difference which really make the comparison striking. One thing, at any rate, is certain about the wood near Athens – it is full of life. The persons that haunt it – though most of them are hardly more than children, and some of them are fairies, and all of them are too agreeable to be true – are nevertheless substantial creatures, whose loves and jokes and quarrels receive our thorough sympathy; and the air they breathe – the lords and the ladies, no less than the mechanics and the elves – is instinct with an exquisite good-humour, which makes us as happy as the night is long. To turn from Theseus and Titania and Bottom to the Enchanted Island, is to step out of a country lane into a conservatory. The roses and the dandelions have vanished before preposterous cactuses, and fascinating orchids too delicate for the open air; and, in the artificial atmosphere, the gaiety of youth has been replaced by the disillusionment of middle age. Prospero is the central figure of *The Tempest*; and it has often been wildly asserted that he is a portrait of the author – an embodiment of that spirit of wise benevolence which is supposed to have thrown a halo over Shakespeare's later life. But, on closer inspection, the portrait seems to be as imaginary as the original. To an irreverent eye, the ex-Duke of Milan would perhaps appear as an unpleasantly crusty personage, in whom a twelve years' monopoly of the conversation had developed an inordinate propensity for talking. These may have been the sentiments of Ariel, safe at the Bermoothes; but to state them is to risk at least ten years in the knotty entrails of an oak, and it is sufficient to point out, that if Prospero is wise, he is also self-opinionated and sour, that his gravity is often another name for pedantic severity, and that there is no character in the play to whom, during some part of it, he is not studiously disagreeable. But his Milanese countrymen are not even disagreeable; they are simply dull. 'This is the silliest stuff that e'er I heard,' remarked Hippolyta of Bottom's amateur theatricals; and one is tempted to wonder what she would have said to the dreary puns and interminable conspiracies of Alonzo, and Gonzalo, and Sebastian, and Antonio, and Adrian, and Francisco, and other shipwrecked noblemen. At all events, there can be little doubt that they would not have had the entrée at Athens.

The depth of the gulf between the two plays is, however, best measured by a comparison of Caliban and his masters with Bottom and his companions. The guileless group of English mechanics, whose sports are interrupted by the mischief of Puck, offers a strange contrast to the hideous trio of the 'jester', the 'drunken butler', and the 'savage and deformed slave', whose designs are thwarted by the magic of Ariel. Bottom was the first of Shake-speare's mastepieces in characterization, Caliban was the last: and what a world of bitterness and horror lies between them! The charming coxcomb it is easy to know and love; but the 'freckled whelp hag-born' moves us mysteriously to pity and to terror, eluding us for ever in fearful allegories, and strange coils of disgusted laughter and phantasmagorical tears. The physical vigour of the presentment is often so remorseless as to shock us. 'I left them,' says Ariel, speaking of Caliban and his crew:

> I' the filthy-mantled pool beyond your cell,
> There dancing up to the chins, that the foul lake
> O'erstunk their feet.

But at other times the great half-human shape seems to swell like the 'Pan' of Victor Hugo, into something unimaginably vast.

> You taught me language, and my profit on't
> Is, I know how to curse.

Is this Caliban addressing Prospero, or Job addressing God? It may be either; but it is not serene, nor benign, nor pastoral, nor 'On the Heights'.

1904

# Sarah Bernhardt

There are many paradoxes in the art of acting. One of them – the discrepancy between the real feelings of the actor and those which he represents – was discussed by Diderot in a famous dialogue. Another – the singular divergence between the art of the stage and the art of the drama – was illustrated very completely by the career of Sarah Bernhardt.

It is clear that the primary business of the actor is to interpret the conception of the dramatist; but it is none the less true that, after a certain degree of excellence has been reached, the merits of an actor have no necessary dependence upon his grasp of the dramatist's meaning. To be a moderately good actor one must understand, more or less, what one's author is up to; but the achievements of Sarah Bernhardt proved conclusively that it was possible to be a very good actor indeed without having the faintest notion, not only of the intentions of particular dramatists, but of the very rudiments of the dramatic art.

No one who saw her in *Hamlet* or in *Lorenzaccio* could doubt that this was so. Her *Hamlet* was a fantastic absurdity which far, far surpassed the permitted limits even of a Gallic miscomprehension of 'le grand Will'. But perhaps even more remarkable was her treatment of *Lorenzaccio*. *Hamlet*, after all, from every point of view, is an extremely difficult play; but the main drift of Musset's admirable tragedy is as plain as a pikestaff. It is a study in disillusionment – the disillusionment of a tyrannicide, who finds that the assassination, which he has contrived and executed with infinite hazard, skill, and difficulty, has merely resulted in a state of affairs even worse than before. Sarah Bernhardt, incredible as it may seem, brought down the final curtain on the murder of the tyrant, and thus made the play, as a play, absolutely pointless. What remained was a series of exciting scenes, strung together by the vivid and penetrating art of a marvellous actress. For art it was, and not mere posturing. Nothing could be further from the truth than to suppose that the great Frenchwoman belonged to that futile tribe of empty-headed impersonators, who, since Irving, have been the particular affliction of the English stage. Dazzling divinity though she was, she was also a serious, a laborious worker, incessantly occupied – not with expensive stage properties, elaborate make-up, and historically accurate scenery – but simply with acting. Sir Herbert Tree was ineffective because he neither knew nor cared how to act; he was content to be a clever entertainer. But Sarah Bernhardt's weakness, if weakness it can be called, arose from a precisely contrary reason – from the very plenitude of her power over all the resources of her craft – a mastery over her medium of so overwhelming a kind as to become an obsession.

The result was that this extraordinary genius was really to be seen at her most characteristic in plays of inferior quality. They gave her what she wanted. She did not want – she did not understand – great drama; what she did want were opportunities for acting; and this was the combination which the *Toscas*, the *Camélias*, and the rest of them, so happily provided. In them the whole of her enormous virtuosity in the representation of passion had full play; she could contrive thrill after thrill, she could seize and tear the nerves of her audience, she could touch, she could terrify, to the very top of her astonishing bent. In them, above all, she could ply her personality to the utmost. All acting must be, to some extent, an exploitation of the personality; but in the acting of Sarah Bernhardt that was the dominating quality – the fundamental element of her art. It was there that her strength, and her weakness, lay. During her best years, her personality remained an artistic instrument; but eventually it became too much for her. It absorbed both herself and her audience; the artist became submerged in the divinity; and what was genuine, courageous, and original in her character was lost sight of in oceans of highly advertised and quite indiscriminate applause.

This, no doubt, was partly due to the age she lived in. It is odd but certainly true that the eighteenth century would have been profoundly shocked by the actress who reigned supreme over the nineteenth. The gay and cynical creatures of the *ancien régime*, who tittered over *La Pucelle*, and whose adventures were reflected

without exaggeration in the pages of *Les Liaisons Dangereuses*, would have recoiled in horror before what they would have called the '*indécence*' of one of Sarah Bernhardt's ordinary scenes. Every age has its own way of dealing with these matters; and the nineteenth century made up for the high tone of its literature and the decorum of its behaviour by the luscious intensity of its theatrical displays. Strict husbands in icy shirt-fronts and lovely epitomes of all the domestic virtues in bustles would sit for hours thrilling with frenzied raptures over intimate and elaborate presentments of passion in its most feverish forms. The supply and the demand, interacting upon one another, grew together. But by the end of the century the fashion had begun to change. The star of Eleonora Duse rose upon the horizon; Ibsen became almost popular; the Théâtre Antoine, the Moscow Art Theatre, introduced a new style of tragic acting – a prose style – surprisingly effective and surprisingly quiet, and subtle with the sinuosities of actual life. Already by the beginning of the twentieth century the bravura of Sarah Bernhardt seemed a magnificent relic of the past. And the generation which was to plunge with reckless fanaticism into the gigantic delirium of the war found its pleasures at the theatre in a meticulous imitation of the significant trivialities of middle-class interiors.

Fortunately, however, Sarah Bernhardt's genius did not spend itself entirely in amazing personal triumphs and the satisfaction of the emotional needs of a particular age. Fortunately the mightier genius of Jean Racine was of such a nature that it was able to lift hers on to its own level of the immortal and the universal. In this case there was no need on her part for an intellectual realization of the dramatist's purpose; Racine had enough intellect for both; all that she had to do was to play the parts he had provided for her to the height of her ability; his supreme art did the rest. Her Hermione was a masterpiece; but certainly the greatest of all her achievements was in *Phèdre*. Tragedy possesses an extraordinary quality, which, perhaps, has given it its traditional place of primacy among all the forms of literature. It is not only immortal; it is also for ever new. There are infinite implications in it which reveal themselves by a mysterious law to each succeeding generation. The *Œdipus* acted yesterday at Cambridge was the identical play that won the prize two thousand years ago; and yet it was a different *Œdipus*, with

meanings for the modern audience which were unperceived by the Athenians. The records show conclusively that the Phèdre of Bernhardt differed as much from that of Rachel as Rachel's differed from Clairon's, and as Clairon's differed from that of the great actress who created the part under the eyes of Racine. But each was Phèdre. Probably the latest of these interpretations was less perfect in all its parts than some of its predecessors; but the great moments, when they came, could never have been surpassed. All through there were details of such wonderful beauty that they return again and again upon the memory – unforgettable delights. The hurried horror of

> Mes yeux le retrouvaient dans les traits de son père;

the slow, expanding, mysterious grandeur of

> Le ciel, tout l'univers, est plein de mes aïeux;

the marvellous gesture with which the words of Œnone, announcing the approach of Thésée, seemed to be pressed back into silence down her 'ill-uttering throat' – such things, and a hundred others, could only have been conceived and executed by a consummate artist in her happiest vein. But undoubtedly the topmost reach came in the fourth act, when the Queen, her reason tottering with passion and jealousy, suddenly turns upon herself in an agony of self-reproach. Sarah Bernhardt's treatment of this passage was extremely original, and it is difficult to believe that it was altogether justified by the text. Racine's words seem to import a violent directness of statement:

> Chaque mot sur mon front fait dresser mes cheveux;

but it was with hysteric irony, with dreadful, mocking laughter, that the actress delivered them. The effect was absolutely overwhelming, and Racine himself could only have bowed to the ground before such a triumphant audacity. Then there followed the invocation to Minos, culminating in the stupendous

> Je crois voir de ta main tomber l'urne terrible.

The secret of that astounding utterance baffles the imagination. The words boomed and crashed with a superhuman resonance which shook the spirit of the hearer like a leaf in the wind. The *voix d'or* has

often been raved over; but in Sarah Bernhardt's voice there was more than gold: there was thunder and lightning; there was Heaven and Hell. But the pitcher is broken at the fountain; that voice is silent now for ever, and the Terror and the Pity that lived in it and purged the souls of mortals have faded into incommunicable dreams.

1923

# The Last Elizabethan

❦

The shrine of Poetry is a secret one; and it is fortunate that this should be the case; for it gives a sense of security. The cult is too mysterious and intimate to figure upon census papers; there are no turnstiles at the temple gates; and so, as all inquiries must be fruitless, the obvious plan is to take for granted a good attendance of worshippers, and to pass on. Yet, if Apollo were to come down (after the manner of deities) and put questions – must we suppose to the Laureate? – as to the number of the elect, would we be quite sure of escaping wrath and destruction? Let us hope for the best; and perhaps, if we were bent upon finding out the truth, the simplest way would be to watch the sales of the new edition of the poems of Beddoes, which Messrs. Routledge have lately added to the 'Muses' Library'. How many among Apollo's pew-renters, one wonders, have ever read Beddoes, or, indeed, have ever heard of him? For some reason or another, this extraordinary poet has not only never received the recognition which is his due, but has failed almost entirely to receive any recognition whatever. If his name is known at all, it is known in virtue of the one or two of his lyrics which have crept into some of the current anthologies. But Beddoes's highest claim to distinction does not rest upon his lyrical achievements, consummate as those achievements are; it rests upon his extraordinary eminence as a master of dramatic blank verse. Perhaps his greatest misfortune was that he was born at the beginning of the nineteenth century, and not at the end of the sixteenth. His proper place was among that noble band of Elizabethans, whose strong and splendid spirit gave to England, in one miraculous generation, the most glorious heritage of drama that the world has known. If Charles Lamb had discovered his tragedies among the folios of the British Museum, and had given extracts from them in the *Specimens of Dramatic Poets*, Beddoes's

140

name would doubtless be as familiar to us now as those of Marlowe and Webster, Fletcher and Ford. As it happened, however, he came as a strange and isolated phenomenon, a star which had wandered from its constellation and was lost among alien lights. It is to very little purpose that Mr Ramsay Colles, his latest editor, assures us that 'Beddoes is interesting as marking the transition from Shelley to Browning'; it is to still less purpose that he points out to us a passage in *Death's Jest Book* which anticipates the doctrines of *The Descent of Man*. For Beddoes cannot be hoisted into line with his contemporaries by such methods as these; nor is it in the light of such after-considerations that the value of his work must be judged. We must take him on his own merits, 'unmixed with seconds'; we must discover and appraise his peculiar quality for its own sake.

> He hath skill in language;
> And knowledge is in him, root, flower, and fruit,
> A palm with winged imagination in it,
> Whose roots stretch even underneath the grave;
> And on them hangs a lamp of magic science
> In his soul's deepest mine, where folded thoughts
> Lie sleeping on the tombs of magi dead.

If the neglect suffered by Beddoes's poetry may be accounted for in more ways than one, it is not so easy to understand why more curiosity has never been aroused by the circumstances of his life. For one reader who cares to concern himself with the intrinsic merit of a piece of writing there are a thousand who are ready to explore with eager sympathy the history of the writer; and all that we know both of the life and the character of Beddoes possesses those very qualities of peculiarity, mystery, and adventure, which are so dear to the hearts of subscribers to circulating libraries. Yet only one account of his career has ever been given to the public; and that account, fragmentary and incorrect as it is, has long been out of print. It was supplemented some years ago by Mr Gosse, who was able to throw additional light upon one important circumstance, and who has also published a small collection of Beddoes's letters. The main biographical facts, gathered from these sources, have been put together by Mr Ramsay Colles, in his introduction to the new edition; but he has added nothing fresh; and we are still in almost complete ignorance as to the details of the last twenty years of Beddoes's existence – full as those years certainly were of interest and even excitement. Nor has the veil been altogether withdrawn from that strange tragedy which, for the strange tragedian, was the last of all.

Readers of Miss Edgeworth's letters may remember that her youngest sister Anne, married a distinguished Clifton physician, Dr Thomas Beddoes. Their eldest son, born in 1803, was named Thomas Lovell, after his father and grandfather, and grew up to be the author of *The Brides' Tragedy* and *Death's Jest Book*. Dr Beddoes was a remarkable man, endowed with high and varied intellectual capacities and a rare independence of character. His scientific attainments were recognized by the University of Oxford, where he held the post of Lecturer in Chemistry, until the time of the French Revolution, when he was obliged to resign it, owing to the scandal caused by the unconcealed intensity of his liberal opinions. He then settled at Clifton as a physician, established a flourishing practice, and devoted his leisure to politics and scientific research. Sir Humphry Davy, who was his pupil, and whose merit he was the first to bring to light, declared that 'he had talents which would have exalted him to the pinnacle of philosophical eminence, if they had been applied with discretion'. The words are curiously suggestive of the history of his son; and indeed the poet affords a striking instance of the hereditary transmission of mental qualities. Not only did Beddoes inherit his father's talents and his father's inability to make the best use of them; he possessed in a no less remarkable degree his father's independence of mind. In both cases, this quality was coupled with a corresponding eccentricity of conduct, which occasionally, to puzzled onlookers, wore the appearance of something very near insanity. Many stories are related of the queer behaviour of Dr Beddoes. One day he astonished the ladies of Clifton by appearing at a tea-party with a packet of sugar in his hand; he explained that it was East Indian sugar, and that nothing would induce him to eat the usual kind, which came from Jamaica and was made by slaves. More extraordinary were his medical prescriptions; for he was in the habit of ordering cows to be conveyed into his patients' bedrooms, in order, as he said, that they might 'inhale the animals' breath'. It is easy to imagine the delight which the singular spectacle of a cow climbing upstairs into an invalid's bedroom must have given to the future author of *Harpagus* and *The Oviparous Tailor*. But 'little Tom', as Miss Edgeworth calls him, was not destined to enjoy for long the benefit of parental example; for Dr Beddoes died in the prime of life, when the child was not yet six years old.

The genius at school is usually a disappointing figure, for, as a rule, one must be commonplace to be a successful boy. In that preposterous world, to be remarkable is to be overlooked; and nothing less vivid than the white-hot blaze of a Shelley will bring with it even a distinguished martyrdom. But Beddoes was an exception, though he was not a martyr. On the contrary, he dominated his fellows as absolutely as if he had been a dullard and a dunce. He was at Charterhouse; and an entertaining account of his existence there has been preserved to us in a paper of school reminiscences, written by Mr C. D. Bevan, who had been his fag. Though his place in the school was high, Beddoes's interests were devoted not so much to classical scholarship as to the literature of his own tongue. Cowley, he afterwards told a friend, had been the first poet he had understood; but no doubt he had begun to understand poetry many years before he went to Charterhouse; and, while he was there, the reading which he chiefly delighted in was the Elizabethan drama. 'He liked acting,' says Mr Bevan, 'and was a good judge of it, and used to give apt though burlesque imitations of the popular actors, particularly Kean and Macready. Though his voice was harsh and his enunciation offensively conceited, he read with so much propriety of expression and manner, that I was always glad to listen: even when I was pressed into the service as his accomplice, his enemy, or his love, with a due accompaniment of curses, caresses, or kicks, as the course of his declamation required. One play in particular, Marlowe's *Tragedy of Dr Faustus*, excited my admiration in this way; and a liking for the old English drama, which I still retain, was created and strengthened by such recitations.' But Beddoes's dramatic performances were not limited to the works of others; when the occasion arose he was able to supply the necessary material himself. A locksmith had incurred his displeasure by putting a bad lock on his bookcase; Beddoes vowed vengeance; and when next the man appeared he was received by a dramatic interlude, representing his last moments, his horror and remorse, his death, and the funeral procession, which was interrupted by fiends, who carried off body and soul to eternal torments. Such was the realistic vigour of the performance that the locksmith, according to Mr Bevan, 'departed in a storm of wrath and execrations, and could not be persuaded, for some time, to resume his work'.

Besides the interlude of the wicked locksmith, Beddoes's school compositions included a novel in the style of Fielding (which has unfortunately disappeared), the beginnings of an Elizabethan tragedy, and much miscellaneous verse. In 1820 he left Charterhouse, and went to Pembroke College, Oxford, where, in the following year, while still a freshman, he published his first volume, *The Improvisatore*, a series of short narratives in verse. The book had been written in part while he was at school; and its immaturity is obvious. It contains no trace of the nervous vigour of his later style; the verse is weak, and the sentiment, to use his own expression, 'Moorish'. Indeed, the only interest of the little work lies in the evidence which it affords that the singular preoccupation which eventually dominated Beddoes's mind had, even in these days, made its appearance. The book is full of death. The poems begin on battle-fields and end in charnel-houses; old men are slaughtered in cold blood, and lovers are struck by lightning into mouldering heaps of corruption. The boy, with his elaborate exhibitions of physical horror, was doing his best to make his readers' flesh creep. But the attempt was far too crude; and in after years, when Beddoes had become a past-master of that difficult art, he was very much ashamed of his first publication. So eager was he to destroy every trace of its existence, that he did not spare even the finely bound copies of his friends. The story goes that he amused himself by visiting their libraries with a penknife, so that, when next they took out the precious volume, they found the pages gone.

Beddoes, however, had no reason to be ashamed of his next publication, *The Brides' Tragedy*, which appeared in 1822. In a single bound, he had reached the threshold of poetry, and was knocking at the door. The line which divides the best and most accomplished verse from poetry itself – that subtle and momentous line which every one can draw, and no one can explain – Beddoes had not yet crossed. But he had gone as far as it was possible to go by the aid of mere skill in the art of writing, and he was still in his twentieth year. Many passages in *The Brides' Tragedy* seem only to be waiting for the breath of inspiration which will bring them into life; and indeed, here and there, the breath has come, the warm, the true, the vital breath of Apollo. No one, surely, whose lips had not tasted of the waters of Helicon, could have uttered such words as these:

> Here's the blue violet, like Pandora's eye,
> When first it darkened with immortal life

or a line of such intense imaginative force as this:

> I've huddled her into the wormy earth;

or this splendid description of a stormy sunrise:

> The day is in its shroud while yet an infant;
> And Night with giant strides stalks o'er the world,
> Like a swart Cyclops, on its hideous front
> One round, red, thunder-swollen eye ablaze.

The play was written on the Elizabethan model, and, as a play, it is disfigured by Beddoes's most characteristic faults: the construction is weak, the interest fluctuates from character to character, and the motives and actions of the characters themselves are for the most part curiously remote from the realities of life. Yet, though the merit of the tragedy depends almost entirely upon the verse, there are signs in it that, while Beddoes lacked the gift of construction, he nevertheless possessed one important dramatic faculty – the power of creating detached scenes of interest and beauty. The scene in which the half-crazed Leonora imagines to herself, beside the couch on which her dead daughter lies, that the child is really living after all, is dramatic in the highest sense of the word; the situation, with all its capabilities of pathetic irony, is conceived and developed with consummate art and absolute restraint. Leonora's speech ends thus:

> . . . Speak, I pray thee, Floribel,
> Speak to thy mother; do but whisper 'aye';
> Well, well, I will not press her; I am sure
> She has the welcome news of some good fortune,
> And hoards the telling till her father comes;
> . . . Ah! She half laughed. I've guessed it then;
> Come tell me, I'll be secret. Nay, if you mock me,
> I must be very angry till you speak.

145

> Now this is silly; some of these young boys
> Have dressed the cushions with her clothes in sport.
> 'Tis very like her. I could make this image
> Act all her greetings; she shall bow her head:
> 'Good-morrow, mother'; and her smiling face
> Falls on my neck. – Oh, heaven, 'tis she indeed!
> I know it all – don't tell me.

The last seven words are a summary of anguish, horror, and despair, such as Webster himself might have been proud to write.

*The Brides' Tragedy* was well received by critics; and a laudatory notice of Beddoes in the *Edinburgh*, written by Bryan Waller Procter – better known then than now under his pseudonym of Barry Cornwall – led to a lasting friendship between the two poets. The connection had an important result, for it was through Procter that Beddoes became acquainted with the most intimate of all his friends – Thomas Forbes Kelsall, then a young lawyer at Southampton. In the summer of 1823 Beddoes stayed at Southampton for several months, and, while ostensibly studying for his Oxford degree, gave up most of his time to conversations with Kelsall and to dramatic composition. It was a culminating point in his life: one of those moments which come, even to the most fortunate, once and once only – when youth, and hope, and the high exuberance of genius combine with circumstance and opportunity to crown the marvellous hour. The spadework of *The Brides' Tragedy* had been accomplished; the seed had been sown; and now the harvest was beginning. Beddoes, 'with the delicious sense', as Kelsall wrote long afterwards, 'of the laurel freshly twined around his head', poured out, in these Southampton evenings, an eager stream of song. 'His poetic composition,' says his friend, 'was then exceedingly facile: more than once or twice has he taken home with him at night some unfinished act of a drama, in which the editor [Kelsall] had found much to admire, and, at the next meeting, has produced a new one, similar in design, but filled with other thoughts and fancies, which his teeming imagination had projected, in its sheer abundance, and not from any feeling, right or fastidious, of unworthiness in its predecessor. Of several of these very striking fragments, large and grand in their aspect as they each started into form,

> Like the red outline of beginning Adam,

. . . the only trace remaining is literally the impression thus deeply cut into their one observer's mind. The fine verse just quoted is the sole remnant, indelibly stamped on the editor's memory, of one of these extinct creations.' Fragments survive of at least four dramas, projected, and brought to various stages of completion, at about this time. Beddoes was impatient of the common restraints; he was dashing forward in the spirit of his own advice to another poet:

> Creep not nor climb,
> As they who place their topmost of sublime
> On some peak of this planet, pitifully.
> Dart eaglewise with open wings, and fly
> Until you meet the gods!

Eighteen months after his Southampton visit, Beddoes took his degree at Oxford, and, almost immediately, made up his mind to a course of action which had the profoundest effect upon his future life. He determined to take up the study of medicine; and with that end in view established himself, in 1825, at the University at Göttingen. It is very clear, however, that he had no intention of giving up his poetical work. He took with him to Germany the beginnings of a new play – 'a very Gothic-style tragedy', he calls it, 'for which I have a jewel of a name – DEATH'S JEST-BOOK; of course,' he adds, 'no one will ever read it'; and, during his four years at Göttingen, he devoted most of his leisure to the completion of this work. He was young; he was rich; he was interested in medical science; and no doubt it seemed to him that he could well afford to amuse himself for half-a-dozen years, before he settled down to the poetical work which was to be the serious occupation of his life. But, as time passed, he became more and more engrossed in the study of medicine, for which he gradually discovered he had not only a taste but a gift; so that at last he came to doubt whether it might not be his true vocation to be a physician, and not a poet after all. Engulfed among the students of Göttingen, England and English ways of life, and even English poetry, became dim to him; 'dir, dem Anbeter der seligen Gottheiten der Musen, u.s.w.,' he wrote to Kelsall, 'was Unterhaltendes kann der Liebhaber von Knochen, der fleissige Botaniker und Phisiolog mittheilen?' In 1830 he was still hesitating between the two alternatives. 'I sometimes wish,' he told the same friend, 'to devote myself exclusively to the study of anatomy and physiology in science, of languages, and dramatic poetry'; his pen had run away with him; and his 'exclusive' devotion turned out to be a double one, directed towards widely different ends. While he was still in this state of mind, a new interest took possession of him – an interest which worked havoc with his dreams of dramatic authorship and scientific research: he became involved in the revolutionary movement which was at that time beginning to agitate Europe. The details of his adventures are unhappily lost to us, for we know nothing more of them than can be learnt from a few scanty references in his rare letters to English friends; but it is certain that the part he played was an active, and even a dangerous one. He was turned out of Würzburg by 'that ingenious Jackanapes', the King of Bavaria; he was an intimate friend of Hegetschweiler, one of the leaders of liberalism in Switzerland; and he was present in Zurich when a body of six thousand peasants, 'half unarmed, and the other half armed with scythes, dungforks and poles, entered the town and overturned the liberal government'. In the tumult Hegetschweiler was killed, and Beddoes was soon afterwards forced to fly the canton. During the following years we catch glimpses of him, flitting mysteriously over Germany and Switzerland, at Berlin, at Baden, at Giessen, a strange solitary figure, with tangled hair and meerschaum pipe, scribbling lampoons upon the King of Prussia, translating Grainger's *Spinal Cord* into German, and Schoenlein's *Diseases of Europeans* into English, exploring Pilatus and the Titlis, evolving now and then some ghostly lyric or some rabelaisian tale, or brooding over the scenes of his 'Gothic-styled tragedy', wondering if it were worthless or inspired, and giving it – as had been his wont for the last twenty years – just one more touch before he sent it to the press. He appeared in England once or twice, and in 1846 made a stay of several months, visiting the Procters in London, and going down to Southampton to be with Kelsall once again. Eccentricity had grown on him; he would shut himself for days in his bedroom, smoking furiously; he would fall into fits of long and deep depression. He shocked some of his relatives by arriving at their country house astride a donkey; and he amazed the Procters by starting out one evening to set fire to Drury Lane Theatre with a lighted five-pound note. After this last visit to England, his history becomes even more obscure than before. It is known that in 1847 he was in Frankfort, where he lived for six months in close companionship with a young baker called Degen – 'a nice-looking young man, nineteen years of age', we are told, 'dressed in a blue blouse, fine in expression, and of a natural dignity of manner'; and that, in the spring of the following year, the two friends went off to Zurich, where Beddoes hired the theatre for a night in order that Degen might appear on the stage in the part of Hotspur. At Basel, however, for some unexplained reason, the friends parted, and Beddoes fell immediately into the profoundest gloom. 'Il a été misérable,' said the waiter at the Cigogne Hotel, where he was staying, 'il a voulu se tuer.' It was true. He inflicted a deep wound in his leg with a razor, in the hope, apparently, of bleeding to death. He was taken to the hospital, where he constantly tore off the bandages, until at last it was necessary to amputate the leg below the knee. The operation was successful, Beddoes began to recover, and, in the autumn, Degen came back to Basel. It seemed as if all were going well; for the poet, with his books around him, and the blue-bloused Degen by his bedside, talked happily of politics and literature, and of an Italian journey in the spring. He walked out twice; was he still happy? Who can tell? Was it happiness, or misery, or what strange impulse, that drove him, on his third walk, to go to a chemist's shop in the town, and to obtain there a phial of deadly poison? On the evening of that day – the 26th of January, 1849 – Dr Ecklin, his physician, was hastily summoned, to find Beddoes lying insensible upon the bed. He never recovered consciousness, and died that night. Upon his breast was found a pencil note, addressed to one of his English friends. 'My dear Philips,' it began, 'I am food for what I am good for – worms.' A few testamentary wishes followed. Kelsall was to have the manuscripts; and – 'W. Beddoes must have a case (50 bottles) of Champagne Moet, 1847 growth, to drink my death in . . . I ought to have been, among other things,' the gruesome document concluded, 'a good poet. Life was too great a bore on one peg, and that a bad one. Buy for Dr Ecklin one of Reade's best stomach-pumps.' It was the last of his additions to Death's Jest Book, and the most *macabre* of all.

Kelsall discharged his duties as literary executor with exemplary care. The manuscripts were fragmentary and confused. There were three distinct drafts of *Death's Jest Book*, each with variations of its own; and from these Kelsall compiled his first edition of the drama, which appeared in 1850. In the following year he brought out the two volumes of poetical works, which remained for forty years the only record of the full scope and power of Beddoes's genius. They contain reprints of *The Brides' Tragedy* and *Death's Jest Book*, together with two unfinished tragedies, and a great number of dramatic fragments and lyrics; and the poems are preceded by Kelsall's memoir of his friend. Of these rare and valuable volumes the Muses' Library edition is almost an exact reprint, except that it omits the memoir and revives *The Improvisatore*. Only one other edition of Beddoes exists – the limited one brought out by Mr Gosse in 1890, and based upon a fresh examination of the manuscripts. Mr Gosse was able to add ten lyrics and one dramatic fragment to those already published by Kelsall; he made public for the first time the true story of Beddoes's suicide, which Kelsall had concealed; and, in 1893, he followed up his edition of the poems by a volume of Beddoes's letters. It is clear, therefore, that there is no one living to whom lovers of Beddoes owe so much as to Mr Gosse. He has supplied most important materials for the elucidation of the poet's history: and, among the lyrics which he has printed for the first time, are to be found one of the most perfect specimens of Beddoes's command of unearthly pathos – *The Old Ghost* – and one of the most singular examples of his vein of grotesque and ominous humour – *The Oviparous Tailor*. Yet it may be doubted whether even Mr Gosse's edition is the final one. There are traces in Beddoes's letters of unpublished compositions which may still come to light. What has happened, one would like to know, to *The Ivory Gate*, that 'volume of prosaic poetry and poetical prose', which Beddoes talked of publishing in 1837? Only a few fine stanzas from it have ever appeared. And, as Mr Gosse himself tells us, the variations in *Death's Jest Book* alone would warrant the publication of a variorum edition of that work – 'if,' he wisely adds, for the proviso contains the gist of the matter – 'if the interest in Beddoes should continue to grow'.

'Say what you will, I am convinced the man who is to awaken the drama must be a bold, trampling fellow – no creeper into worm-holes – no reviver even – however good. These re-animations are vampire-cold.' The words occur in one of Beddoes's letters, and they are usually quoted by critics, on the rare occasions on which his poetry is discussed, as an instance of the curious incapacity of artists to practise what they preach. But the truth is that Beddoes was not a 'creeper into worm-holes', he was not even a 'reviver'; he was a reincarnation. Everything that we know of him goes to show that the laborious and elaborate effort of literary reconstruction was quite alien to his spirit. We have Kelsall's evidence as to the ease and abundance of his composition; we have the character of the man, as it shines forth in his letters and in the history of his life – records of a 'bold, trampling fellow', if ever there was one; and we have the evidence of his poetry itself. For the impress of a fresh and vital intelligence is stamped unmistakably upon all that is best in his work. His mature blank verse is perfect. It is not an artificial concoction galvanized into the semblance of life; it simply lives. And, with Beddoes, maturity was precocious, for he obtained complete mastery over the most difficult and dangerous of metres at a wonderfully early age. Blank verse is like the Djin in the Arabian Nights; it is either the most terrible of masters, or the most powerful of slaves. If you have not the magic secret, it will take your best thoughts, your bravest imaginations, and change them into toads and fishes; but, if the spell be yours, it will turn into a flying carpet and lift your simplest utterance into the highest heaven. Beddoes had mastered the 'Open, Sesame' at an age when most poets are still mouthing ineffectual wheats and barleys. In his twenty-second year, his thoughts filled and moved and animated his blank verse as easily and familiarly as a hand in a glove. He wishes to compare, for instance, the human mind, with its knowledge of the past, to a single eye receiving the light of the stars; and the object of the comparison is to lay stress upon the concentration on one point of a vast multiplicity of objects. There could be no better exercise for a young verse-writer than to attempt his own expression of this idea, and then to examine these lines by Beddoes – lines where simplicity and splendour have been woven together with the ease of accomplished art.

> How glorious to live! Even in one thought
> The wisdom of past times to fit together,
> And from the luminous minds of many men
> Catch a reflected truth; as, in one eye,
> Light, from unnumbered worlds and farthest planets
> Of the star-crowded universe, is gathered
> Into one ray.

The effect is, of course, partly produced by the diction; but the diction, fine as it is, would be useless without the phrasing – that art by which the two forces of the metre and the sense are made at once to combat, to combine with, and to heighten each other. It is, however, impossible to do more than touch upon this side – the technical side – of Beddoes's genius. But it may be noticed that in his mastery of phrasing – as in so much besides – he was a true Elizabethan. The great artists of that age knew that without phrasing dramatic verse was a dead thing; and it is only necessary to turn from their pages to those of an eighteenth-century dramatist – Addison, for instance – to understand how right they were.

Beddoes's power of creating scenes of intense dramatic force, which had already begun to show itself in *The Brides' Tragedy*, reached its full development in his subsequent work. The opening act of *The Second Brother* – the most nearly complete of his unfinished tragedies – is a striking example of a powerful and original theme treated in such a way that, while the whole of it is steeped in imaginative poetry, yet not one ounce of its dramatic effectiveness is lost. The duke's next brother, the heir to the dukedom of Ferrara, returns to the city, after years of wandering, a miserable and sordid beggar – to find his younger brother, rich, beautiful, and reckless, leading a life of gay debauchery, with the assurance of succeeding to the dukedom when the duke dies. The situation presents possibilities for just those bold and extraordinary contrasts which were so dear to Beddoes's heart. While Marcello, the second brother, is meditating over his wretched fate, Orazio, the third, comes upon the stage, crowned and glorious, attended by a train of singing revellers, and with a courtesan upon either hand. 'Wine in a ruby!' he exclaims, gazing into his mistress's eyes:

> I'll solemnize their beauty in a draught
> Pressed from the summer of an hundred vines.

Meanwhile Marcello pushes himself forward, and attempts to salute his brother.

> *Orazio.*   Insolent beggar!
> *Marcello.*                   Prince! But we must shake hands.
>     Look you, the round earth's like a sleeping serpent,
>     Who drops her dusky tail upon her crown
>     Just here. Oh, we are like two mountain peaks

> Of two close planets, catching in the air:
> You, King Olympus, a great pile of summer,
> Wearing a crown of gods; I, the vast top
> Of the ghosts' deadly world, naked and dark,
> With nothing reigning on my desolate head
> But an old spirit of a murdered god,
> Palaced within the corpse of Saturn's father.

They begin to dispute, and at last Marcello exclaims –

> Aye, Prince, you have a brother –
> *Orazio.*   The Duke – he'll scourge you.
> *Marcello.*                              Nay, *the second*, sir,
> Who, like an envious river, flows between
> Your footsteps and Ferrara's throne. . . .
> *Orazio.*                              Stood he before me there,
> By you, in you, as like as you're unlike,
> Straight as you're bowed, young as you are old,
> And many years nearer than him to Death,
> The falling brilliancy of whose white sword
> Your ancient locks so silverly reflect,
> I would deny, outswear, and overreach,
> And pass him with contempt, as I do you.
> Jove! How we waste the stars: set on, my friends.

And so the revelling band pass onward, singing still, as they vanish down the darkened street:

> Strike, you myrtle-crownèd boys,
> Ivied maidens, strike together! . . .

and Marcello is left alone:

>                              I went forth
> Joyfully, as the soul of one who closes
> His pillowed eyes beside an unseen murderer,
> And like its horrible return was mine,
> To find the heart, wherein I breathed and beat,
> Cold, gashed, and dead. Let me forget to love,
> And take a heart of venom: let me make
> A staircase of the frightened breasts of men,
> And climb into a lonely happiness!
> And thou, who only art alone as I,
> Great solitary god of that one sun,
> I charge thee, by the likeness of our state,

Undo these human veins that tie me close
To other men, and let your servant griefs
Unmilk me of my mother, and pour in
Salt scorn and steaming hate!

A moment later he learnt that the duke has suddenly died, and that
the dukedom is his. The rest of the play affords an instance of
Beddoes's inability to trace out a story, clearly and forcibly, to an
appointed end. The succeeding acts are crowded with beautiful
passages, with vivid situations, with surprising developments, but
the central plot vanishes away into nothing, like a great river
dissipating itself among a thousand streams. It is, indeed, clear
enough that Beddoes was embarrassed with his riches, that his
fertile mind conceived too easily, and that he could never resist the
temptation of giving life to his imaginations, even at the cost of
killing his play. His conception of Orazio, for instance, began by
being that of a young Bacchus, as he appears in the opening scene.
But Beddoes could not leave him there; he must have a romantic
wife, whom he has deserted; and the wife, once brought into being,
must have an interview with her husband. The interview is an
exquisitely beautiful one, but it shatters Orazio's character, for, in
the course of it, he falls desperately in love with his wife; and
meanwhile the wife herself has become so important and interesting a figure that she must be given a father, who in his turn becomes
the central character in more than one exciting scene. But, by this
time, what has happened to the second brother? It is easy to believe
that Beddoes was always ready to begin a new play rather than
finish an old one. But it is not so certain that his method was quite as
inexcusable as his critics assert. To the reader, doubtless, his faulty
construction is glaring enough; but Beddoes wrote his plays to be
acted, as a passage in one of his letters very clearly shows. 'You are,
I think,' he writes to Kelsall, 'disinclined to the stage: now I confess
that I think this is the highest aim of the dramatist, and should be
very desirous to get on it. To look down on it is a piece of
impertinence, as long as one chooses to write in the form of a play,
and is generally the result of one's own inability to produce
anything striking and affecting in that way.' And it is precisely upon
the stage that such faults of construction as those which disfigure
Beddoes's tragedies matter least. An audience, whose attention is

held and delighted by a succession of striking incidents clothed in splendid speech, neither cares nor knows whether the effect of the whole, as a whole, is worthy of the separate parts. It would be foolish, in the present melancholy condition of the art of dramatic declamation, to wish for the public performance of *Death's Jest Book*; but it is impossible not to hope that the time may come when an adequate representation of that strange and great work may be something more than 'a possibility more thin than air'. Then, and then only, shall we be able to take the true measure of Beddoes's genius.

Perhaps, however, the ordinary reader finds Beddoes's lack of construction a less distasteful quality than his disregard of the common realities of existence. Not only is the subject-matter of the greater part of his poetry remote and dubious; his very characters themselves seem to be infected by their creator's delight in the mysterious, the strange, and the unreal. They have no healthy activity; or, if they have, they invariably lose it in the second act; in the end, they are all hypochondriac philosophers, puzzling over eternity and dissecting the attributes of Death. The central idea of *Death's Jest Book* – the resurrection of a ghost – fails to be truly effective, because it is difficult to see any clear distinction between the phantom and the rest of the characters. The duke, saved from death by the timely arrival of Wolfram, exclaims, 'Blest hour!' and then, in a moment, begins to ponder, and agonize, and dream:

> And yet how palely, with what faded lips
> Do we salute this unhoped change of fortune!
> Thou art so silent, lady; and I utter
> Shadows of words, like to an ancient ghost,
> Arisen out of hoary centuries
> Where none can speak his language.

Orazio, in his brilliant palace, is overcome with the same feelings:

> Methinks, these fellows, with their ready jests,
> Are like to tedious bells, that ring alike
> Marriage or death.

And his description of his own revels applies no less to the whole atmosphere of Beddoes's tragedies:

> Voices were heard, most loud, which no man owned:

There were more shadows too than there were men;
And all the air more dark and thick than night
Was heavy, as 'twere made of something more
Than living breaths.

It would be vain to look, among such spectral imaginings as
these, for guidance in practical affairs, or for illuminating views on
men and things, or for a philosophy, or, in short, for anything
which may be called a 'criticism of life'. If a poet must be a critic of
life, Beddoes was certainly no poet. He belongs to the class of
writers of which, in English literature, Spenser, Keats, and Milton
are the dominant figures – the writers who are great merely because
of their art. Sir James Stephen was only telling the truth when he
remarked that Milton might have put all that he had to say in
*Paradise Lost* into a prose pamphlet of two or three pages. But who
cares about what Milton had to say? It is his way of saying it that
matters; it is his expression. Take away the expression from the
*Satires* of Pope, or from *The Excursion*, and, though you will
destroy the poems, you will leave behind a great mass of thought.
Take away the expression from *Hyperion*, and you will leave
nothing at all. To ask which is the better of the two styles is like
asking whether a peach is better than a rose, because, both being
beautiful, you can eat the one and not the other. At any rate,
Beddoes is among the roses: it is in his expression that his greatness
lies. His verse is an instrument of many modulations, of exquisite
delicacy, of strange suggestiveness, of amazing power. Playing on
it, he can give utterance to the subtlest visions, such as this:

Just now a beam of joy hung on his eyelash;
But, as I looked, it sunk into his eye,
Like a bruised worm writhing its form of rings
Into a darkening hole.

Or to the most marvellous of vague and vast conceptions, such as
this:

I begin to hear
Strange but sweet sounds, and the loud rocky dashing
Of waves, where time into Eternity
Falls over ruined worlds.

Or he can evoke sensations of pure loveliness, such as these:

So fair a creature! of such charms compact
As nature stints elsewhere: which you may find
Under the tender eyelid of a serpent,
Or in the gurge of a kiss-coloured rose,
By drops and sparks: but when she moves, you see,
Like water from a crystal overfilled,
Fresh beauty tremble out of her and lave
Her fair sides to the ground.

Or he can put into a single line all the long memories of adoration:

My love was much;
My life but an inhabitant of his.

Or he can pass in a moment from tiny sweetness to colossal turmoil:

I should not say
How thou art like the daisy in Noah's meadow,
On which the foremost drop of rain fell warm
And soft at evening: so the little flower
Wrapped up its leaves, and shut the treacherous water
Close to the golden welcome of its breast,
Delighting in the touch of that which led
The shower of oceans, in whose billowy drops
Tritons and lions of the sea were warring,
And sometimes ships on fire sunk in the blood,
Of their own inmates; others were of ice,
And some had islands rooted in their waves,
Beasts on their rocks, and forest-powdering winds,
And showers tumbling on their tumbling self,
And every sea of every ruined star
Was but a drop in the world-melting flood.

He can express alike the beautiful tenderness of love, and the hectic, dizzy, and appalling frenzy of extreme rage:—

... What shall I do? I speak all wrong,
And lose a soul-full of delicious thought
By talking. Hush! Let's drink each other up
By silent eyes. Who lives, but though and I
My heavenly wife? ...
I'll watch thee thus, till I can tell a second
By thy cheek's change.

In that, one can almost feel the kisses; and, in this, one can almost hear the gnashing of the teeth. 'Never!' exclaims the duke to his son Torrismond:

> There lies no grain of sand between
> My loved and my detested! Wing thee hence,
> Or thou dost stand to-morrow on a cobweb
> Spun o'er the well of clotted Acheron,
> Whose hydrophobic entrails stream with fire!
> And may this intervening earth be snow,
> And my step burn like the mid coal of Ætna,
> Plunging me, through it all, into the core,
> Where in their graves the dead are shut like seeds,
> If I do not – O, but he is my son!

Is not that tremendous? But, to find Beddoes in his most characteristic mood, one must watch him weaving his mysterious imagination upon the woof of mortality. One must wander with him through the pages of *Death's Jest Book*, one must grow accustomed to the dissolution of reality, and the opening of the nettled lips of graves; one must learn that 'the dead are most and merriest', one must ask – 'Are the ghosts eaves-dropping?' – one must realize that 'murder is full of holes'. Among the ruins of his Gothic cathedral, on whose cloister walls the Dance of Death is painted, one may speculate at ease over the fragility of existence, and, within the sound of that dark ocean,

> Whose tumultuous waves
> Are heaped, contending ghosts,

one may understand how it is that

> Death is mightier, stronger, and more faithful
> To man than Life.

Lingering there, one may watch the Deaths come down from their cloister, and dance and sing amid the moonlight; one may laugh over the grotesque contortions of skeletons; one may crack jokes upon corruption; one may sit down with phantoms, and drink to the health of Death.

In private intercourse Beddoes was the least morbid of human beings. His mind was like one of those Gothic cathedrals of which he was so fond – mysterious within, and filled with a light at once richer and less real than the light of day; on the outside, firm, and towering, and immediately impressive; and embellished, both inside and out, with grinning gargoyles. His conversation, Kelsall tells us, was full of humour and vitality, and untouched by any trace of egoism or affection. He loved discussion, plunging into it with fire, and carrying it onward with high dexterity and good-humoured force. His letters are excellent: simple, spirited, spicy, and as original as his verse; flavoured with that vein of rattling open-air humour which had produced his school-boy novel in the style of Fielding. He was a man whom it would have been a rare delight to know. His character, so eminently English, compact of courage, of originality, of imagination, and with something coarse in it as well, puts one in mind of Hamlet: not the melodramatic sentimentalist of the stage; but the real Hamlet, Horatio's Hamlet, who called his father's ghost old truepenny, who forged his uncle's signature, who fought Laertes, and ranted in a grave, and lugged the guts into the neighbour room. His tragedy, like Hamlet's, was the tragedy of an overpowerful will – a will so strong as to recoil upon itself, and fall into indecision. It is easy for a weak man to be decided – there is so much to make him so; but a strong man, who can do anything, sometimes leaves everything undone. Fortunately Beddoes, though he did far less than he might have done, possessed so rich a genius that what he did, though small in quantity, is in quality beyond price. 'I might have been among other things, a good poet,' were his last words. 'Among other things'! Aye, there's the rub. But, in spite of his own 'might have been', a good poet he was. Perhaps for him, after all, there was very little to regret; his life was full of high nobility; and what other way of death would have befitted the poet of death? There is a thought constantly recurring throughout his writings – in his childish as in his most mature work – the thought of the beauty and the supernal happiness of soft and quiet death. He had visions of 'rosily dying', of 'turning to daisies gently in the grave', of a 'pink reclining death', of death coming like a summer cloud over the soul. 'Let her deathly life pass into death,' says one of his earliest characters, 'like music on the night wind.' And, in *Death's Jest Book*, Sibylla has the same thoughts:

> O Death! I am thy friend,
> I struggle not with thee, I love thy state:
> Thou canst be sweet and gentle, be so now;
> And let me pass praying away into thee,
> As twilight still does into starry night.

Did his mind, obsessed and overwhelmed by images of death, crave at last for the one thing stranger than all these – the experience of it? It is easy to believe so, and that, ill, wretched, and abandoned by Degen at the miserable Cigogne Hotel, he should seek relief in the gradual dissolution which attends upon loss of blood. And then, when he had recovered, when he was almost happy once again, the old thoughts, perhaps, came crowding back upon him – thoughts of the futility of life, and the supremacy of death and the mystical whirlpool of the unknown, and the long quietude of the grave. In the end, Death had grown to be something more than Death to him – it was, mysteriously and transcendentally, Love as well.

> Death's darts are sometimes Love's. So Nature tells,
> When laughing waters close o'er drowning men;
> When in flowers' honied corners poison dwells;
> When Beauty dies: and the unwearied ken
> Of those who seek a cure for long despair
> Will learn . . .

What learning was it that rewarded him? What ghostly knowledge of eternal love?

> If there are ghosts to raise,
>     What shall I call,
> Out of hell's murky haze,
>     Heaven's blue pall?
> – Raise my loved long-lost boy
> To lead me to his joy.–
>     There are no ghosts to raise;
>     Out of death lead no ways;
>         Vain is the call.
>
>     – Know'st thou not ghosts to sue?
>         No love thou hast.
>     Else lie, as I will do,
>         And breathe thy last.
> So out of Life's fresh crown
> Fall like a rose-leaf down.
>     Thus are the ghosts to woo;
>     Thus are all dreams made true,
>         Ever to last!

1907

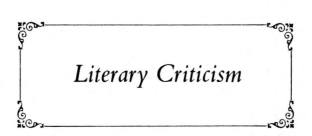

*Literary Criticism*

# Pope[1]

❦

Among the considerations that might make us rejoice or regret that
we did not live in the eighteenth century, there is one that to my
mind outbalances all the rest – if we had, we might have known
Pope. At any rate, we have escaped that. We may lament that
flowered waistcoats are forbidden us, that we shall never ride in a
sedan-chair, and that we shall never see good Queen Anne taking
tea at Hampton Court: but we can at least congratulate ourselves
that we run no danger of waking up one morning to find ourselves
exposed, both now and for ever, to the ridicule of the polite world
– that we are hanging by the neck, and kicking our legs, on the
elegant gibbet that has been put up for us by the little monster of
Twit'nam. And, on the other hand, as it is, we are in the happy
position of being able, quite imperturbably, to enjoy the fun. There
is nothing so shamelessly selfish as posterity. To us, after two
centuries, the agonies suffered by the victims of Pope's naughtiness
are a matter of indifference; the fate of Pope's own soul leaves us
cold. We sit at our ease, reading those *Satires* and *Epistles*, in which
the verses, when they were written, resembled nothing so much as
spoonfuls of boiling oil, ladled out by a fiendish monkey at an
upstairs window upon such of the passers-by whom the wretch had
a grudge against – and we are delighted. We would not have it
otherwise: whatever is, is right.

In this there is nothing surprising; but what does seem strange is
that Pope's contemporaries should have borne with him as they
did. His attacks were by no means limited to Grub Street. He fell
upon great lords and great ladies, duchesses and statesmen, noble
patrons and beautiful women of fashion, with an equal ferocity;
and such persons, in those days, were very well able to defend

[1] The Leslie Stephen Lecture for 1925.

themselves. In France, the fate suffered by Voltaire, at that very time, and on far less provocation, is enough to convince us that such a portent as Pope would never have been tolerated on the other side of the Channel. The monkey would have been whipped into silence and good manners in double quick time. But in England it was different. Here, though 'the Great', as they were called, were all-powerful, they preferred not to use their power against a libellous rhymer, who was physically incapable of protecting himself, and who, as a Roman Catholic, lay particularly open to legal pressure. The warfare between Pope and Lady Mary Wortley Montagu illustrates the state of affairs. The origin of their quarrel is uncertain. According to the lady, it was caused by her bursting into fits of laughter upon a declaration of passion from the poet. Another and perhaps more probable story traces the origin of the discord to a pair of sheets, borrowed by Lady Mary from old Mrs Pope, the poet's mother, and returned by her ladyship, after a fortnight, unwashed. But whatever may have been the hidden cause of the quarrel, its results were obvious enough. Pope, in one of his *Imitations of Horace*, made a reference to 'Sappho', whom all the world knew to be Lady Mary, in a couplet of extraordinary scurrility. Always a master of the art of compression, he asserted, in a single line of ten syllables, that his enemy, besides being a slanderous virago, was a debauched woman afflicted with a disgraceful malady. If, after this, Lady Mary had sent her friends or her footmen to inflict a personal chastisement upon the poet, or if she had used her influence with the government to have him brought to his senses, nobody could have been very much surprised. But she did nothing of the sort. Instead, she consulted with Lord Hervey, whom Pope had also attacked, and the two together decided to pay back their tormentor in his own coin. Accordingly they decocted and published a lampoon, in which they did their best to emulate both the style and the substance of the poet. 'None', they declared,

> thy crabbed numbers can endure,
> Hard as thy heart, and as thy birth obscure.

It shows, they said,

> the Uniformity of Fate
> That one so odious should be born to hate.

And if

> Unwhipt, unblanketed, unkick'd, unslain,
> That wretched little carcase you retain,
> The reason is, not that the world wants eyes,
> But thou'rt so mean, they see and they despise.

After sixty lines of furious abuse, they wound up with a shrug of the shoulders, which was far from convincing.

> You strike unwounding, we unhurt can laugh,

they asseverated. But for the unhurt this was certainly very odd laughter. It was also quite ineffective. Pope's first reply was a prose pamphlet, in which there is at least one amusing passage – 'It is true, my Lord, I am short, not well shaped, generally ill-dressed, if not sometimes dirty. Your Lordship and Ladyship are still in bloom, your figures such as rival the Apollo of Belvedere and the Venus of Medicis, and your faces so finished that neither sickness nor passion can deprive them of colour.' But, of course, he reserved his most poisonous shafts for his poetry. Henceforth, his readers might be sure that in any especially unsavoury couplet the name of Sappho would be found immortally embedded; while, as for Lord Hervey, he met his final doom in the Character of Sporus – the most virulent piece of invective in the English language.

Lady Mary and Lord Hervey, clever as they were, had been so senseless as to try to fight Pope on his own ground, and, naturally enough, their failure was dismal. But why had they committed this act of folly? Their own explanation was the exact reverse of the truth. Far from despising the poet, they profoundly admired him. Hypnotized by his greatness, they were unable to prevent themselves from paying him the supreme compliment of an inept and suicidal imitation. And in this they were typical of the society in which they lived. That society was perhaps the most civilized that our history has known. Never, at any rate, before or since, has literature been so respected in England. Prior wrote well, and he became an ambassador. Addison wrote well, and he was made a Secretary of State. The Duke of Wharton gave Young £2,000 for having written a poem on the Universal Passion. Alderman Barber's great ambition was to be mentioned favourably by Pope.

He let it be understood that he would be willing to part with £4,000 if the poet would gratify him; a single couplet was all he asked for; but the Alderman begged in vain. On the other hand, Pope accepted £1,000 from the old Duchess of Marlborough in return for the suppression of an attack upon the late Duke. Pope cancelled the lines; but soon afterwards printed an envenomed character of the Duchess. And even the terrific Sarah herself – such was the overwhelming prestige of the potentate of letters – was powerless in face of this affront.

For the first time in our history, a writer, who was a writer and nothing more – Shakespeare was an actor and a theatrical manager – had achieved financial independence. Pope effected this by his translation of Homer, which brought him £9,000 – a sum equivalent to about £30,000 today. The immense success of this work was a sign of the times. Homer's reputation was enormous: was he not the father of poetry? The literary snobbery of the age was profoundly impressed by that. Yes, it was snobbery, no doubt; but surely it was a noble snobbery which put Homer so *very* high in the table of precedence – probably immediately after the Archbishop of Canterbury. Yet, there were difficulties. It was not only hard to read Homer, it was positively dangerous. Too close an acquaintance might reveal that the mythical figure sweeping along so grandly in front of the Archbishop of York was something of a blackguard – an alarming barbarian, with shocking tastes, small knowledge of the rules and altogether far from correct. Pope solved these difficulties in a masterly manner. He supplied exactly what was wanted. He gave the eighteenth century a Homer after its own heart – a Homer who was the father – not quite of poetry, indeed, but of something much more satisfactory – of what the eighteenth century believed poetry to be; and, very properly, it gave him a fortune in return.

The eighteenth century has acquired a reputation for scepticism; but this is a mistake. In truth there has never been a less sceptical age. Its beliefs were rigid, intense, and imperturbable. In literature, as in every other department of life, an unquestioning orthodoxy reigned. It was this extraordinary self-sufficiency that gave the age its force; but the same quality caused the completeness of its downfall. When the reaction came, the absolute certainty of the past epoch seemed to invest it with the maximum degree of odium and absurdity. The romantics were men who had lost their faith; and they rose against the old dispensation with all the zeal of rebels and heretics. Inevitably, their fury fell with peculiar vehemence upon Pope. The great idol was overturned amid shouts of execration and scornful laughter. The writer who, for three generations, had divided with Milton the supreme honour of English poetry, was pronounced to be shallow, pompous, monotonous, meretricious, and not a poet at all.

Now that we have perhaps emerged from romanticism, it is time to consider the master of the eighteenth century with a more impartial eye. This is not altogether an easy task. Though we may be no longer in the least romantic, are we not still – I hesitate to suggest it – are we not still slightly Victorian? Do we not continue to cast glances of furtive admiration towards the pontiffs of that remarkable era, whose figures, on the edge of our horizon, are still visible, so lofty, and so large? We can discount the special pleadings of Wordsworth; but the voice of Matthew Arnold, for instance, still sounds with something like authority upon our ears. Pope, said Matthew Arnold, is not a classic of our poetry, he is a classic of our prose. He was without an 'adequate poetic criticism of life'; his criticism of life lacked 'high seriousness'; it had neither largeness, freedom, insight, nor benignity. Matthew Arnold was a poet, but his conception of poetry reminds us that he was also an inspector of schools. That the essence of poetry is 'high seriousness' is one of those noble platitudes which commend themselves immediately as both obvious and comfortable. But, in reality, obviousness and comfort have very little to do with poetry. It is not the nature of poetry to be what anyone expects; on the contrary, it is its nature to be surprising, to be disturbing, to be impossible. Poetry and high seriousness! Of course, to Dr Arnold's son, they seemed to be inevitably linked together; and certainly had the world been created by Dr Arnold they actually would have been. But – perhaps fortunately – it was not. If we look at the facts, where do we find poetry? In the wild fantasies of Aristophanes, in the sordid lusts of Baudelaire, in the gentle trivialities of La Fontaine.

> Dreadful was the din
> Of hissing through the hall, thick swarming now
> With complicated monsters, head and tail,
> Scorpion, and asp, and amphisbaena dire,

> Cerastes horn'd, hydrus, and ellops drear,
> And dipsas –

That is not high seriousness; it is a catalogue of curious names; and it is poetry. There is poetry to be found lurking in the metaphysical system of Epicurus, and in the body of a flea. And so need we be surprised if it invests a game of cards, or a gentleman sneezing at Hampton Court? –

> Just where the breath of life his nostrils drew,
> A charge of snuff the wily virgin threw;
> The gnomes direct, to every atom just,
> The pungent grains of titillating dust.
> Sudden, with starting tears each eye o'erflows,
> And the high dome re-echoes to his nose.

Pope, we are told, was not only without 'high seriousness'; he lacked no less an 'adequate poetic criticism of life'. What does this mean? The phrase is ambiguous; it signifies at once too much and too little. If we are to understand – as the context seems to imply – that, in Matthew Arnold's opinion, no poetic criticism of life can be adequate unless it possesses largeness, freedom, and benignity, we must certainly agree that Pope's criticism of life was far from adequate; for his way of writing was neither large nor free, and there was nothing benignant about him. But the words will bear another interpretation; and in this sense it may turn out that Pope's poetic criticism of life was adequate to an extraordinary degree.

Let us examine for a moment the technical instrument which Pope used – I mean the heroic couplet.

When he was a young man, the poet Walsh gave Pope a piece of advice. 'We have had great poets,' he said, 'but never one great poet that was correct. I recommend you to make your leading aim – correctness.' Pope took the advice, and became the most correct of poets. This was his chief title to glory in the eighteenth century; it was equally the stick that he was most frequently and rapturously beaten with, in the nineteenth. Macaulay, in his essay on Byron, devotes several pages of his best forensic style to an exposure and denunciation of the absurd futility of the 'correctness' of the school of Pope. There is in reality, he declared, only one kind of correctness in literature – that which 'has its foundation in truth and in the principles of human nature'. But Pope's so-called correctness was something very different. It consisted simply in a strict obedience to a perfectly arbitrary set of prosodic rules. His couplet was a purely artificial structure – the product of mere convention; and, so far from there being any possible poetic merit in the kind of correctness which it involved, this 'correctness' was in fact only 'another name for dullness and absurdity'. A short time ago, the distinguished poet, M. Paul Valéry, demolished Macaulay's argument – no doubt quite unconsciously – in an essay full of brilliant subtlety and charming wit. He showed conclusively the essentially poetic value of purely arbitrary conventions. But, for our purposes, so drastic a conclusion is unnecessary. For Macaulay was mistaken, not only in his theory, but in his facts. The truth is that the English classical couplet – unlike the French – had nothing conventional about it. On the contrary, it was the inevitable, the logical, the natural outcome of the development of English verse.

The fundamental element in the structure of poetry is rhythmical repetition. In England, the favourite unit of this repetition very early became the ten-syllabled iambic line. Now it is clear that the treatment of this line may be developed in two entirely different directions. The first of these developments is blank verse. Milton's definition of blank verse is well known, and it cannot be bettered: it consists, he says, 'in apt numbers, fit quantity of syllables, and the sense variously drawn out from one verse into another'. Its essence, in other words, is the combination formed by rhythmical variety playing over an underlying norm; and it is easy to trace the evolution of this wonderful measure from the primitive rigidity of Surrey to the incredible virtuosity of Shakespeare's later plays, where blank verse reaches its furthest point of development – where rhythmical variety is found in unparalleled profusion, while the underlying regularity is just, still, miraculously preserved. After Shakespeare, the combination broke down; the element of variety became so excessive that the underlying norm disappeared, with the result that the blank verse of the latest Elizabethans is virtually indistinguishable from prose.

But suppose the ten-syllabled iambic were treated in precisely the contrary manner. Suppose, instead of developing the element of variety to its maximum, the whole rhythmical emphasis were put upon the element of regularity. What would be the result? This was the problem that presented itself to the poets of the seventeenth century, when it appeared to them that the possibilities of blank verse were played out. (In reality they were not played out, as Milton proved; but Milton was an isolated and unique phenomenon.) Clearly, the most effective method of emphasizing regularity is the use of rhyme; and the most regular form of rhyme is the couplet. Already, in the splendid couplets of Marlowe and in the violent couplets of Donne, we can find a foretaste of what the future had in store for the measure. Shakespeare, indeed, as if to show that there were no limits either to his comprehension or to his capacity, threw off a few lines which might have been written by Pope, and stuck them into the middle of *Othello*.[2] But it was not until the collapse of blank verse, about 1630, that the essential characteristics which lay concealed in the couplet began to be exploited. It was Waller who first fully apprehended the implications of regularity; and it is to this fact that his immense reputation during the succeeding hundred years was due. Waller disengaged the heroic couplet from the beautiful vagueness of Elizabethanism. He perceived what logically followed from a rhyme. He saw that regularity implied balance, that balance implied antithesis; he saw that balance also implied simplicity, that simplicity implied clarity and that clarity implied exactitude. The result was a poetical instrument contrary in every particular to blank verse – a form which instead of being varied, unsymmetrical, fluid, complex, profound, and indefinite, was regular, balanced, antithetical, simple, clear, and exact. But, though Waller was its creator, the heroic couplet remained, with him, in an embryonic state. Its evolution was slow; even Dryden did not quite bring it to perfection. That great genius, with all his strength and all his brilliance, lacked one quality without which no mastery of the couplet could be complete – the elegance of perfect finish. This was possessed by Pope. The most correct of poets – Pope was indeed that; it is his true title to glory. But the phrase does not mean that he

---

[2] She that in wisdom never was so frail
　To change the cod's head for the salmon's tail;
　She that could think, and ne'er disclose her mind;
　See suitors following, and not look behind;
　She was a wight, if ever such wight were,
　To suckle fools and chronicle small beer.

obeyed more slavishly than anybody else a set of arbitrary rules. No, it means something entirely different: it means that the system of versification of which the principle is regularity reached in Pope's hands the final plenitude of its nature – its ultimate significance – its supreme consummation.

That Pope's verse is artificial there can be no doubt. But then there is only one kind of verse that is not artificial, and that is, bad verse. Yet it is true that there is a sense in which Pope's couplet is more artificial than, let us say, the later blank verse of Shakespeare – it has less resemblance to nature. It is regular and neat; but nature is 'divers et ondoyant'; and so is blank verse. Nature and blank verse are complicated; and Pope's couplet is simplicity itself. But what a profound art underlies that simplicity! Pope's great achievement in English literature was the triumph of simplification. In one of his earliest works, the *Pastorals*, there is simplicity and nothing else; Pope had understood that if he could once attain to a perfect simplicity, all the rest would follow in good time –

> O deign to visit our forsaken seats,
> The mossy fountains, and the green retreats!
> Where'er you walk, cool gales shall fan the glade;
> Trees, where you sit, shall crowd into a shade;
> Where'er you tread, the blushing flow'rs shall rise,
> And all things flourish where you turn your eyes.

The lines flow on with the most transparent limpidity –

> But see, the shepherds shun the noon-day heat,
> The lowing herds to murm'ring brooks retreat,
> To closer shades the panting flocks remove;
> Ye Gods! and is there no relief for love?

Everything is obvious. The diction is a mass of clichés, the epithets are the most commonplace possible; the herds low, the brooks murmur, the flocks pant and remove, the retreats are green, and the flowers blush. The rhythm is that of a rocking-horse; and the sentiment is mere sugar. But what a relief! What a relief to have escaped for once from *le mot propre*, from subtle elaboration of diction and metre, from complicated states of mind, and all the profound obscurities of Shakespeare and Mr T. S. Eliot! How delightful to have no trouble at all – to understand so very, very easily every single thing that is said!

This is Pope at his most youthful. As he matured, his verse matured with him. Eventually, his couplets, while retaining to the full their early ease, polish, and lucidity, became charged with an extraordinary weight. He was able to be massive, as no other wielder of the measure has ever been –

> Lo! thy dread empire, Chaos! is restored;
> Light dies before thy uncreating word;
> Thy hand, great Anarch! lets the curtain fall,
> And universal Darkness buries All.

Here the slow solemnity of the effect is produced by a most learned accumulation of accents and quantities; in some of the lines all the syllables save two are either long or stressed. At other times, he uses a precisely opposite method; in line after line he maintains, almost completely, the regular alternation of accented and un-accented syllables; and so conveys a wonderful impression of solidity and force –

> Proceed, great days! till learning fly the shore,
> Till Birch shall blush with noble blood no more,
> Till Thames see Eton's sons for ever play,
> Till Westminster's whole year be holiday,
> Till Isis' Elders reel, their pupils' sport,
> And Alma Mater lie dissolved in Port!

Perhaps the most characteristic of all the elements in the couplet is antithesis. Ordinary regularity demands that the sense should end with every line – that was a prime necessity; but a more scrupulous symmetry would require something more – a division of the line itself into two halves, whose meanings should correspond. And yet a further refinement was possible: each half might be again divided, and the corresponding divisions in the two halves might be so arranged as to balance each other. The force of neatness could no further go; and thus the most completely evolved type of the heroic line is one composed of four main words arranged in pairs, so as to form a double antithesis.

> Willing to wound, and yet afraid to strike

is an example of such a line, and Pope's poems are full of them. With astonishing ingenuity he builds up these exquisite structures, in which the parts are so cunningly placed that they seem to interlock spontaneously, and, while they are all formed on a similar model, are yet so subtly adjusted that they produce a fresh pleasure as each one appears. But that is not all. Pope was pre-eminently a satirist. He was naturally drawn to the contemplation of human beings, their conduct in society, their characters, their motives, their destinies; and the feelings which these contemplations habitually aroused in him were those of scorn and hatred. Civilization illumined by animosity – such was his theme; such was the passionate and complicated material from which he wove his patterns of balanced precision and polished clarity. Antithesis penetrates below the structure; it permeates the whole conception of his work. Fundamental opposites clash, and are reconciled. The profundities of persons, the futilities of existence, the rage and spite of genius – these things are mixed together, and presented to our eyes in the shape of a Chinese box. The essence of all art is the accomplishment of the impossible. This cannot be done, we say; and it *is* done. What has happened? A magician has waved his wand. It is impossible that Pope should convey to us his withering sense of the wretchedness and emptiness of the fate of old women in society, in five lines, each containing four words, arranged in pairs, so as to form a double antithesis. But the magician waves his wand, and there it is –

> See how the world its veterans rewards!
> A youth of frolics, an old age of cards;
> Fair to no purpose, artful to no end,
> Young without lovers, old without a friend,
> A fop their passion, and their prize a sot;
> Alive ridiculous, and dead forgot!

And now, perhaps, we have discovered what may truly be said to have been Pope's 'poetic criticism of life'. His poetic criticism of life was, simply and solely, the heroic couplet.

Pope was pre-eminently a satirist; and so it is only natural that his enemies should take him to task for not being something else. He had no benignity; he had no feeling for sensuous beauty; he took no interest in nature; he was pompous – did he not wear a wig? Possibly; but if one is to judge poets by what they are without, where is one to end? One might point out that Wordsworth had no sense of humour, that Shelley did not understand human beings, that Keats could not read Greek, and that Matthew Arnold did not wear a wig. And, if one looks more closely, one perceives that there were a good many things that Pope could do very well – when he wanted to. Sensuous beauty, for instance –

> Die of a rose in aromatic pain.

If that is not sensuously beautiful, what is? Then, we are told, he did not 'compose with his eye on the object'. But once Pope looked at a spider, and this was what he composed –

> The spider's touch, how exquisitely fine!
> Feels at each thread, and lives along the line.

Could Wordsworth have done better? It is true that he did not often expatiate upon the scenery; but, when he chose, he could call up a vision of nature which is unforgettable –

> Lo! where Mæotis sleeps, and hardly flows
> The freezing Tanais thro' a waste of snows.

We see, and we shiver. It cannot be denied that Pope wore a wig; it must even be confessed that there are traces, in his earlier work especially, of that inexpressive ornament in the rococo style, which was the bane of his age; but the true Pope was not there. The true Pope threw his wig into the corner of the room, and used all the plainest words in the dictionary. He used them carefully, no doubt, very carefully, but he used them – one-syllabled, Saxon words, by no means pretty – they cover his pages; and some of his pages are among the coarsest in English literature. There are passages in the *Dunciad* which might agitate Mr James Joyce. Far from being a scrupulous worshipper of the noble style, Pope was a realist – in thought and in expression. He could describe a sordid interior as well as any French novelist –

> In the worst inn's worst room, with mat half-hung,
> The floors of plaster, and the walls of dung,
> On once a flock-bed, but repair'd with straw,
> With tape-tied curtains, never meant to draw,
> The George and Garter dangling from that bed
> Where tawdry yellow strove with dirty red,
> Great Villiers lies. . . .

But these are only the outworks of the citadel. The heart of the man was not put into descriptions of physical things; it was put into descriptions of people whom he disliked. It is in those elaborate Characters, in which, through a score of lines or so, the verse rises in wave upon wave of malice, to fall at last with a crash on the devoted head of the victim – in the sombre magnificence of the denunciation of the great dead Duke, in the murderous insolence of the attack on the great living Duchess, in the hooting mockery of Bufo, in the devastating analysis of Addison – it is here that Pope's art comes to its climax. With what a relish, with what a thrill, we behold once more the impossible feat – the couplet, that bed of Procrustes, fitted exactly and eternally with the sinuous egoism of Addison's spirit, or the putrescent nothingness of Lord Hervey's. In the Character of Sporus, says the great critic and lexicographer, in memory of whom I have had the honour of addressing you today, Pope 'seems to be actually screaming with malignant fury'. It is true.

> Let Sporus tremble! – What? that thing of silk,
> Sporus, that mere white curd of ass's milk?
> Satire or sense, alas! can Sporus feel?
> Who breaks a butterfly upon a wheel?
> – Yet let me flap this bug with gilded wings,
> This painted child of dirt, that stinks and stings;
> Whose buzz the witty and the fair annoys,
> Yet wit ne'er tastes, and beauty ne'er enjoys:
> So well-bred spaniels civilly delight
> In mumbling of the game they dare not bite.
> Eternal smiles his emptiness betray,
> As shallow streams run dimpling all the way.
> Whether in florid impotence he speaks,
> And, as the prompter breathes, the puppet squeaks,
> Or at the ear of Eve, familiar toad,
> Half froth, half venom, spits himself abroad
> In puns, or politics, or tales, or lies,
> Or spite, or smut, or rhymes, or blasphemies.
> His wit all see-saw, between that and this,
> Now high, now low, now master up, now miss,
> And he himself one vile antithesis.
> Amphibious thing! that acting either part,
> The trifling head, or the corrupted heart,

Fop at the toilet, flatterer at the board,
Now trips a lady, and now struts a lord.
Eve's tempter thus the Rábbins have expressed,
A cherub's face, a reptile all the rest;
Beauty that shocks you, parts that none can trust,
Wit that can creep, and pride that licks the dust.

It is true: Pope *seems* to be actually screaming; but let us not mistake. It is only an appearance; actually, Pope is not screaming at all; for these are strange impossible screams, unknown to the world of fact – screams endowed with immortality. What has happened then? Pope has waved his wand. He has turned his screams into poetry, with the enchantment of the heroic couplet.

1925

# A Victorian Critic

To the cold and youthful observer there is a strange fascination about the Age of Victoria. It has the odd attractiveness of something which is at once very near and very far off; it is like one of those queer fishes that one sees behind glass at an aquarium, before whose grotesque proportions and sombre menacing agilities one hardly knows whether to laugh or to shudder; when once it has caught one's eye, one cannot tear oneself away. Probably its reputation will always be worse than it deserves. Reputations, in the case of ages no less than of individuals, depend, in the long run, upon the judgments of artists; and artists will never be fair to the Victorian Age. To them its incoherence, its pretentiousness, and its incurable lack of detachment will always outweigh its genuine qualities of solidity and force. They will laugh and they will shudder, and the world will follow suit. The Age of Victoria was, somehow or other, unæsthetic to its marrow-bones; and so we may be sure it will never loom through history with the glamour that hangs about the Age of Pericles or the brilliance that sparkles round the eighteenth century. But if men of science and men of action were not inarticulate, we should hear a different story.

The case of Matthew Arnold is a case in point. And who has not heard of Matthew Arnold? Certainly, out of every hundred who have, you would not find more than forty who could tell you anything of his contemporary, Lyell, for instance, who revolutionized geology, or more than twenty who would attach any meaning whatever to the name of another of his contemporaries, Dalhousie, who laid the foundations of modern India. Yet, compared to the work of such men as these, how feeble, how insignificant was Matthew Arnold's achievement! But he was a literary man; he wrote poetry, and he wrote essays discussing other poets and dabbling in general reflections. And so his fame has gone out to the ends of the earth, and now the Clarendon Press have done him the honour of bringing out a cheap collection of his essays,[1] so that even the working-man may read him and find out the heights that could be reached, in the way of criticism, during the golden years of the 'sixties. Surely, before it is too late, a club should be started – an Old Victorian Club – the business of whose members would be to protect the reputation of their Age and give it a fair chance with the public. Perhaps such a club exists already – in some quiet corner of Pimlico; but if so, it has sadly neglected one of its most pressing duties – the hushing-up of Matthew Arnold.

For here in this collection of essays there lies revealed what was really the essential and fatal weakness of the Victorian Age – its incapability of criticism. If we look at its criticism of literature alone, was there ever a time when the critic's functions were more grievously and shamelessly mishandled? When Dryden or Johnson wrote of literature, they wrote of it as an art; but the Victorian critic had a different notion of his business. To him literature was always an excuse for talking about something else. From Macaulay, who used it as a convenient peg for historical and moral disquisitions, to Leslie Stephen, who frankly despised the whole business, this singular tradition holds good. In what other age would it have been possible for a literary critic to begin an essay on Donne, as Leslie Stephen once did, with the cool observation that, as he was not interested in Donne's poetry, he would merely discuss his biography? An historian might as well preface an account of Columbus with the remark that, as he was not interested in Columbus's geographical discoveries, he would say nothing about that part of his career. It was their ineradicable Victorian instinct for action and utility which drove these unfortunate writers into so strangely self-contradictory a position. 'No one in his senses,' they always seem to be saying, 'would discuss anything so impalpable and frivolous as a work of art; and yet it is our painful duty to do so; therefore we shall tell you all we can about the moral lessons we can draw from it, and the period at which it was produced, and the curious adventures of the man who produced it; and so, as you must admit, we shall have done our duty like the Englishmen that we are.'

This was not quite Matthew Arnold's way; he went about his

[1] *Essays by Matthew Arnold.* Oxford University Press.

business with more subtlety. He was a man, so he keeps assuring us, of a refined and even fastidious taste; it was his mission to correct and enlighten the barbarism of his age; he introduced the term 'philistine' into England, and laughed at Lord Macaulay. Yet it is curious to observe the flagrant ineptitudes of judgment committed by a writer of his pretensions directly he leaves the broad flat road of traditional appreciation. On that road he is safe enough. He has an unbounded admiration for Shakespeare, Dante, and Sophocles; he considers Virgil a very fine writer, though marred by melancholy; and he has no doubt that Milton was a master of the grand style. But when he begins to wander on to footpaths of his own, how extraordinary are his discoveries! He tells us that Molière was one of the five or six supreme *poets* of the world; that Shelley will be remembered for his essays and letters rather than for his poetry; that Byron was a greater poet than Coleridge or Shelley or Keats; that the French alexandrine is an inefficient poetical instrument; that Heine was an 'incomparably more important figure' in European poetry than Victor Hugo. As to his taste, a remarkable instance of it occurs in his Lectures on translating Homer. Describing the Trojan encampments by night on the plains of Troy, with their blazing watch-fires as numerous as the stars, Homer concludes with one of those astonishingly simple touches which, for some inexplicable reason, seem to evoke an immediate vision of thrilling and magical romance: 'A thousand fires were kindled in the plain; and by each one there sat fifty men in the light of the blazing fire. And the horses, munching white barley and rye, and standing by the chariots, waited for the bright-throned Morning.' Such was Homer's conception – it was the horses who were waiting for the morning. But Matthew Arnold will not have it so. 'I want to show you,' he says, 'that it is possible in a plain passage of this sort to keep Homer's simplicity without being heavy and dull'; and accordingly he renders the passage thus:

> By their chariots stood the steeds, and champ'd the
>     white barley,
> While their masters sate by the fire and waited for
>     Morning.

'I prefer,' he explains, 'to attribute this expectation of Morning to the master and not to the horse.' *I prefer!* Surely, if ever the word 'philistine' were applicable, this is the occasion for it. And, indeed, Arnold himself seems to have felt a twinge of conscience. 'Very likely,' he adds, with a charming ingenuousness, 'in this particular, as in any other particular, I may be wrong.'

One of the surest signs of a man's taste being shaky is his trying to prop it up by artificial supports. Matthew Arnold was always doing this. He had a craving for Academies. He thought that if we could only have a Literary Academy in England we should all be able to tell what was good and what was bad without any difficulty; for, of course, the Academy would tell us. He had a profound reverence for the French Academy – a body which has consistently ignored every manifestation of original genius; and no doubt the annual exhibitions of the Royal Academy gave him exquisite satisfaction. He even had dreams of a vast international Academy; carried away by the vision, he seemed almost to imagine that it was already in existence. 'To be recognised by the verdict of such a confederation,' he exclaims, 'is indeed glory; a glory which it would be difficult to rate too highly. For what could be more beneficent, more salutary? The world is forwarded by having its attention fixed on the best things; and here is a tribunal, free from all suspicion of national and provincial partiality, putting a stamp on the best things, and recommending them for general honour and acceptance.' But, failing this, failing the impartial tribunal which shall put 'a stamp on the best things', one can fall back upon other devices. If one is in doubt as to the merit of a writer, the best course one can take is to make him, so to speak, run the gauntlet of 'the great masters'. We must 'lodge well in our minds' lines and expressions of the great masters – 'short passages, even single lines will serve our turn quite sufficiently' – and these we shall find 'an infallible touchstone' for testing the value of all other poetry. The plan is delightfully simple; there is, indeed, only one small difficulty about it: it cannot come into operation until we have decided the very question which it is intended to solve – namely, who 'the great masters' are.

'The world is forwarded by having its attention fixed on the best things.' Yes; *the world is forwarded*. Here, plainly enough, is the tip of the Victorian ear peeping forth from under the hide of the æsthetic lion; the phrase might have come straight from Mr Roebuck or the *Daily Telegraph* – those perpetual targets for Matthew Arnold's raillery. But when he proceeds to suggest yet another test for literature, when he asserts that, in order to decide upon the value of any piece of writing, what we must do is to ask ourselves whether or not it is a 'Criticism of Life' – then, indeed, all concealment is over; the whole head of the animal is out. There is something pathetic about the eager persistence with which Matthew Arnold enunciates this doctrine. How pleased with himself he must have been when he thought of it! How beautifully it fitted in with all his needs! How wonderfully it soothed away all the difficulties of his situation! For, of course, he was nothing if not a critic, a man whose nature it was to look at literature from the detached and disinterested standpoint of a refined – a fastidious – æsthetic appreciation; and yet . . . and yet . . . well, after all (but please don't say so), how *could* anyone, at this time of day, in the 'sixties, be expected to take literature seriously, for its own sake? The contradiction was obvious, and it was reconciled by that ingenious godsend, the theory of the Criticism of Life. By means of that theory it became possible to serve God and Mammon at the same time. Life, as everyone knew, was the one serious affair in the world – active, useful life; but then literature, it turned out – or rather, all literature that was worth anything – was a criticism of life; and so, after all, Matthew Arnold was justified in writing about it, and the public were justified in reading what Matthew Arnold wrote, for they were not merely reading about literature – who would do that? – they were reading about the Criticism of Life. And it is singular to see the shifts to which Matthew Arnold was put in order to carry out this theory consistently. He had somehow to bring all 'the great masters' into line with it. Shakespeare was easy enough, for he will fit into any theory; and Sophocles, of course, saw life steadily and saw it whole; but Dante and Milton – a queer kind of criticism of life they give us, surely! But they were so elevated, so extremely elevated, that they would pass; as for Sappho and Catullus, it was convenient not to mention them. Of course Matthew Arnold was careful to give no very exact explanation of his famous phrase, and one is always being puzzled by his use of it. Pope, one would have thought, with those palpitating psychological portraits of his, in which are concentrated the experience and passion of one of the sharpest and most sensitive observers who ever lived – Pope might well be considered a critic of life; but for some reason or other Pope would not do. Byron, on the other hand – not the Byron of *Don Juan*, but the Byron of *Childe Harold* and *Manfred* – did very well indeed. But we must remember that Byron was still fashionable in the 'sixties, and that Pope was not.

Certainly it is a curious and instructive case, that of Matthew Arnold: all the more so since no one could suppose that he was a stupid man. On the contrary, his intelligence was above the average, and he could write lucidly, and he got up his subjects with considerable care. Unfortunately, he mistook his vocation. He might, no doubt, if he had chosen, have done some excellent and lasting work upon the movements of glaciers or the fertilization of plants, or have been quite a satisfactory collector in an up-country district in India. But no; he *would* be a critic.

1914

# A Russian Humorist

❧

'Look well at the face of Dostoievsky, half a Russian peasant's face, half a criminal physiognomy, flat nose, small penetrating eyes beneath lids that quiver with a nervous affection; look at the forehead, lofty, thoroughly well formed; the expressive mouth, eloquent of numberless torments, of abysmal melancholy, of infinite compassion and envy! – An epileptic genius, whose exterior speaks of the mild milk of human kindness, with which his temperament was flooded, and of the depth of an almost maniacal acuteness which mounted to his brain.' These words of Dr Brandes, which occur in a letter to Nietzsche, written in 1888, express with force and precision the view of Dostoievsky, both as a man and as a writer, which probably every reader of the extraordinary works now being translated by Mrs Garnett[1] would naturally be inclined to take. To the English reader, no less than to the Norwegian critic, what must first be apparent in those works is the strange and poignant mixture which they contain of 'an almost maniacal acuteness' with 'the mild milk of human kindness' – of the terrible, febrile agitations reflected in those penetrating eyes and their quivering lids, with the serene nobility and 'infinite compassion' which left their traces in the expressive mouth and the lofty brow. These conflicting and mingling qualities are, in fact, so obvious wherever Dostoievsky's genius reveals itself in its truly characteristic form, that there is some danger of yet another, and a no less important, element in this complex character escaping the notice which it deserves – the element of humour. That Dostoievsky was a humorist – and a humorist of a remarkable and original type – has

---

[1] *The Novels of Fyodor Dostoievsky.* Translated from the Russian by Constance Garnett. Vol. II., *The Idiot.* Vol. III., *The Possessed.* London: William Heinemann.

not been sufficiently emphasized by critics. Perhaps this may be partly explained by the fact that his most famous and widely read work, *Crime and Punishment*, happens to contain less of this particular quality than any of his other books. But to conclude from a perusal of *Crime and Punishment* that Dostoievsky had no humour would be as fallacious as to suppose that Shakespeare had none because he had written *Othello*. Indeed, just as a perspicacious reader, unacquainted with the rest of Shakespeare, might infer from the massive breadth and the penetrating vision of *Othello* the possibility of the early comedies, so the amazing psychological sympathy of *Crime and Punishment* almost suggests a similar phase of work in Dostoievsky. And, as a matter of fact, such work exists. The group of novels (not at present translated into English) of which *Uncle's Dream*, *The Eternal Husband*, and *Another's* are typical examples show Dostoievsky in a mood of wild gaiety, sometimes plunging into sheer farce, but more often reminiscent of the Molière of *Le Médecin Malgré Lui* and *Georges Dandin*, in the elaborate concentration of his absurdities, the brilliance of his satire, and his odd combination of buffoonery and common sense. This mood of pure comedy disappears in *The Double* – a singular and highly interesting work, containing a study of the growth of madness in a feeble intellect overcome by extreme self-consciousness – where the ridicule is piled up till it seems to topple over upon itself, and the furious laughter ends in a gnashing of teeth. Then we have *Crime and Punishment*, in which the humorous faculty is almost entirely suspended; and at last, in *The Idiot* and *The Possessed* (the two latest volumes of Mrs Garnett's complete translation), Dostoievsky's humour appears in its final and most characteristic form, in which it dominates and inspires all his other qualities – his almost fiendish insight into the human heart, his delight in the extraordinary and the unexpected, his passionate love of what is noble in man, his immense creative force – and endows them with a new and wonderful significance.

The truth is that it is precisely in such cases as Dostoievsky's that the presence or the absence of humour is of the highest importance. With some writers it hardly occurs to us to consider whether they are humorous or not. It makes very little difference to us, for instance, that Tolstoy should scarcely show any signs of humour at all. And the reason for this is clear. Tolstoy is one of those writers who present their imaginary world to us with such calmness, with such exactness, with such an appearance at least of judicial impartiality, that we are immediately satisfied and ask for nothing more. But the imaginary world of a Dostoievsky strikes our senses in a very different fashion; it comes to us amid terror and exorbitance – not in the clear light of day, but in the ambiguous glare of tossing torches and meteors streaming through the heavens. Now writing of that kind may have many advantages: it may arouse the curiosity, the excitement, and the enthusiasm of the reader to a high degree; but there is one great risk that it runs – the risk of unreality. The beckoning lights may turn out to be will-o'-the-wisps, the mysterious landscape nothing but pasteboard scenery. And against that risk the only really satisfactory safeguard is a sense of humour. An author with a sense of humour puts, as it were, a stiff stout walking-stick into the hand of his reader, and bids him lean on that, and, when he is in doubt of the way he is going, feel with it the solid earth under his feet. Balzac is a case in point. He had wit, but no humour; his readers are without that invaluable walking-stick, and the consequence is that they are constantly being tripped up by pieces of stage carpentry, or plunging up to their necks in the bogs of melodrama. If Dostoievsky had been simply what Dr Brandes describes and nothing more – a genius of excessive acuteness and excessive sensibility – we should have been in the same predicament in his pages. But it was not so. He had humour; and so it happens that, by virtue of that magic power, his wildest fancies have something real and human in them, and his moments of greatest intensity are not melodramatic but tragic. In *The Idiot*, for instance, the unchecked passions of Rogozhin and Nastasya, the morbid agonies of such a figure as Ippolit, the unearthly and ecstatic purity of the Prince – all these things are controlled and balanced by the sheer fun of a hundred incidents, by the ludicrousness of Lebedyev and General Ivolgin, and, above all, by the masterly creation of Madame Epanchin – the sharp-witted, impulsive, irascible old lady, who storms and snorts and domineers through the book with all the vigour of a substantial and familiar reality. Madame Epanchin had many worries, and her daughters were the cause of nearly all of them. Adelaïda, it is true, was engaged to be married, but Alexandra! –

'Sometimes she thought the girl was "utterly hopeless". "She is

twenty-five, so she will be an old maid; and with her looks!"
Lizaveta Prokofievna positively shed tears at night thinking of her,
while Alexandra herself lay sleeping tranquilly. "What is one to
make of her? Is she a Nihilist or simply a fool?" That she was not a
fool even Lizaveta Prokofievna had no doubt; she had the greatest
respect for Alexandra's judgment and was fond of asking her
advice. But that she was a *poule mouillée* she did not doubt for a
moment; "so calm there's no making her out. Though it's true
*poules mouillées* are not calm – foo, I am quite muddled over
them." '

The irritatingly phlegmatic Alexandra had a habit which
particularly annoyed her mother – she *would* dream the most inept
dreams. One day the climax was reached when it transpired that
Alexandra had dreamt of nine hens the night before – simply nine
hens, and that was all. Madame Epanchin was furious. Such
pleasant visions of domestic life are certainly not what one would
expect from the inspired epileptic of Dr Brandes's description; but
they are in truth typical of Dostoievsky's art. The thought of those
nine hens in Alexandra's dream gives one, somehow, a sense of
security amid the storm and darkness of that strange history; one
feels that one has one's walking-stick.

But Dostoievsky's humour serves another purpose besides that
of being a make-weight to those intense and extreme qualities in his
composition which would otherwise have carried him into mere
extravagance; it is also the key to his sympathetic treatment of
character. There are many ways of laughing at one's fellow-
creatures. One may do so with the savage fury of Swift, or the
barbed mockery of Voltaire, or the caressing mischief of Jane
Austen; but Dostoievsky, in his latest works, uses another sort of
laughter – the laughter of lovingkindness. Such laughter is very
rare in literature; Shakespeare has some for Falstaff (though there it
is complicated by feelings of genuine contempt); it inspired Sterne
when he created Uncle Toby, and, of course, there is the classic
instance of Don Quixote. Dostoievsky's mastery of this strange
power of ridicule, which, instead of debasing, actually ennobles and
endears the object upon which it falls, is probably the most
remarkable of all his characteristics. *The Idiot* is full of it. It falls in
gay cataracts over Madame Epanchin; it lends a humanity to the
absurd old General, fallen on evil times, whose romancings drift

into imbecility, and who remembers at last quite distinctly that he was one of Napoleon's pages in 1814. But the most elaborate use of it occurs in *The Possessed*, where the figure of Stepan Trofimovitch, the old idealistic Liberal who comes to his ruin among the hideous realities of modern Nihilism, is presented to us through an iridescent veil of shimmering laughter and tears. The final passage describing his death inevitably recalls the famous pages of Cervantes; and, while it would be rash to say that the Russian writer surpasses his Spanish predecessor in native force, it cannot be doubted that he is the superior in subtlety. Stepan Trofimovitch is a nineteenth-century Quixote – a complex creature of modern civilization, in whom the noblest aspirations are intertwined with the pettiest personal vanities, in whom cowardice and heroism, folly and wisdom, are inextricably mixed. So consummate is the portraiture that one seems to see the whole nature of the man spread out before one like a piece of shot silk, shifting every moment from silliness to saintliness, from meanness to dignity, from egoism to abnegation. This marvellous synthesis is the work of humour, but of humour which has almost transcended itself – a smile felt so profoundly that it is only shown in the eyes.

1914

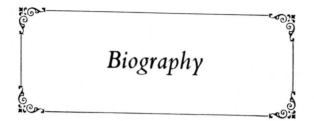

*Biography*

# Mr Creevey

Clio is one of the most glorious of the Muses; but, as everyone knows, she (like her sister Melpomene) suffers from a sad defect: she is apt to be pompous. With her buskins, her robes, and her airs of importance she is at times, indeed, almost intolerable. But fortunately the Fates have provided a corrective. They have decreed that in her stately advances she should be accompanied by certain apish, impish creatures, who run round her tittering, pulling long noses, threatening to trip the good lady up, and even sometimes whisking to one side the corner of her drapery, and revealing her undergarments in a most indecorous manner. They are the diarists and letter-writers, the gossips and journalists of the past, the Pepyses and Horace Walpoles and Saint-Simons, whose function it is to reveal to us the littleness underlying great events and to remind us that history itself was once real life. Among them is Mr Creevey. The Fates decided that Mr Creevey should accompany Clio, with appropriate gestures, during that part of her progress which is measured by the thirty years preceding the accession of Victoria; and the little wretch did his job very well.

It might almost be said that Thomas Creevey was 'born about three of the clock in the afternoon, with a white head and something a round belly'. At any rate, we know nothing of his youth, save that he was educated at Cambridge, and he presents himself to us in the early years of the nineteenth century as a middle-aged man, with a character and a habit of mind already fixed and an established position in the world. In 1803 we find him what he was to be for the rest of his life – a member of Parliament, a familiar figure in high society, an insatiable gossip with a rattling tongue. That he should have reached and held the place he did is a proof of his talents, for he was a very poor man; for the greater part of his life his income was less than £200 a year. But those were the days of patrons and jobs, pocket-boroughs and sinecures; they were the days, too, of vigorous, bold living, torrential talk, and splendid hospitality; and it was only natural that Mr Creevey, penniless and immensely entertaining, should have been put into Parliament by a Duke, and welcomed in every great Whig House in the country with open arms. It was only natural that, spending his whole political life as an advanced Whig, bent upon the destruction of abuses, he should have begun that life as a member for a pocket-borough and ended it as the holder of a sinecure. For a time his poverty was relieved by his marriage with a widow who had means of her own; but Mrs Creevey died, her money went to her daughters by her previous husband, and Mr Creevey reverted to a possessionless existence – without a house, without servants, without property of any sort – wandering from country mansion to country mansion, from dinner-party to dinner-party, until at last in his old age, on the triumph of the Whigs, he was rewarded with a pleasant little post which brought him in about £600 a year. Apart from these small ups and downs of fortune, Mr Creevey's life was static – static spiritually, that is to say; for physically he was always on the move. His adventures were those of an observer, not of an actor; but he was an observer so very near the centre of things that he was by no means dispassionate; the rush of great events would whirl him round into the vortex, like a leaf in an eddy of wind; he would rave, he would gesticulate, with the fury of a complete partisan; and then, when the wind dropped, he would be found, like the leaf, very much where he was before. Luckily, too, he was not merely an agitated observer, but an observer who delighted in passing on his agitations, first with his tongue, and then – for so the Fates had decided – with his pen. He wrote easily, spicily, and persistently; he had a favourite stepdaughter, with whom he corresponded for years; and so it happens that we have preserved to us, side by side with the majestic march of Clio (who, of course, paid not the slightest attention to him), Mr Creevey's exhilarating *pas de chat*.

Certainly he was not over-given to the praise of famous men. There are no great names in his vocabulary – only nicknames: George III is 'Old Nobs', the Regent 'Prinney', Wellington 'the Beau', Lord John Russell 'Pie and Thimble', Brougham, with whom he was on friendly terms, is sometimes 'Bruffam', sometimes 'Beelzebub', and sometimes 'Old Wickedshifts'; and Lord Durham, who once remarked that one could 'jog along on £40,000 a year', is 'King Jog'. The latter was one of the great Whig potentates, and it was characteristic of Creevey that his scurrility should have been poured out with a special gusto over his own leaders. The Tories were villains, of course – Canning was all perfidy and 'infinite meanness', Huskisson a mass of 'intellectual confusion and mental dirt', Castlereagh . . . But all that was obvious and hardly worth mentioning; what was really too exacerbating to be borne was the folly and vileness of the Whigs. 'King Jog', the 'Bogey', 'Mother Cole', and the rest of them – they were either knaves or imbeciles. Lord Grey was an exception; but then Lord Grey, besides passing the Reform Bill, presented Mr Creevey with the Treasurership of the Ordnance, and in fact was altogether a most worthy man.

Another exception was the Duke of Wellington, whom, somehow or other, it was impossible not to admire. Creevey, throughout his life, had a trick of being 'in at the death' on every important occasion; in the House, at Brooks's, at the Pavilion, he invariably popped up at the critical moment; and so one is not surprised to find him at Brussels during Waterloo. More than that, he was the first English civilian to see the Duke after the battle, and his report of the conversation is admirable; one can almost hear the 'It has been a damned serious business. Blücher and I have lost 30,000 men. It has been a damned nice thing – the nearest run thing you ever saw in your life', and the 'By God! I don't think it would have done if I had not been there.' On this occasion the Beau spoke, as was fitting, 'with the greatest gravity all the time, and without the least approach to anything like triumph or joy'. But at other times he was jocular, especially when 'Prinney' was the subject. 'By God! you never saw such a figure in your life as he is. Then he speaks and swears so like old Falstaff, that damn me if I was not ashamed to walk into the room with him.'

When, a few years later, the trial of Queen Caroline came on, it was inevitable that Creevey should be there. He had an excellent seat in the front row, and his descriptions of 'Mrs. P.', as he preferred to call her Majesty, are characteristic:

Two folding doors within a few feet of me were suddenly thrown open, and in entered her Majesty. To describe to you her appearance and manner is far beyond my powers. I had been taught to believe she was as much improved in looks as in dignity of manners; it is therefore with much pain I am obliged to observe that the nearest resemblance I can recollect to this much injured Princess is a toy which you used to call Fanny Royds (a Dutch doll). There is another toy of a rabbit or a cat, whose tail you squeeze under its body, and then out it jumps in half a minute off the ground into the air. The first of these toys you must suppose to represent the person of the Queen; the latter the manner by which she popped all at once into the House, made a *duck* at the throne, another to the Peers, and a concluding jump into the chair which was placed for her. Her dress was black figured gauze, with a good deal of trimming, lace, &c., her sleeves white, and perfectly episcopal; a handsome white veil, so thick as to make it very difficult to me, who was as near to her as anyone, to see her face; such a back for variety and inequality of ground as you never beheld; with a few straggling ringlets on her neck, which I flatter myself from their appearance were not her Majesty's own property.

Mr Creevey, it is obvious, was not the man to be abashed by the presence of Royalty.

But such public episodes were necessarily rare, and the main stream of his life flowed rapidly, gaily, and unobtrusively through the fat pastures of high society. Everywhere and always he enjoyed himself extremely, but his spirits and his happiness were at their highest during his long summer sojourns at those splendid country houses whose hospitality he chronicles with indefatigable *verve*. 'This house,' he says at Raby, 'is itself *by far* the most magnificent and unique in several ways that I have ever seen. . . . As long as I have heard of anything, I have heard of being driven into the hall of this house in one's carriage, and being set down by the fire. You can have no idea of the magnificent perfection with which this is accomplished.' At Knowsley 'the new dining-room is opened; it is 53 feet by 37, and such a height that it destroys the effect of all the other apartments. . . . There are two fireplaces; and the day we dined there, there were 36 wax candles over the table, 14 on it, and ten great lamps on tall pedestals about the room.' At Thorp Perrow 'all the living rooms are on the ground floor, one a very handsome one about 50 feet long, with a great bow furnished with rose-coloured satin, and the whole furniture of which cost £4000.' At Goodwood the rooms were done up in 'brightest yellow satin', and at Holkham the walls were covered with Genoa velvet, and there was gilding worth a fortune on 'the roofs of all the rooms and the doors'. The fare was as sumptuous as the furniture. Life passed amid a succession of juicy chops, gigantic sirloins, plump fowls, pheasants stuffed with pâté de foie gras, gorgeous Madeiras, ancient Ports. Wine had a double advantage: it made you drunk; it also made you sober: it was its own cure. On one occasion, when Sheridan, after days of riotous living, showed signs of exhaustion, Mr and Mrs Creevey pressed upon him 'five or six glasses of light French wine' with excellent effect. Then, at midnight, when the talk began to flag and the spirits grew a little weary, what could be more rejuvenating than to ring the bell for a broiled bone? And one never rang in vain – except, to be sure, at King Jog's. There, while the host was guzzling, the guests starved. This was too much for Mr Creevey, who, finding he could get nothing for breakfast, while King Jog was 'eating his own fish as comfortably as could be', fairly lost his temper.

My blood beginning to boil, I said: 'Lambton, I wish you could tell me what quarter I am to apply to for some fish.' To which he replied in the most impertinent manner: 'The servant, I suppose.' I turned to Mills and said pretty loud: 'Now, if it was not for the fuss and jaw of the thing, I would leave the room and the house this instant'; and dwelt on the damned outrage. Mills said: 'He hears every word you say': to which I said: 'I hope he does.' It was a regular scene.

A few days later, however, Mr Creevey was consoled by finding himself in a very different establishment, where 'everything is of a piece – excellent and plentiful dinners, a fat service of plate, a fat butler, a table with a barrel of oysters and a hot pheasant, &c., wheeled into the drawing-room every night at half-past ten.'

It is difficult to remember that this was the England of the Six Acts, of Peterloo, and of the Industrial Revolution. Mr Creevey, indeed, could hardly be expected to remember it, for he was utterly unconscious of the existence – of the possibility – of any mode of living other than his own. For him, dining-rooms 50 feet long, bottles of Madeira, broiled bones, and the brightest yellow satin were as necessary and obvious a part of the constitution of the universe as the light of the sun and the law of gravity. Only once in his life was he seriously ruffled; only once did a public question present itself to him as something alarming, something portentous, something more than a personal affair. The occasion is significant. On March 16, 1825, he writes:

> I have come to the conclusion that our Ferguson is *insane*. He quite foamed at the mouth with rage in our Railway Committee in support of this infernal nuisance – the loco-motive Monster, carrying *eighty tons* of goods, and navigated by a tail of smoke and sulphur, coming thro' every man's grounds between Manchester and Liverpool.

His perturbation grew. He attended the committee assiduously, but in spite of his efforts it seemed that the railway Bill would pass. The loco-motive was more than a joke. He sat every day from 12 to 4; he led the opposition with long speeches. 'This railway,' he exclaims on May 31, 'is the devil's own.' Next day, he is in triumph: he had killed the Monster.

> Well – this devil of a railway is strangled at last. . . . To-day we had a clear majority in committee in our favour, and the promoters of the Bill withdrew it, and took their leave of us.

With a sigh of relief he whisked off to Ascot, for the festivities of which he was delighted to note that 'Prinney' had prepared 'by having 12 oz. of blood taken from him by cupping'.

Old age hardly troubled Mr Creevey. He grew a trifle deaf, and he discovered that it was possible to wear woollen stockings under his silk ones; but his activity, his high spirits, his popularity, only seemed to increase. At the end of a party ladies would crowd round him. 'Oh, Mr Creevey, how agreeable you have been!' 'Oh thank you, Mr Creevey! how useful you have been!' 'Dear Mr Creevey, I laughed out loud last night in bed at one of your stories.' One would like to add (rather late in the day, perhaps) one's own praises. One feels almost affectionate; a certain sincerity, a certain immediacy in his response to stimuli, are endearing qualities; one quite understands that it was natural, on the pretext of changing house, to send him a dozen of wine. Above all, one wants him to go on. Why should he stop? Why should he not continue indefinitely telling us about 'Old Salisbury' and 'Old Madagascar'? But it could not be.

> Le temps s'en va, le temps s'en va, Madame;
> Las! Le temps non, mais nous, nous en allons.

It was fitting that, after fulfilling his seventy years, he should catch a glimpse of 'little Vic' as Queen of England, laughing, eating, and showing her gums too much at the Pavilion. But that was enough: the piece was over; the curtain had gone down; and on the new stage that was preparing for very different characters, and with a very different style of decoration, there would be no place for Mr Creevey.

1919

# James Boswell

It would be difficult to find a more shattering refutation of the lessons of cheap morality than the life of James Boswell. One of the most extraordinary successes in the history of civilization was achieved by an idler, a lecher, a drunkard, and a snob. Nor was this success of that sudden explosive kind which is frequent enough with youthful genius – the inspired efflorescence of a Rimbaud or a Swinburne; it was essentially the product of long years of accumulated energy; it was the supreme expression of an entire life. Boswell triumphed by dint of abandoning himself, through fifty years, to his instincts. The example, no doubt, is not one to be followed rashly. Self-indulgence is common, and Boswells are rare. The precise character of the rarity we are now able, for the first time, to estimate with something like completeness. Boswell's nature and inner history cannot be fully understood from the works published by himself. It is only in his letters that the whole man is revealed. Professor Tinker, by collecting together Boswell's correspondence and editing it with scholarly exactitude, has done a great service to English literature.[1] There is, in fact, only one fault to be found with this admirable book. Professor Tinker shows us more of Boswell than any previous editor, but he does not show us all that he might. Like the editors of Walpole's Letters and Pepys's Diary, while giving himself credit for rehabilitating the text of his author, he admits in the same breath that he has mutilated it. When will this silly and barbarous prudery come to an end?

Boswell's career was completely dominated by his innate characteristics. Where they came from it is impossible to guess. He was the strangest sport: the descendant of Scotch barons and

---

[1] *Letters of James Boswell.* Collected and edited by Chauncey Brewster Tinker. 2 vols. (Oxford: Clarendon Press.)

country gentlemen, the son of a sharp lowland lawyer, was an artist, a spendthrift, a buffoon, with a passion for literature, and without any dignity whatever. So he was born, and so he remained; life taught him nothing – he had nothing to learn; his course was marked out, immutably, from the beginning. At the age of twenty-three he discovered Dr Johnson. A year later he was writing to him, at Wittenberg, 'from the tomb of Melancthon': 'My paper rests upon the gravestone of that great and good man. . . . At this tomb, then, my ever dear and respected friend! I vow to thee an eternal attachment.' The rest of Boswell's existence was the history of that vow's accomplishment. But his connection with Dr Johnson was itself only the crowning instance of an overwhelming predisposition, which showed itself in a multitude of varied forms. There were other great men, for instance – there was Mr Wilkes, and General Paoli, and Sir David Dalrymple. One of Professor Tinker's most delightful discoveries is a series of letters from the youthful Boswell to Jean-Jacques Rousseau, in which all the writer's most persistent qualities – his literary skill, his psychological perspicacity, his passion for personalities and his amazing aptitude for self revelation – are exquisitely displayed. 'Dites-moi,' he asked the misanthropic sentimentalist, 'ne ferai-je bien de m'appliquer véritablement à la musique, jusques à un certain point? Dites-moi quel doit être mon instrument. C'est tard je l'avoue. Mais n'aurai-je le plaisir de faire un progrès continuel, et ne serai-je pas capable d'adoucir ma vieillesse par les sons de ma lyre?' Rousseau was completely melted. The elder Pitt, however, was made of sterner stuff. When Boswell appeared before him in the costume of a Corsican chieftain, 'Lord Chatham,' we are told, 'smiled, but received him very graciously in his Pompous manner' – and there the acquaintance ended; in spite of Boswell's modest suggestion that the Prime Minister should 'honour me now and then with a letter. . . . To correspond with a Paoli and with a Chatham is enough to keep a young man ever ardent in the pursuit of virtuous fame.'

Fame – though perhaps it was hardly virtuous – Boswell certainly attained; but his ardent pursuit of it followed the track of an extraordinary zigzag which could never have had anything in common with letters from Lord Chatham. His own letters to his friend Temple lay bare the whole unique peregrination, from start to finish. To confess is the desire of many; but it is within the power of few. A rare clarity of vision, a still rarer candour of expression – without these qualities it is vain for a man to seek to unburden his heart. Boswell possessed them in the highest degree; and, at the same time, he was untroubled by certain other qualities, which, admirable though they be in other connections, are fatal for this particular purpose. He had no pride, no shame, and no dignity. The result was that a multitude of inhibitions passed him by. Nevertheless he was by no means detached. His was not the method of the scientific observer, noting his introspections with a cold exactness – far from it; he was intimately fascinated by everything to do with himself – his thoughts, his feelings, his reactions; and yet he was able to give expression to them all with absolute ingenuousness, without a shade of self-consciousness, without a particle of reserve. Naturally enough the picture presented in such circumstances is full of absurdities, for no character which had suppressed its absurdities could possibly depict itself so. Boswell was *ex hypothesi* absurd: it was his absurdity that was the essential condition of his consummate art.

It was in the description of his love affairs that this truly marvellous capacity found its fullest scope. The succession of his passions, with all their details, their variations, their agitations, and their preposterousnesses, fill the letters to Temple (a quiet clergyman in the depths of Devonshire) with a constant effervescence of delight. One progresses with wonderful exhilaration from Miss W———t ('just such a young lady as I could wish for the partner of my soul') to Zelide ('upon my soul, Temple, I must have her'), and so to the Signora, and the Moffat woman ('can I do better than keep a dear infidel for my hours of Paphian bliss?'), and the Princess ('here every flower is united'), and the gardener's daughter, and Mrs D., and Miss Bosville, and La Belle Irlandaise ('just sixteen, formed like a Grecian nymph, with the sweetest countenance, full of sensibility, accomplished, with a Dublin education'), and Mrs Boswell ('I am fully sensible of my happiness in being married to so excellent a woman'), and Miss Silverton ('in the fly with me, an amiable creature who has been in France. I can unite little fondnesses with perfect conjugal love'), and Miss Bagnal ('*a Ranelagh girl*, but of excellent principles, in so much that she reads prayers to the servants in her father's family, every Sunday evening. "Let me see such a woman," cried I'), and Miss Milles ('*d'une certaine âge*, and with a fortune of £10,000'), and – but the catalogue is endless. These are the pages which record the sunny hours of Boswell's chequered day. Light and warmth sparkle from them; but, even in the noon of his happiness, there were sudden clouds. Hypochondria seized him; he would wake in the night 'dreading annihilation, or being thrown into some horrible state of being'. His conscience would not leave him alone; he was attacked by disgraceful illnesses; he felt 'like a man ordered for ignominious execution'; he feared that his infidelities to Mrs Boswell would not be excused hereafter. And then his vital spirits rushed to his rescue, and the shadow fled. Was he not the friend of Paoli? Indeed he was; and he was sitting in a library forty feet long, dressed in green and gold. The future was radiant. 'My warm imagination looks forward with great complacency on the sobriety, the healthfulness, and the worth of my future life.' As for his infidelities, were they so reprehensible after all? 'Concubinage is almost universal. If it was *morally* wrong, why was it permitted to the pious men under the Old Testament? Why did our Saviour never say a word against it?'

As his life went on, however, the clouds grew thicker and more menacing, and the end was storm and darkness. The climax came with the death of his wife. Boswell found himself at the age of fifty alone in the world with embarrassed fortunes, a family of young children to bring up, and no sign that any of the 'towering hopes' of his youth had been realized. Worse still, he had become by this time a confirmed drunkard. His self-reproaches were pitiable; his efforts at amendment never ceased; he took a vow of sobriety under 'a venerable yew'; he swore a solemn oath that he would give up drinking altogether – that he would limit himself to four glasses of wine at dinner and a pint afterwards; but it was all in vain. His way of life grew more and more disorderly, humiliating, and miserable. If he had retired to Scotland, and lived economically on his estate, he might have retrieved his position; but that was what he could not do; he could not be out of London. His ambitions seemed to multiply with his misfortunes. He exchanged the Scotch bar for the English, and lost all his professional income at a blow. He had wild hopes of becoming a Member of Parliament, if only he toadied Lord Lonsdale sufficiently; and Lord Lonsdale promised much, asked him to his castle, made a butt of him, hid his wig, was gravely concerned, and finally threw him off after 'expressing himself in the most degrading manner in presence of a low man from Carlisle and one of his menial servants'. Consolations now were few indeed. It was something, no doubt, to be able to go to Court. 'I was the *great man* at the late drawing-room in a suit of imperial blue lined with rose-coloured silk, and ornamented with rich gold-wrought buttons. What a motley scene is life!' And at Eton, where he was 'carried to dine at the Fellows' table', it was pleasant enough to find that in spite of a Scotch education one could still make a creditable figure. 'I had my classical quotations very ready.' But these were fleeting gleams. 'Your kindness to me,' he burst out to Temple, in April, 1791, 'fairly makes me shed tears. Alas, I fear that my constitutional melancholy, which returns in such dismal fits and is now aggravated by the loss of my valuable wife, must prevent me from any permanent felicity in this life. I snatch *gratifications*; but have no *comfort*, at least very little. . . . I get bad rest in the night, and then I brood over all my complaints – the *sickly mind* which I have had from my early years – the disappointment of my hopes of success in life – the irrevocable separation between me and that excellent woman who was my cousin, my friend, and my wife – the embarrassment of my affairs – the disadvantage to my children in having so wretched a father – nay, the want of *absolute certainty* of being happy after death, the *sure prospect* of which is *frightful*. No more of this.'

The tragedy was closing; but it was only superficially a sordid one. Six weeks later the writer of these lines published, in two volumes quarto, the *Life of Dr. Johnson*. In reality, Boswell's spirit had never failed. With incredible persistence he had carried through the enormous task which he had set himself thirty years earlier. Everything else was gone. He was burnt down to the wick, but his work was there. It was the work of one whose appetite for life was insatiable – so insatiable that it proved in the end self-destructive. The same force which produced the *Life of Johnson* plunged its author into ruin and desperation. If Boswell had been capable of retiring to the country and economizing we should never have heard of him. It was Lord Lonsdale's butt who reached immortality.

1925

# Lady Hester Stanhope

The Pitt nose has a curious history. One can watch its transmigrations through three lives. The tremendous hook of old Lord Chatham, under whose curve Empires came to birth, was succeeded by the bleak upward-pointing nose of William Pitt the younger – the rigid symbol of an indomitable *hauteur*. With Lady Hester Stanhope came the final stage. The nose, still with an upward tilt in it, had lost its masculinity; the hard bones of the uncle and the grandfather had disappeared. Lady Hester's was a nose of wild ambitions, of pride grown fantastical, a nose that scorned the earth, shooting off, one fancies, towards some eternally eccentric heaven. It was a nose, in fact, altogether in the air.

Noses, of course, are aristocratic things; and Lady Hester was the child of a great aristocracy. But, in her case, the aristocratic impulse, which had carried her predecessors to glory, had less fortunate results. There has always been a strong strain of extravagance in the governing families of England; from time to time they throw off some peculiarly ill-balanced member, who performs a strange meteoric course. A century earlier, Lady Mary Wortley Montagu was an illustrious example of this tendency: that splendid comet, after filling half the heavens, vanished suddenly into desolation and darkness. Lady Hester Stanhope's spirit was still more uncommon; and she met with a most uncommon fate.

She was born in 1776, the eldest daughter of that extraordinary Earl Stanhope, Jacobin and inventor, who made the first steamboat and the first calculating machine, who defended the French Revolution in the House of Lords and erased the armorial bearings – 'damned aristocratical nonsense' – from his carriages and his plate. Her mother, Chatham's daughter and the favourite sister of Pitt, died when she was four years old. The second Lady Stanhope, a frigid woman of fashion, left her stepdaughters to the care of futile governesses, while 'Citizen Stanhope' ruled the household from his laboratory with the violence of a tyrant. It was not until Lady Hester was twenty-four that she escaped from the slavery of her father's house, by going to live with her grandmother, Lady Chatham. On Lady Chatham's death, three years later, Pitt offered her his protection, and she remained with him until his death in 1806.

Her three years with Pitt, passed in the very centre of splendid power, were brilliant and exciting. She flung herself impetuously into the movement and the passion of that vigorous society; she ruled her uncle's household with high vivacity; she was liked and courted; if not beautiful, she was fascinating – very tall, with a very fair and clear complexion, and dark-blue eyes, and a countenance of wonderful expressiveness. Her talk, full of the trenchant nonchalance of those days, was both amusing and alarming: 'My dear Hester, what are you saying?' Pitt would call out to her from across the room. She was devoted to her uncle, who warmly returned her affection. She was devoted, too – but in a more dangerous fashion – to the intoxicating Antinous, Lord Granville Leveson Gower. The reckless manner in which she carried on this love-affair was the first indication of something overstrained, something wild and unaccountable, in her temperament. Lord Granville, after flirting with her outrageously, declared that he could never marry her, and went off on an embassy to St. Petersburg. Her distraction was extreme: she hinted that she would follow him to Russia; she threatened, and perhaps attempted, suicide; she went about telling everybody that he had jilted her. She was taken ill, and then there were rumours of an accouchement, which, it was said, she took care to *afficher*, by appearing without rouge and fainting on the slightest provocation. In the midst of these excursions and alarums there was a terrible and unexpected catastrophe. Pitt died. And Lady Hester suddenly found herself a dethroned princess, living in a small house in Montague Square on a pension of £1200 a year.

She did not abandon society, however, and the tongue of gossip continued to wag. Her immediate marriage with a former lover, Mr Hill, was announced; 'il est bien bon', said Lady Bessborough. Then it was whispered that Canning was 'le régnant' – that he was with her 'not only all day, but almost all night'. She quarrelled with

Canning and became attached to Sir John Moore. Whether she was actually engaged to marry him – as she seems to have asserted many years later – is doubtful; his letters to her, full as they are of respectful tenderness, hardly warrant the conclusion; but it is certain that he died with her name on his lips. Her favourite brother, Charles, was killed beside him; and it was natural that under this double blow she should have retired from London. She buried herself in Wales; but not for long. In 1810 she set sail for Gibraltar with her brother James, who was rejoining his regiment in the Peninsula. She never returned to England.

There can be no doubt that at the time of her departure the thought of a lifelong exile was far from her mind. It was only gradually, as she moved further and further eastward, that the prospect of life in England – at last even in Europe – grew distasteful to her; as late as 1816 she was talking of a visit to Provence. Accompanied by two or three English fellow travellers, her English maid, Mrs Fry, her private physician, Dr Meryon, and a host of servants, she progressed, slowly and in great state, through Malta and Athens, to Constantinople. She was conveyed in battleships, and lodged with governors and ambassadors. After spending many months in Constantinople, Lady Hester discovered that she was 'dying to see Napoleon with her own eyes', and attempted accordingly to obtain passports to France. The project was stopped by Stratford Canning, the English Minister, upon which she decided to visit Egypt, and, chartering a Greek vessel, sailed for Alexandria in the winter of 1811. Off the island of Rhodes a violent storm sprang up; the whole party were forced to abandon the ship, and to take refuge upon a bare rock, where they remained without food or shelter for thirty hours. Eventually, after many severe privations, Alexandria was reached in safety; but this disastrous voyage was a turning-point in Lady Hester's career. At Rhodes she was forced to exchange her torn and dripping raiment for the attire of a Turkish gentleman – a dress which she never afterwards abandoned. It was the first step in her orientalization.

She passed the next two years in a triumphal progress. Her appearence in Cairo caused the greatest sensation, and she was received in state by the Pasha, Mehemet Ali. Her costume on this occasion was gorgeous: she wore a turban of cashmere, a brocaded waistcoat, a priceless pelisse, and a vast pair of purple velvet pantaloons embroidered all over in gold. She was ushered by chamberlains with silver wands through the inner courts of the palace to a pavilion in the harem, where the Pasha, rising to receive her, conversed with her for an hour. From Cairo she turned northwards, visiting Jaffa, Jerusalem, Acre, and Damascus. Her travelling dress was of scarlet cloth trimmed with gold, and, when on horseback, she wore over the whole a white-hooded and tasselled burnous. Her maid, too, was forced, protesting, into trousers, though she absolutely refused to ride astride. Poor Mrs Fry had gone through various and dreadful sufferings – shipwreck and starvation, rats and black-beetles unspeakable – but she retained her equanimity. Whatever her Ladyship might think fit to be, *she* was an Englishwoman to the last, and Philippaki was Philip Parker and Mustapha Mr Farr.

Outside Damascus, Lady Hester was warned that the town was the most fanatical in Turkey, and that the scandal of a woman entering it in man's clothes, unveiled, would be so great as to be dangerous. She was begged to veil herself, and to make her entry under cover of darkness. 'I must take the bull by the horns,' she replied, and rode into the city unveiled at midday. The population were thunderstruck; but at last their amazement gave way to enthusiasm, and the incredible lady was hailed everywhere as Queen, crowds followed her, coffee was poured out before her, and the whole bazaar rose as she passed. Yet she was not satisfied with her triumphs; she would do something still more glorious and astonishing; she would plunge into the desert and visit the ruins of Palmyra, which only half-a-dozen of the boldest travellers had ever seen. The Pasha of Damascus offered her military escort, but she preferred to throw herself upon the hospitality of the Bedouin Arabs, who, overcome by her horsemanship, her powers of sight, and her courage, enrolled her a member of their tribe. After a week's journey in their company, she reached Palmyra, where the inhabitants met her with wild enthusiasm, and under the Corinthian columns of Zenobia's temple crowned her head with flowers. This happened in March 1813; it was the apogee of Lady Hester's life. Henceforward her fortunes gradually but steadily declined.

The rumour of her exploits had spread through Syria, and from the year 1813 onwards, her reputation was enormous. She was received everywhere as a royal, almost as a supernatural, personage:

she progressed from town to town amid official prostrations and popular rejoicings. But she herself was in a state of hesitation and discontent. Her future was uncertain; she had grown scornful of the West – must she return to it? The East alone was sympathetic, the East alone was tolerable – but could she cut herself off for ever from the past? At Laodicea she was suddenly struck down by the plague, and, after months of illness, it was borne in upon her that all was vanity. She rented an empty monastery on the slopes of Mount Lebanon, not far from Sayda (the ancient Sidon), and took up her abode there. Then her mind took a new surprising turn; she dashed to Ascalon, and, with the permission of the Sultan, began excavations in a ruined temple with the object of discovering a hidden treasure of three million pieces of gold. Having unearthed nothing but an antique statue, which, in order to prove her disinterestedness, she ordered her appalled doctor to break into little bits, she returned to her monastery. Finally, in 1816, she moved to another house, further up Mount Lebanon, and near the village of Djoun; and at Djoun she remained until her death, more than twenty years later.

Thus, almost accidentally as it seems, she came to the end of her wanderings, and the last, long, strange, mythical period of her existence began. Certainly the situation that she had chosen was sublime. Her house, on the top of a high bare hill among great mountains, was a one-storeyed group of buildings, with many ramifying courts and outhouses, and a garden of several acres surrounded by a rampart wall. The garden, which she herself had planted and tended with the utmost care, commanded a glorious prospect. On every side but one the vast mountains towered, but to the west there was an opening, through which, in the far distance, the deep blue Mediterranean was revealed. From this romantic hermitage, her singular renown spread over the world. European travellers who had been admitted to her presence brought back stories full of Eastern mystery; they told of a peculiar grandeur, a marvellous prestige, an imperial power. The precise nature of Lady Hester's empire was, indeed, dubious; she was in fact merely the tenant of her Djoun establishment, for which she paid a rent of £20 a year. But her dominion was not subject to such limitations. She ruled imaginatively, transcendentally; the solid glory of Chatham had been transmuted into the fantasy of an Arabian Night. No doubt she herself believed that she was something more than a chimerical Empress. When a French traveller was murdered in the desert, she issued orders for the punishment of the offenders; punished they were, and Lady Hester actually received the solemn thanks of the French Chamber. It seems probable, however, that it was the Sultan's orders rather than Lady Hester's which produced the desired effect. In her feud with her terrible neighbour, the Emir Beshyr, she maintained an undaunted front. She kept the tyrant at bay; but perhaps the Emir, who, so far as physical force was concerned, held her in the hollow of his hand, might have proceeded to extremities if he had not received a severe admonishment from Stratford Canning at Constantinople. What is certain is that the ignorant and superstitious populations around her feared and loved her, and that she, reacting to her own mysterious prestige, became at last even as they. She plunged into astrology and divination; she awaited the moment when, in accordance with prophecy, she should enter Jerusalem side by side with the Mahdi, the Messiah; she kept two sacred horses, destined, by sure signs, to carry her and him to their last triumph. The Orient had mastered her utterly. She was no longer an Englishwoman, she declared; she loathed England; she would never go there again; and if she went anywhere, it would be to Arabia, to 'her own people'.

Her expenses were immense – not only for herself but for others, for she poured out her hospitality with a noble hand. She ran into debt, and was swindled by the moneylenders; her steward cheated her, her servants pilfered her; her distress was at last acute. She fell into fits of terrible depression, bursting into dreadful tears and savage cries. Her habits grew more and more eccentric. She lay in bed all day, and sat up all night, talking unceasingly for hour upon hour to Dr Meryon, who alone of her English attendants remained with her, Mrs Fry having withdrawn to more congenial scenes long since. The doctor was a poor-spirited and muddle-headed man, but he was a good listener; and there he sat while that extraordinary talk flowed on – talk that scaled the heavens and ransacked the earth, talk in which memories of an abolished past – stories of Mr Pitt and of George III, vituperations against Mr Canning, mimicries of the Duchess of Devonshire – mingled phantasmagorically with doctrines of Fate and planetary influence, and speculations on the Arabian origin of the Scottish clans, and lamentations over the wickedness of servants; till the unaccountable figure, with its robes and its long pipe, loomed through the tobacco-smoke like some vision of a Sibyl in a dream. She might be robbed and ruined, her house might crumble over her head; but she talked on. She grew ill and desperate; yet still she talked. Did she feel that the time was coming when she should talk no more?

Her melancholy deepened into a settled gloom when the news came of her brother James's death. She had quarrelled with all her English friends, except Lord Hardwicke – with her eldest brother, with her sister, whose kind letters she left unanswered; she was at daggers drawn with the English consul at Alexandria, who worried her about her debts. Ill and harassed, she hardly moved from her bedroom, while her servants rifled her belongings and reduced the house to a condition of indescribable disorder and filth. Three dozen hungry cats ranged through the rooms, filling the courts with frightful noises. Dr Meryon, in the midst of it all, knew not whether to cry or laugh. At moments the great lady regained her ancient fire; her bells pealed tumultuously for hours together; or she leapt up, and arraigned the whole trembling household before her, with her Arab war-mace in her hand. Her finances grew more and more involved – grew at length irremediable. It was in vain that the faithful Lord Hardwicke pressed her to return to England to settle her affairs. Return to England, indeed! To England, that ungrateful, miserable country, where, so far as she could see, they had forgotten the very name of Mr Pitt! The final blow fell when a letter came from the English authorities threatening to cut off her pension for the payment of her debts. Upon that, after despatching a series of furious missives to Lord Palmerston, to Queen Victoria, to the Duke of Wellington, she renounced the world. She commanded Dr Meryon to return to Europe, and he – how could he have done it? – obeyed her. Her health was broken, she was over sixty, and, save for her vile servants, absolutely alone. She lived for nearly a year after he left her – we know no more. She had vowed never again to pass through the gate of her house; but did she sometimes totter to her garden – that beautiful garden which she had created, with its roses and its fountains, its alleys and its bowers – and look westward at the sea? The end came in June 1839. Her servants immediately possessed themselves of every movable object in the house. But Lady Hester cared no longer: she was lying back in her bed – inexplicable, grand, preposterous, with her nose in the air.

1919

# Sir John Harington

An old miniature shows a young man's face, whimsically Elizabethan, with tossed-back curly hair, a tip-tilted nose, a tiny point of
a beard, and a long single earring, falling in sparkling drops over a
ruff of magnificent proportions. Such was John Harington, as he
appeared in the happy fifteen-eighties, at Greenwich, or at
Nonesuch – a courtier, a wit, a scholar, a poet, and a great favourite
with the ladies. Even Gloriana herself usually unbent when he
approached her. She liked the foolish fellow. She had known him
since he was a child; he was her godson – almost, indeed, a family
connection, for his father's first wife had been a natural daughter of
her own indefatigable sire. Through this lady the young man had
inherited his fine Italian house at Kelston, in Somersetshire, where
one day Elizabeth, on her way to Bath, paid him the honour of an
extremely expensive visit. He had felt himself obliged to rebuild
half the house to lodge his great guest fittingly; but he cared little
for that – he wrote a rhyming epigram about it all, which amused
the ladies of the bedchamber. He wrote, he found, with extraordinary ease and pleasure; the words came positively running off the
end of his pen; and so – to amuse the ladies again, or to tease them –
he translated the twenty-eighth book of Ariosto's *Orlando Furioso*,
in which the far from decorous history of the fair Fiammetta is told.
The Queen soon got wind of this. She read the manuscript and sent
for the poet. She was shocked, she said, by this attempt to
demoralize her household; and she banished the offender from
Court until – could there be a more proper punishment? – he
should have completed the translation of the whole poem.
Harington hurried off to Kelston, worked away for a month or
two, and returned with a fine folio containing the entire *Orlando* in
English, together with notes, a life of Ariosto, 'a general allegory of
the whole', and 'apologie of Poetrie', an 'epistle dedicatorie to the

211

Queenes Majestie', and an engraved title-page with the portrait of himself and his dog Bungay. The book was printed in 1591. The exquisite elegance and mature serenity of the original are nowhere to be found in it; but Harington himself, bringing with him the natural abundance, the charming ingenuousness, the early morning freshness of his wonderful generation, comes to us delightfully on every page.

The translation was well received, and the gay young man looked about for new worlds to conquer. Not to be talked of was his only fear. A curious notion struck him. His nose was sensitive as well as impudent, and he had been made to suffer agonies by the sanitary arrangements in the houses of the great. Suddenly inspired, he invented the water-closet. Then, seizing his pen, he concocted a pamphlet after the manner of Rabelais – or, as he preferred to call him 'the reverent Rabbles' – in which extravagant spirits, intolerable puns, improper stories, and sly satirical digs at eminent personages were blended together into a preposterous rhapsody, followed by an appendix – written, of course, by his servant – could a gentleman be expected to discuss such details? – containing a minute account, with measurements, diagrams and prices, of the new invention. *The Metamorphosis of Ajax* – for so the book with a crowningly deplorable pun, [1] was entitled – created some sensation. Queen Elizabeth was amused. But then some malicious courtier told her that one of the satirical digs was aimed at the memory of Leicester, whereupon her smiles changed to frowns, the Star Chamber was talked of, and Harington made a strategic retreat to Somersetshire. 'The merry poet, my godson,' the Queen declared, 'must not come to Greenwich, till he hath grown sober and leaveth the ladies' sports and frolics.' But before very long she relented. With her supreme sense of the practical, she saw that, as she put it, 'the marrow of the book' was not entirely ludicrous; she sent down word to the poet that she approved of his invention; and eventually she set the fashion for the new contrivances by installing one of them in Richmond Palace, with a copy of the *Ajax* hanging from the wall.

Harington's next adventure was more serious. He was summoned by Essex to join his ill-fated expedition to Ireland, in command of a troop of horse. In Ireland, with a stretch of authority

[1] = 'a jakes' (eds.)

212

which was bitterly resented by the Queen, Harington was knighted by the rash Lord Deputy, and afterwards, when disaster came thick upon disaster, he followed his patron back to London. In fear and trembling, he presented himself before the enraged Elizabeth. 'What!' she cried, 'did the fool bring you too?' The terrified poet fell upon his knees, while the Queen, as he afterwards described it, 'chafed much, walked fastly to and fro, and looked with discomposure in her visage'. Then, suddenly rushing towards him, she caught hold of his girdle. 'By God's Son,' she shouted, 'I am no Queen, and that man is above me!' His stammering excuses were cut short with a 'Go back to your business!' uttered in such a tone that Sir John, not staying to be bidden twice, fled out of the room, and fled down to Kelston, 'as if all the Irish rebels had been at his heels'.

It is clear that poor Harington never quite recovered from the shock of that terrific scene. The remainder of his life passed in ineffectiveness and disillusionment. In the bosom of his family he did his best to forget the storms and shipwrecks of 'the Essex coast'; he wrote incessantly; he cracked scandalous jokes with his mother-in-law, old Lady Rogers; he busied himself over the construction of a curious lantern for King James of Scotland. But his happy vein had deserted him. His *Discourse shewing that Elyas must personally come before the Day of Judgment* could never get finished, and he threw aside his *Treatise on Playe* as a failure. His epigrams, no doubt, were more successful; he scribbled them down on every possible occasion, and the most scurrilous he invariably despatched to old Lady Rogers. She roared with laughter, but omitted to leave him a legacy. He dashed into her house as she was dying, broke open the chests, tried to get possession of everything, and was at last ignominiously ejected by his brother-in-law. King James was equally disappointing. Even the curious lantern, even a learned, elaborate, and fantastic dissertation *On the Succession to the Crown*, failed to win him. After he had been a year in London, the new King granted Sir John an interview, but, though his Majesty was polite, he was not impressed. 'Sir John,' he said, with much gravity, 'do you truly understand why the Devil works more with ancient women than others?' And, unluckily, on that, Sir John 'could not refrain from a scurvy jest'. Nevertheless, though he felt that he had made no headway, he would not despair; a little later, the Lord

Chancellorship of Ireland and the Archbishopric of Dublin fell vacant, and the author of *Ajax* bravely requested that he should be appointed to both offices. Oddly enough, his application received no answer. He solaced himself with an endeavour to win the good graces of the young Prince Henry, to whom he addressed a discourse, full of pleasant anecdotes, concerning all the bishops of his acquaintance, followed by a letter describing 'the good deedes and straunge feats' of his 'rare Dogge', Bungay – how he used to carry messages from London to Kelston, and how, on one occasion, he took a pheasant from a dish at the Spanish Ambassador's table, and then returned it to the very same dish, at a secret sign from his master.

But in truth the days of Bungay were over, and the new times were uncomfortable and strange. 'I ne'er did see such lack of good order, discretion, and sobriety.' There had been jollities and junketings, no doubt, in his youth, but surely they were different. He remembered the 'heroicall dames', the 'stately heroyns' whom he had celebrated aforetime –

> These entertayn great Princes; these have learned
>   The tongues, toys, tricks of Rome, of Spayn, of Fraunce;
>   These can correntos and lavoltas daunce,
> And though they foote it false 'tis ne'er discerned.

More and more his thoughts reverted to his old mistress. 'When she smiled, it was a pure sunshine, that everyone did choose to bask in, if they could, but anon came a storm from a sudden gathering of clouds, and the thunder fell in wondrous manner on all alike.' Yes! Those were great times indeed! And now . . . he was 'olde and infirme'; he was forty-five; he must seek a quiet harbour and lay up his barque. He lingered at Kelston, impoverished, racked by various diseases; he vainly took the Bath waters; he became 'stricken of a dead palsy'; until, in 1612, at the age of fifty-one, he passed into oblivion. And in oblivion he has remained. Nobody reads his *Orlando*; his letters are known to none but a few learned historians; his little books of epigrams lie concealed in the grim recesses of vast libraries; and Englishmen today, reflecting on many things, as they enjoy the benefits of a sanitary system unknown to the less fortunate inhabitants of other countries, give never a thought to Sir John Harington.

1923

# Muggleton

Never did the human mind attain such a magnificent height of self-assertiveness as in England about the year 1650. Then it was that the disintegration of religious authority which had begun with Luther reached its culminating point. The Bible, containing the absolute truth as to the nature and the workings of the Universe, lay open to all; it was only necessary to interpret its assertions; and to do so all that was wanted was the decision of the individual conscience. In those days the individual conscience decided with extraordinary facility. Prophets and prophetesses ranged in crowds through the streets of London, proclaiming, with complete certainty, the explanation of everything. The explanations were extremely varied: so much the better – one could pick and choose. One could become a Behmenist, a Bidellian, a Coppinist, a Salmonist, a Dipper, a Traskite, a Tryonist, a Philadelphian, a Christadelphian, or a Seventh Day Baptist, just as one pleased. Samuel Butler might fleer and flout at

> petulant, capricious sects,
> The maggots of corrupted texts;

but he, too, was deciding according to the light of his individual conscience. By what rule could men determine whether a text was corrupted, or what it meant? The rule of the Catholic Church was gone, and henceforward Eternal Truth might with perfect reason be expected to speak through the mouth of any fish-wife in Billingsgate.

Of these prophets the most famous was George Fox; the most remarkable was Lodowick Muggleton. He was born in 1609, and was brought up to earn his living as a tailor. Becoming religious, he threw over a charming girl, with whom he was in love and whom he was engaged to marry, on the ground that her mother kept a pawnbroker's shop and that usury was sinful. He was persuaded to this by his puritan friends, among whom was his cousin, John Reeve, a man of ardent temperament, fierce conviction, and unflinching holiness. Some years later, in 1650, two peculiar persons, John Tawny and John Robins, appeared in London. Tawny declared that he was the Lord's high priest, that it was his mission to lead the Jews back to Jerusalem, and that, incidentally, he was the King of France. Robins proclaimed that he was something greater; he was Adam, he was Melchizedek, he was the Lord himself. He had raised Jeremiah, Benjamin, and many others from the dead, and did they not stand there beside him, admitting that all he said was true? Serpents and dragons appeared at his command; he rode upon the wings of the wind; he was about to lead 144,000 men and women to the Mount of Olives through the Red Sea, on a diet of dry bread and raw vegetables. These two men, 'greater than prophets', made a profound impression upon Muggleton and his cousin Reeve. A strange melancholy fell upon them, and then a more strange exaltation. They heard mysterious voices; they were holy; why should not they too be inspired? Greater than prophets ... ? Suddenly Reeve rushed into Muggleton's room and declared that they were the chosen witnesses of the Lord, whose appearance had been prophesied in the Book of Revelation, xi. 3. Muggleton agreed that it was so. As for Tawny and Robins, they were devilish impostors, who must be immediately denounced. Sentence of eternal damnation should be passed upon them. The cousins hurried off on their mission, and discovered Robins in gaol, where he had been lodged for blasphemy. The furious embodiment of Adam, Melchizedek, and the Lord glared out at them from a window, clutching the bars with both hands. But Reeve was unabashed. 'That body of thine,' he shouted, pointing at his victim, 'which was thy heaven, must be thy hell; and that proud spirit of thine, which said it was God, must be thy Devil. The one shall be as fire, and the other as brimstone, burning together to all eternity. This is the message of the Lord.' The effect was instantaneous: Robins, letting go the bars, fell back, shattered. 'It is finished,' he groaned; 'the Lord's will be done.' He wrote a letter to Cromwell, recanting; was released from prison, and retired into private life, in the depths of the country. Tawny's fate was equally impressive. Reeve wrote on a piece of paper, 'We pass sentence upon you of eternal damnation,' and left it in his room. The wretched man fled to Holland, in a small boat, *en route* for Jerusalem, and was never heard of again.

After this the success of the new religion was assured. But Reeve did not live long to enjoy his glory. In a few months his fiery spirit had worn itself away, and Muggleton was left alone to carry on the work. He was cast in a very different mould. Tall, thick-set, vigorous, with a great head, whose low brow, high cheekbones, and projecting jowl almost suggested some simian creature, he had never known a day's illness, and lived to be eighty-eight. Tough and solid, he continued, year after year, to earn his living as a tailor, while the words flowed from him which were the final revelation of God. For he preached and he wrote with an inexhaustible volubility. He never ceased, in sermons, in letters, in books, in pamphlets, to declare to the world the divine and absolute truth. His revelations might be incomprehensible, his objurgations frenzied, his argumentations incoherent – no matter; disciples gathered round him in ever-thickening crowds, learning, to their amazement and delight, that there is no Devil but the unclean Reason of men, that Angels are the only beings of Pure Reason, that God is of the stature of a man and made of flesh and bone, that Heaven is situated beyond the stars and six miles above the earth. Schismatics might arise, but they were crushed, cast forth, and sentenced to eternal damnation. Inquiring magistrates were browbeaten with multitudinous texts. George Fox, the miserable wretch, was overwhelmed – or would have been had he not obtained the assistance of the Devil – by thick volumes of intermingled abuse and Pure Reason. The truth was plain – it had been delivered to Muggleton by God; and henceforward, until the Day of Judgment, the Deity would hold no further communication with his creatures. Prayer, therefore, was not only futile, it was blasphemous; and no form of worship was admissible, save the singing of a few hymns of thanksgiving and praise. All that was required of the true believer was that he should ponder upon the Old and the New Testaments, and upon 'The Third and Last Testament of Our Lord Jesus Christ', by Muggleton.

The English passion for compromise is well illustrated by the attitude of Charles II's Government towards religious heterodoxy. There are two logical alternatives for the treatment of heretics – to let them alone, or to torture them to death; but English public opinion recoiled – it still recoils – from either course. A compromise was the obvious, the comfortable solution; and so it was, decided that heretics should be tortured – not to death, oh no! – but ... to some extent. Accordingly, poor Muggleton became a victim, for years, to the small persecutions of authority. He was badgered by angry justices, he was hunted from place to place, his books were burnt, he was worried by small fines and short imprisonments. At last, at the age of sixty-eight, he was arrested and tried for blasphemy. In the course of the proceedings, it appeared that the prosecution had made a serious blunder: since the publication of the book on which the charge was based an Act of Indemnity had been passed. Thereupon the Judge instructed the jury that, as there was no reason to suppose that the date on the book was not a false imprint, the Act of Indemnity did not apply; and Muggleton was condemned to the pillory. He was badly mauled, for it so happened that the crowd was hostile and pelted the old man with stones. After that, he was set free; his tribulations were at last over. The Prophet spent his closing years writing his autobiography, in the style of the Gospels; and he died in peace.

His doctrines did not die with him. Two hundred and fifty Muggletonians followed him to the grave, and their faith has been handed down, unimpaired through the generations, from that day to this. Still, in the very spot where their founder was born, the chosen few meet together to celebrate the two festivals of their religion – the Great Holiday, on the anniversary of the delivery of the Word to Reeve, and the Little Holiday, on the day of Muggleton's final release from prison.

> I do believe in God alone,
> Likewise in Reeve and Muggleton.

So they have sung for more than two hundred years.

> This is the Muggletonians' faith,
> This is the God which we believe;
> None salvation-knowledge hath,
> But those of Muggleton and Reeve.
> Christ is the Muggletonians' king,
> With whom eternally they'll sing.

It is an exclusive faith, certainly; and yet, somehow or other, it disarms criticism. Even though one may not be of the elect oneself, one cannot but wish it well; one would be sorry if the time ever came when there were no more Muggletonians. Besides, one is happy to learn that with the passage of years they have grown more gentle. Their terrible offensive weapon – which, in early days, they wielded so frequently – has fallen into desuetude: no longer do they pass sentence of eternal damnation. The dreaded doom was pronounced for the last time on a Swedenborgian, with great effect, in the middle of the nineteenth century.

1924

# The Life, Illness, and Death
# of Dr North

John North was a man of eminence in his day – a prebend of Westminster, Professor of Greek at Cambridge, Master of Trinity College, and Clerk of the King's Closet: now totally forgotten. Only the curious inquirer, chancing on the obscure and absurd memoir of him by his admiring younger brother, Roger, catches a glimpse of the intense individual existence of this no longer distinguished man. In the sight of God, we used to be told, a thousand years are as a day; possibly; but notions of the deity are not what they were in the days of King David and Sir Isaac Newton; Evolution, the Life Force, and Einstein have all intervened; so that whether the dictum is still one to which credence should be attached is a problem that must be left to Professor Whitehead (who has studied the subject very carefully) to determine. However that may be, for mortal beings the case is different. In their sight (or perhaps one should say their blindness) a thousand years are too liable to be not as a day but as just nothing. The past is almost entirely a blank. The indescribable complexities, the incalculable extravagances, of a myriad consciousnesses have vanished for ever. Only by sheer accident, when some particular drop from the ocean of empty water is slipped under the microscope – only when some Roger North happens to write a foolish memoir, which happens to survive, and which we happen to open – do we perceive for an amazed moment or two the universe of serried and violent sensations that lie concealed so perfectly in the transparency of oblivion.

Born in 1645, the younger son of an impecunious peer, John North was one of those good little boys who, in the seventeenth century, were invariably destined to Learning, the Universities, and the Church. His goodness, his diligence, his scrupulosity, were perhaps, it is true, the result of a certain ingrained timidity rather than anything else; but that could not be helped. Fear is not easily exorcised. As an undergraduate at Cambridge the youth was still afraid of ghosts in the dark, and slept with the bedclothes over his head. 'For some time,' we are told, 'he lay with his Tutor, who once, coming home, found the Scholar in bed with only his Crown visible. The Tutor, indiscreetly enough, pulled him by the Hair; whereupon the Scholar sunk down, and the Tutor followed, and at last, with a great Outcry, the Scholar sprung up, expecting to see an enorm Spectre.' But in spite of such contretemps the young man pursued his studies with exemplary industry. He was soon a Fellow of his college and a Doctor of Divinity. He continued to work and work; collected a vast library; read the Classics until 'Greek became almost vernacular to him'; wrestled with Hebrew, dived deep into Logic and Metaphysics, and was even 'a Friend to, though no great Scholar in, the Mathematicks'. Unwilling to waste a moment of time, the Doctor found means for turning the most ordinary conversations into matter for improvement, but 'he could not be pleased with such insipid Pastime as Bowls, or less material Discourse, such as Town Tales, Punning, and the Like'. At last his fame as a prodigy of learning spread over the land. He preached before King Charles II, and the great Duke of Lauderdale became his patron. At the early age of twenty-seven, his talents and virtues were rewarded by the Professorship of Greek in the University of Cambridge.

His talents and virtues were indeed great; but still they were informed and dominated by an underlying apprehensiveness. Meticulous, in the true sense of the word, was the nature of the Doctor. An alarmed exactitude kept him continually on the stretch. He was in fear alike for the state of his soul and for his reputation with posterity. He published only one small volume – a commentary on some of Plato's Dialogues; all the rest of the multitudinous fruits of his labours – notes, sermons, treatises, lectures, dissertations – were burnt, by his direction, after his death. A small notebook alone survived by accident, containing the outline of a great work against Socinians, Republics, and Hobbes. But the Doctor had taken care to write on the first page of it – 'I beshrew his heart, that gathers my opinion from anything he finds wrote here.' Nor was this strange diffidence merely literary; it extended to his person as well. He would never allow his portrait to be painted, in spite of the entreaties of Sir Peter Lely; 'and, what was very odd, he would not leave the Print in his Bed, where he had lain, remain undefaced'.

Curiously enough, his appearance seemed to belie his character. His complexion was florid, his hair flaxen, and, 'as some used to jest, his Features were scandalous, as showing rather a Madam *entravestie* than a Book-Worm'. At times, indeed, it almost appeared as if his features were a truer index to his soul than the course of his life. His friends were surprised to see that, among his pupils, he 'affected to refresh himself with the society of the young Noblemen', who gathered round him, in fits of laughter, 'like Younglings about old *Silenus*'. He was arch, too, with the ladies, plying them with raillery. 'Of all the Beasts of the Field,' he said, 'God Almighty thought Woman the fittest Companion for Man'; and the ladies were delighted. But unfortunately no corresponding specimen of his jests with the young noblemen has been preserved.

In 1677, when he was thirty-two, his career reached its climax and he was made Master of Trinity. The magnificent appointment proved to be his ruin. Faced with the governance of the great college over which the omniscient Barrow had lately ruled and which the presence of Newton still made illustrious, the Doctor's sense of responsibility, of duty, and of inadequacy became almost pathological. His days and his nights passed in one ceaseless round of devotion, instruction, and administration, reading, writing, and abstemiousness. He had no longer any time for the young and the fair; no time for a single particle of enjoyment; no time even for breakfast. His rule was strict beyond all measure and precedent. With relentless severity he pursued the undergraduates through their exercises and punished them for their peccadilloes. His unpopularity became intense: he was openly jeered at in the Cloisters, and one evening a stone came whizzing through the window of the room in the Lodge where he was sitting, and fell in the fire at his feet. Nor was he consoled by the friendship of his equals. The Senior Fellows were infuriated by his sour punctilio; a violent feud sprang up; there were shocking scenes at the council meetings. 'Let me be buried in the ante-chapel,' exclaimed the Master in his desperation, 'so that they may trample on me dead as they have living.'

And death was always before his eyes; for now a settled

hypochondria was added to his other miseries. He was a prey to constant nightmare. He had little doubt that he would perish of the stone. Taking upon himself the functions of the Wise Woman, he displayed before his embarrassed friends the obvious symptoms of fatal disorder. 'Gravel! Red gravel!' he gasped. In reality his actual weakness lay in quite another direction. One day he caught cold, it grew worse, his throat was affected, his uvula swelled. The inflammation continued, and before long the unhappy Doctor became convinced that his uvula would have to be cut off. All the physicians of the University were summoned, and they confessed that the case was grave. It was the age of Molière, and the practitioners of Cambridge might well have figured in the *Malade Imaginaire*. Their prescriptions were terrific and bizarre: drenches, 'enough to purge a strong man from off his legs', accompanied by amber, to be smoked like tobacco in pipes, with astringent powders blown into the mouth through quills. The Doctor, who, with all his voluminous reading, had never heard of Diafoirus, believed every word he was told, and carried out the fearful orders with elaborate conscientiousness. The result was plain to all; in a few weeks his health was completely shattered, and his friends, to their amazement, saw him 'come helmeted in Caps upon Caps, and meagre as one newly crope out of a Fever'. They privately consulted the great Dr Lower in London. He threw up his hands. 'I would undertake,' he said, 'by the smoak of Amber alone, to put the soundest Man in the World into Convulsion Fits.' But it was too late to intervene; the treatment was continued, while the Doctor struggled on with the duties of his office. Two scholars were to be publicly admonished for scandalous conduct; the fellows assembled; the youths stood trembling; the Master appeared. Emaciated, ghastly, in his black gown, and with a mountain of caps upon his head, the extraordinary creature began a tirade of bitter and virulent reproof; when suddenly his left leg swerved beneath him, and he fell in a fit upon the ground. It was apoplexy. He was carried to his bed, where the physicians clustered round him. The one thing, they declared, that was essential was that he should never lose consciousness; if he did he would never regain it; and they therefore ordered that a perpetual noise should be made about his ears. Whereupon 'there was a Consort of Tongs, Firegrate, Wainscote-Drum, and dancing of Curtains and Curtain Rings, such as would have made a sound Man mad'. At that moment, old Lady North, the patient's mother and a formidable dowager, appeared upon the scene. She silenced the incredible tintin-nabulation; she even silenced the faculty; and she succeeded in nursing her son back from death.

Yet there were some who averred that it would have been better had she never done so. For now the strangest of the Doctor's transformations came upon him. His recovery was not complete; his body was paralysed on the left side; but it was in his mind that the most remarkable change had occurred. His fears had left him. His scrupulosity, his diffidence, his seriousness, even his morality – all had vanished. He lay on his bed, in reckless levity, pouring forth a stream of flippant observations, and naughty stories, and improper jokes. While his friends hardly knew which way to look, he laughed consumedly, his paralysed features drawn up into a curiously distorted grin. He sent for a gay young scholar of the college, Mr Warren, to sit by him and regale him with merry tales and readings from light romances. And there was worse still to follow. Attacked by epileptic seizures, he declared that the only mitigation of his sufferings lay in the continued consumption of wine. He, who had been so noted for his austerities, now tossed off, with wild exhilaration, glass after glass of the strongest sherry; the dry ascetic had become a convert to the golden gospel of *la dive bouteille*. In the depth of the night, the studious precincts of the Great Court of Trinity were disturbed by peculiar sounds – the high, triumphant, one-sided cackle of the Master, as he lay, with his flagon in his hand and young Mr Warren beside him, absorbed in the abandoned, exuberant fantasies of the Curé of Meudon.

After four years of this strange existence, the Doctor died in his sleep. He was buried, as he had directed, in the ante-chapel of the college, where, under a small square stone, engraved with the initials 'J.N.', so many singular agitations came to their final rest. In his brother Roger's opinion, 'the Consciousness of a well-spent Life was of great service to him', for otherwise he 'might have fallen into Melancholy, Dejections, Despair, and Misconstructions of Providence'. And probably Roger was right; conscientiousness is apt, in however devious a manner, to have its reward in this world. Whether it also has it in any other is another of those questions that must be referred to Professor Whitehead.                1927

# Introduction to 'Warren Hastings, Cheyt Sing and the Begums of Oude'

❦

The history of India has been strangely neglected by English historians, and Hastings's Administration has suffered in this general neglect. The great mass of original materials which throw light upon his life and work remains almost entirely unexplored. The current biographies of Hastings are either too short to present an adequate view of his career, or are merely compilations from well-known printed sources. There is only one full and detailed account of his Administration: that contained in the third, fourth and fifth volumes of James Mill's *History of India*.

Before entering into a discussion of Mill's characteristics as a historian, mention must be made of a far more famous and potent work – Macaulay's Essay on Warren Hastings. There can be no doubt that the popular conception of Hastings is based upon the view of his career and his character expressed with such consummate skill in Macaulay's brilliant sketch. The great historian has lavished upon his subject all the resources of his art – his incisive clarity, his powers of splendid description and masterly narrative, his easy wit, his vast knowledge, the rhetoric of his darkest and most dazzling colours; and he has produced a picture which, once seen, is seen for ever. To the ordinary Englishman, uninstructed in Indian history, the figure of Hastings stands out as Macaulay painted it – a Satanic embodiment of wickedness and power, a creature endowed with a mighty intellect and an indomitable will, who perverted these noble qualities to the hideous uses of violence, rapacity, ruthlessness and fraud. The portrait is a masterpiece; but it is a masterpiece of imagination, and not of history. Under the clear light of impartial inquiry, the fascinating spectre which Macaulay conjured up vanishes into air, or rather takes its place, once and for all, among the villains of romance. Nevertheless, the impartial inquirers have very little to boast of. For one man who reads the

225

results of their researches there are a hundred who read Macaulay. In general, books are read solely for the pleasure that they give; and the mixture of a lie doth ever add pleasure. Macaulay will triumph, until there arises a greater master of the art of writing, who will choose to invest the facts of Indian history with the glamour of literature, and make the truth more attractive than even fiction itself.

But the blame for having given currency to a totally false view of Hastings's administration does not rest with Macaulay alone; the great criminal was James Mill. Every important statement in the Essay is taken from Mill's work; and it is clear that Macaulay entertained no doubts as to the value of the authority upon which he so implicitly relied. The truth is that no historian was ever less worthy of trust. It is equally true that no historian appears more certainly to deserve it. In style, Mill's history is the precise antithesis of Macaulay's Essay. It is crabbed, cold, and dull; and the general impression which it produces is that the writer has sacrificed every grace of language and every audacity of thought for the sake of a meticulous accuracy. Yet the more Mill's work is examined the more delusive this general impression turns out to be: its dryness is nothing more than the cloak for a multitude of errors. And inaccuracy is not the only fault of which Mill was guilty. It has been clearly shown that his transgressions were far more serious, that he misrepresented facts, that he suppressed material evidence, and that his whole treatment of his subject was impregnated with acrimonious prejudice. ...

Mill's attitude, however, cannot be rightly understood without reference to a great mass of literature which had come into existence forty years before he wrote, and formed the real foundation for his history. I refer to the accusatory writings and speeches which culminated in the impeachment of Hastings. The nature of these compositions is extremely various; some were the outcome of personal malignity, others of party feeling, others of rhetorical sentiment, others of noble indignation, and most of prejudice and ignorance. There is, however, one characteristic which is common to them all. Whether one examines the Reports of the Committee of the Commons upon Indian affairs, or the speeches of Hastings's antagonists in the House, or the articles of accusation drawn up for the Impeachment, or the speeches of the

Managers in the Impeachment itself – in all these productions it is impossible to discover one the motive for whose composition was simply a desire to state the truth. The articles of impeachment have been described by Sir James Stephen in the following words:

Instead of being short, full, pointed, and precise, they are bulky pamphlets sprinkled over with imitations of legal phraseology. They are full of invective, oratorical matter, needless recitals, arguments, statements of evidence – everything in fact which can possibly serve to make an accusation difficult to understand and to meet. They are, moreover, extremely tricky, being full of insinuations, and covering, by their profusion of irrelevant matter, the total and no doubt designed absence of averments essential to the conclusion which they are meant to support. In short, they are as shuffling and disingenuous in substance, as they are clumsy, awkward, and intricate in form.

This description might be applied with equal truth to the whole set of compositions of which the articles of impeachment were a part. But, for some of these works, the description would not be complete. The prime mover in the prosecution of Hastings was Burke; and his utterances stand out from among the rest in virtue both of their hideous violence of language and their splendid elevation of thought. The scintillating wisdom, the passionate nobility, the gorgeous rhetoric, which characterize Burke's speeches against Hastings, have given them a place in literature which they would certainly have ill deserved if sanity, clarity, and accuracy were the sole tests of literary merit. The speeches are, in truth, disfigured not only by bad taste, by sophistry, and by intolerable longueurs, but also by an overweening and implacable spirit of rage and hatred which manifests itself in an unending stream of reckless insinuations and unbridled abuse. Burke seems to have believed that every charge of which his imagination was capable, however vague and however unsubstantiated, was good enough to fling at Hastings, and that no conceivable invective, however frantic and however filthy, could possibly be out of place. 'Un enthousiaste ignorant', says Condorcet, 'est le plus dangereux des bêtes féroces'; and too many of Burke's periods put one in mind of the aphorism. It would, of course, be senseless, and worse than senseless, to suppose that Burke's conduct was actuated by any motives save the purest and best. Ignoble indeed must be the man to whom a study of that vast and high intelligence does not bring feelings of respect and admiration, which come near to love. But it was Burke's misfortune that the press and passion of his most resplendent qualities let loose a wild beast within him, which drove him headlong into the paths of frenzy and folly; so that we would willingly turn away our eyes from the spectacle of such virtue brought to such a miserable pass. And, in respect of his utterances on Indian questions, there was, besides the natural infirmities of his temper, an additional cause for error: his ignorance of the facts. He plunged into his crusade against Hastings under the influence of a vague enthusiasm; he soon fell into the hands of Philip Francis, the most rancorous and unscrupulous of Hastings's enemies; and the whole of his knowledge of the actual circumstances of Indian politics came to him from that poisoned source. As early as 1782 he had irrevocably committed himself, by his succession of accusatory Reports on Indian affairs (drawn up by him, with the aid of Francis, as Chairman of the Select Committee of the House of Commons appointed to inquire into Indian affairs)[1] to a policy of uncompromising hostility towards Hastings and all his acts; and it was not until ten years later, when the Impeachment had been accomplished, and the trial itself was half way through, that the real strength of Hastings's position was put before the world. The first, and indeed (with a few exceptions) the only, detailed exposition of the facts of Hastings's administration was that made in the speeches of his Counsel (in the year 1792) at Westminster Hall. There can, I think, be little doubt that if Burke, before the time at which he came under the influence of Francis, had been acquainted with the facts upon which these speeches were based, his attitude towards Indian affairs would have been entirely different. As it was, the fragmentary information which by degrees reached him from the East, was easily susceptible of every vile construction which the suggestions of Francis, crouching like the toad beside the ear of Eve, poured into his mind. Thus it happened that Burke never had the opportunity of coming to an independent judgment upon Hastings: the judgment which he did make was arrived at before he knew the facts; and when he knew the facts it was too late to revise

[1] For the important part taken by Francis in the composition not only of these Reports, but of many other of Burke's Indian writings and speeches, see Merivale's *Life of Francis*, Vol. II, p. 289. (*Strachey's footnote*)

his judgment. Prejudice and ignorance lay at the root of all his virtuous rage. And, the guilt of Hastings once granted, what indignation could be too furious, what punishment too heavy, for such atrocious crimes? It is clear that Burke, possessed of the certainty that Hastings was the greatest criminal on the face of the earth, believed that this enormity of wickedness justified methods of prosecution which, in ordinary cases, would have been inexcusable. In ordinary cases, it was unfair deliberately to create prejudice against an accused person, to endeavour to overwhelm him by inflammatory appeals to popular sentiment, to cover the dubious points in an indictment by ambiguous insinuations and shifting arguments, to pile upon an Ossa of accusations a Pelion of abuse. But this was not an ordinary case; this was a case in which virtue itself was struggling for existence against the machinations of the 'captain general of iniquity'; this was the impeachment of Warren Hastings. Such was Burke's view of the situation, and it dominated the whole conduct of the trial. The Lords were not called upon to decide upon the proofs of certain criminal acts; they were asked to declare Hastings guilty of all the vague and vast enormities which could be conceived by the most prolific imagination of the age. They acquitted him; and it is to their honour that they did; but for seven years they had listened to a torrent of accusations, such as no man could make good and no man could rebut. On the whole, the trial of Hastings is a dark stain upon the history of English Justice.

Burke was a public accuser; he was not bound to be judicial; it was his duty to attack. But it was also his duty to attack fairly; and, since he attacked with gross unfairness, he committed a grievous fault. Very different was the position of James Mill, a historian, whose sole business was to examine the evidence impartially, to discover the truth, and to tell it; who was, as it were, on the judicial bench. His fault was even more grievous than Burke's, for his prejudice and acrimony were as great, and he had not Burke's excuse. How far Mill was deliberate in what he did, it is difficult to say. Sir James Stephen does not hesitate to accuse him of 'bad faith', which can only mean that, in Sir James Stephen's opinion, Mill wrote what was false in order to deceive, and knew that he was doing so. No graver charge could be made against a historian, and the fact that it was made by a man of such high intelligence and weighty judgment as Sir James Stephen adds immensely to its gravity. The question is a psychological one, to be determined by knowledge of the human mind in general, and of the historical mind in particular, rather than by the sifting of specific facts; and, in so difficult a matter, many may be content to bow to the authority of a great judge. Yet it is, I think, at least possible to account for Mill's conduct without resorting to the imputation of deliberate falsehood; and, if we can do that, ought we not, in charity, to acquit him of this worst of charges, or, at any rate, to bring in a verdict of 'not proven'? It must be allowed that Mill's falsification of the evidence with which he was dealing – his suppressions, his distortions, his confusions, his insidious additions, his unwarrantable inferences – admit of no exaggeration; the question is whether it is conceivable that a man who told so many untruths could by any possibility have been anything but a liar. I think it is conceivable, if we assume, not only that Mill was prejudiced, but that his prejudice was inordinately great; that he was completely obsessed by the *a priori* belief that all methods of government, except his own, were infamous; and that his mind had fallen into such a state that he was unable to imagine an Englishman in India acting from any other motives than those of cruelty and rapaciousness. Such assumptions as these make it surely possible to suppose that Mill, utterly blinded by preconceived theories and hatreds, did honestly believe that his history was impartial, candid, and accurate; that his treatment of the evidence – and, in all history, the evidence must be 'treated' – was really calculated to produce an impression of the truth. Upon this view, his case resembles that of the Spanish Inquisitors; he distorted facts just as they burnt heretics – believing, without reservation, that it was right to do so; and everyone knows that to determine the precise degree of guilt attaching to the Spanish Inquisitors is one of the most delicate problems of ethics. Curiously enough, however, James Mill himself entertained no doubts upon this point; 'he would not have accepted', his son tells us, 'as a plea in mitigation for inquisitors, that they sincerely believed burning heretics to be an obligation of conscience.'

But the problem presented by Mill's faults is, after all, one of merely minor interest; it is his history, and not his conscience, which is important now. That work, published in 1817–18 remained the undisputed authority upon the history of the British in India, until in 1840–8 Professor Wilson brought out a new edition of it, in which he pointed out the gravest of Mill's errors in a series of notes. Wilson's work, however, was necessarily slight; it was confined to a small space and had no pretensions to a detailed examination of the evidence; it was little more than a running fire of protest against the prejudice and misrepresentation of the text. It was not until Sir James Stephen, in 1885, published his work on the Trial of Nuncomar and the Impeachment of Impey, that the true nature of Mill's transgressions became obvious. In 1892, Sir John Strachey did for the Rohilla War what Sir James Stephen had done for the Trial of Nuncomar. These two books, based upon independent research, have revealed, not only the errors of Mill, but the true history of two important incidents in Hastings's career. But how much more remains to be done! How little we still know of the authentic history of those great events, those wise and wondrous actions, those portentous revolutions, which, from the time of Clive to the time of Dalhousie, have gone to the making of our vast, our mysterious, our noble Empire of India! So far as Hastings is concerned, by far the greater part of his career is still obscured by the Cimmerian darkness of Mill's malevolence. The current biographies, though they do not subscribe to the calumnies of Mill, have an almost equally serious defect; for— except in their accounts of the Rohilla War and the Trial of Nuncomar – they are not based upon any thorough and scientific examination of the facts. Thus a student of Indian history finds himself face to face with a grave anomaly. He finds that the only history of Hastings's administration which is confessedly based upon documentary research must be rejected as worthless; and that the entirely contrary view of Hastings's career, expressed in his modern biographies, is unsupported by adequate evidence. . . .

It is not surprising that the forces combined against the reputation of Hastings – the blazing rhetoric of Burke's speeches, the sober and punctilious falsehoods of Mill's history, the fascinating melodrama of Macaulay's Essay – should have exercised an overwhelming effect upon the public mind. The 'man in the street', though he may admit that any specific charge against Hastings is devoid of foundation, continues firmly to believe that, on the whole, and in general, Hastings was a thoroughly unscrupulous character. But upon what does this general impression of unscrupulousness depend for its validity? Simply upon the truth of those very charges which will not bear the test of scientific examination. You cannot acquit a man upon every count, and condemn him on the whole indictment. You cannot say 'all that we *know* about Hastings's career is to his credit; every accusation against him which has been accurately and impartially examined, has proved to be baseless; and yet we consider him a bad man'. But this, in effect, is the attitude with regard to him, not only of the ordinary reading public, but of writers of learning and weight. It is indeed discouraging, for instance, to find an authority so distinguished as Sir Alfred Lyall asserting, in the same breath, both that Nuncomar was fairly tried and justly executed, and that Hastings had conspired with Impey to bring about his death; and to find an historian, no less influential that Lord Morley, producing edition after edition of his life of Burke, in which, without a word of qualification or explanation, he gives currency to the disproved calumny about Hastings 'selling English troops to assist in the extermination' of the people of Rohilkhand. Hastings's own prophecy upon the matter has been justified by the event. 'Let this business end as it will', he wrote at the time of the impeachment, 'a great portion of mankind will think they judge with candour, if, unable to comprehend any part of the accusations, they acquit me, at a guess, of some, and conclude that where so much is alleged against me, much of it must be necessarily true.'

1905

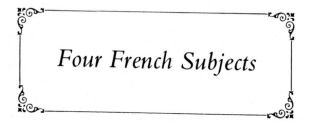

*Four French Subjects*

# Mademoiselle de Lespinasse

'Oh! je m'en vais vous paraître folle: je vais vous parler avec la fran-
chise et l'abandon qu'on aurait, si l'on croyait mourir le lendemain;
écoutez-moi donc avec cette indulgence et cet intérêt qu'on a pour
les mourants.' So wrote Mademoiselle de Lespinasse; and the words
might well be taken as a motto for the volume of letters which has
made her name imperishable. The book, for all its tenderness and
pathos, is in many ways a terrible one; it is gloomy, morbid, and
remorseless; after one has read it, it is horrible to think that it is true.
Yet it is its truth – its uncompromising truth – which gives it an
immense and unique value: it is the most complete analysis the
world possesses of a passion which actually existed in a human
mind. Thus, when one thinks of Mademoiselle de Lespinasse, it is
towards passion, and all the fearful accompaniments of passion, that
one's imagination naturally turns. One is apt to forget that she was
not merely 'une amante insensée', that she was also a brilliant and
fascinating woman of the world. The Marquis de Ségur, in the
biography of her which he has recently published,[1] has been careful
to avoid this error. He has drawn a full-length portrait of Julie de
Lespinasse; and he has drawn it with a subtlety and a sympathy
which compels a delighted attention. His book is enriched with a
great mass of information never before made public; his researches
have been rewarded with the discovery of authentic documents of
the deepest interest; and every reader of the present volume will
await with anxious expectation the publication, which he promises
us, of a new and enlarged edition of the Letters themselves. One of
the most important results of M. de Ségur's labours is the additional
knowledge which they have given us upon the subject of the
Comte de Guibert, to whom the letters were addressed. This alone

[1]Marquis de Ségur. *Julie de Lespinasse*. Paris: Calmann-Lévy.

235

would have made the book indispensable to any one who is interested in Mademoiselle de Lespinasse. But it would be idle to attempt to recapitulate all the fresh points of importance which M. de Ségur has brought out; it were best to go to the book itself. In the meantime, it may be worth while to trace, however rapidly and imperfectly, the outline of that tragical history which M. de Ségur has done so much to put in its proper light.

Julie de Lespinasse was born at Lyons on November 9, 1732. She was the illegitimate daughter of the Comtesse d'Albon, a lady of distinguished family, who, some years earlier, had separated from her husband and established herself in the neighbourhood of Lyons in the château of Avauges. So much is certain; but the obscurity which hung over Julie's birth has never been completely withdrawn. Who was her father? According to the orthodox tradition, she was the child of Cardinal de Tencin, whose sister, the famous Madame de Tencin, was the mother of d'Alembert. This story has the advantage of discovering a strange and concealed connection between two lives which were afterwards to be intimately bound together; but it has the disadvantage of not being true. M. de Ségur shows conclusively that, whoever else may have been the father of Mademoiselle de Lespinasse, Cardinal de Tencin was not; and he produces some weighty reasons for believing that Julie was the niece, not of Madame de Tencin, but of a woman equally remarkable and equally celebrated – Madame du Deffand. If M. de Ségur's hypothesis be correct – and the evidence which he adduces is, I think, conclusive – the true history of Julie's parentage is even more extraordinary than the orthodox one. Besides Julie herself, Madame d'Albon had two legitimate children, one of whom was a daughter; this daughter married, in 1739, the Comte Gaspard de Vichy, the eldest brother of Madame du Deffand. The Comte de Vichy was the father of Mademoiselle de Lespinasse. Once or twice, in her correspondence, she touches upon the strange circumstances of her early life. Her history, she said, outdid the novels of Prévost and of Richardson; it proved that 'le vrai n'est souvent pas vraisemblable'; it was 'un composé de circonstances funestes', which would produce, in the mind of her correspondent, 'une grande horreur pour l'espèce humaine'. These phrases lose their appearance of exaggeration in the light of the Marquis de

Ségur's theory. 'Ce sont des horreurs!' exclaimed Gaspard's son, when his mother had told him all. Even for the eighteenth century, there was something horrible in Julie's situation. When, at the age of sixteen, she lost Madame d'Albon, she was obliged to take up her abode with her sister and the Comte de Vichy. They treated her as a dependant, as a governess for their children, as some one to be made use of and kept in place. There, in her father's strange old castle, with its towers and its terraces and its moat, amid the quiet Macon country, neglected, wretched, alone, Julie de Lespinasse grew up into womanhood; she was waiting for her fate.

Her fate came in the shape of Madame du Deffand. That great lady was entering upon the final stage of her long career. She was beginning to grow old, she was beginning to grow blind, and, in spite of her glory and her dominion, she was beginning to grow tired of Paris. Disgusted and ill, she fled into the depths of the country; she spent a summer with the Vichys, and became acquainted with Mademoiselle de Lespinasse. The two women seem to have felt almost at once that they were made for one another. Julie was now twenty-one; she was determined to escape at all hazards from an intolerable position; and she confided in the brilliant and affectionate marquise. With all her cynicism and all her icy knowledge of the world, Madame du Deffand was nothing if not impulsive. Julie had every virtue and every accomplishment; she was 'ma reine'; with her, it would be once more possible to exist; she must come to Paris; it was the only thing to do. For a year Julie hesitated, and then she took the final plunge. In April, 1754, she went to Paris, to live with Madame du Deffand in her apartments in the Convent of St. Joseph.

The famous salon was now reaching the highest point of its glory. Nowhere else in Paris were the forces of intellect and the forces of the world so completely combined. That was Madame du Deffand's great achievement: she was able to mingle every variety of distinction into an harmonious whole. Her drawing-room was filled with eminent diplomatists, with beautiful women of fashion, with famous men of letters; it was the common meeting-place for great ladies like the Duchesse de Choiseul, for politicians like Turgot, for arbiters of taste like the Maréchale de Luxembourg, for philosophers like d'Alembert. Amid these brilliant assemblies, Mademoiselle de Lespinasse very soon obtained an established place. She possessed all the qualities necessary for success in such a society; she had tact, refinement, wit and penetration; she was animated and she was sympathetic; she could interest and she could charm. Madame du Deffand's experiment seemed to be amply justified by the event. Yet, after ten years, Julie's connection with the Convent of St. Joseph came to a sudden and violent termination. The story of the quarrel is sufficiently well known: the informal and surreptitious gatherings in Julie's private room, the discovery of the secret, the fury of the blind old woman, the cold hostility of the younger one, the eternal separation – these things need no further description here. M. de Ségur dwells on them with his usual insight; and his account is peculiarly valuable because it makes quite clear what had always been ambiguous before – the essential points of the situation. The discovery of the secret salon only brought to a head a profound disagreement which had been gathering strength for years; Julie's flight was not the result of a vulgar squabble, it was the outcome of an inherent antagonism pregnant with inevitable disaster. The two women were too much alike for a tolerable partnership; they were both too clever, too strong, and too fond of their own will. In the drawing-room of St. Joseph it was a necessary condition that Julie should play second fiddle; and how could she do that? She was born – it was clear enough – to be nothing less than the leader of an orchestra. Thus the question at issue was a question of spiritual domination; and the dilemma was a tragic one, because it was insoluble except by force. The struggle – the long, the desperate struggle – centred round d'Alembert, who, supreme alike in genius and in conversation, was the keystone of Madame du Deffand's elaborate triumphal arch. When the time came, it was for him to make the momentous decision. He did not hesitate. He knew well how much he owed to Madame du Deffand – fifteen years of unwavering friendship and his position in the world; but his indebtedness to Julie – her sympathy, her attachment, her affection – these things surpassed his computations; and, in exchange, he had given her his heart. He followed where she led, carrying with him in his defection the whole body of the encyclopædists. The salon of St. Joseph was shattered; it became a wilderness, and, in the eyes of its ruler, life itself grew waste. To the miserable lady, infinitely disillusioned and eternally alone, it must have seemed that she at any rate had experienced the last humiliation. She was wrong. She was yet to know, in what remained to her of life, a suffering far deeper than any that had gone before. She – but this is not the history of Madame du Deffand.

Julie was victorious and free. Her friends closed round her, gallantly subscribed towards her maintenance, established her in a little set of rooms on the upper storey of a house in the rue Saint-Dominique. The years which followed were the happiest of her life. They passed in a perpetual round of visits and conversations, of theatres and operas, of gaiety and success. Her drawing-room became the intellectual centre of Paris, perhaps of the world. Every evening, from six to ten, there assembled within it a circle of illustrious persons. D'Alembert was always there; Condorcet and Turgot constantly, sometimes Malesherbes and Diderot, often Chastellux and Suard and Marmontel. One might find there the charming Duchesse de Châtillon, and the amazing Comtesse de Boufflers, and even sometimes the great Madame Geoffrin herself. In addition, there were the distinguished strangers – Caraccioli, the Neapolitan ambassador, the witty and inexhaustible Galiani, the penetrating Lord Shelburne, and the potentate of potentates, David Hume. Oh! It was a place worth visiting – the little salon in the rue Saint-Dominique. And, if one were privileged to go there often, one found there what one found nowhere else – a sense of freedom and intimacy which was the outcome of a real equality, a real understanding, a real friendship such as have existed, before or since, in few societies indeed. Mademoiselle de Lespinasse, inspiring and absorbing all, was the crowning wonder, the final delight. To watch the moving expressions of her face was to watch the conversation itself, transmuted to a living thing by the glow of an intense intelligence. 'There is a flame within her!' was the common exclamation of her friends. Nor were they mistaken; she burnt with an inward fire. It was a steady flame, giving out a genial warmth, a happy brilliance. What wind could shake it? What sudden gust transform it to an instrument of devastation? whirl it, with horror and with blindness, into the path of death?

About two years after Julie's establishment in the rue Saint-Dominique, the Marquis de Mora, a young Spaniard of rank and fortune, paid a visit to Paris. He was handsome, clever, and *sensible*; he delighted the French *philosophes*, he fascinated the French ladies;

among his conquests was Mademoiselle de Lespinasse. He departed, returned two years later, renewed acquaintance with Julie, and, this time, fell deeply in love. All that is known of him goes to show that he was a man of high worth, endowed with genuine talents, and capable of strong and profound emotions. To Julie, then and ever afterwards, he appeared to be a perfect being, a creature of almost superhuman excellence. She returned his passion with all the force of her nature; her energies had suddenly carried her into a new and splendid universe; she loved him with the intensity of a woman who has lost her youth, and loves for the first time. In spite of the disparity of age, of wealth, and of position, Mora had determined upon marriage. There was only one bar to the completion of their happiness – his ill-health, which perpetually harassed him and was beginning to display the symptoms of consumption. At last, after four years of waiting, everything was prepared; they were about to take the final step; and at that very moment Mora was stricken down by a violent attack of illness. He was obliged to depart from Paris, and return to his native air. The separation was terrible. Julie, worn out with anxiety and watching, her nerves shattered, her hopes crushed, was ready to presage the worst. Yet, however dreadful her fears may have been, they fell far short of the event. After a few weeks of collapse, she managed to pull herself together. She dragged herself to a garden party, in the hope of meeting some of her friends. She met the Comte de Guibert, and her fate was sealed.

The Comte de Guibert was at that moment at the height of his celebrity. A wonderful book on military tactics – now, alas! known no more – had made him the fashion; every one was at his feet; even ladies, in their enthusiasm, read (or pretended to read) his great work. 'Oh, M. de Guibert,' said one of them, 'que votre tic-tac est admirable!' But it was not only his book, it was the compelling charm of his manner and his conversation which secured him his distinguished place in the Parisian world. His talk was copious, brilliant, and extraordinarily impressive; one came away from him wondering what splendid future was in store for so remarkable a man. In addition, he was young, and gallant in every sense of the word. Mademoiselle de Lespinasse, wandering and dejected, came upon him suddenly, and, with a flash of intuition, recognized his qualities as precisely those of which she stood most in need. He seemed to her a tower of strength and sympathy; she felt him to be something she might cling to for support. She showed it, and he was flattered, attracted, at last charmed. They very soon became friends. Before long she had poured out to him the whole history of her agitations and her sorrows; and when, after a few months of constant intercourse, he left Paris to make a tour in Germany, she immediately continued the stream of her confidence in a series of letters. Thus began the famous and terrible correspondence which has made her immortal. The opening letters are charged with dramatic import and premonitions of approaching disaster. They are full of Mora; but, as they succeed one another, it is easy to observe in them a latent uneasiness rising gradually to the surface – a growing, dreadful doubt. As one peers into their depths, one can see forming itself ever more and more distinctly, the image of the absent Guibert, the intruding symbol of a new, inexplicable desire. The mind of Julie, lonely, morbid, and hysterical, was losing itself among its memories and imaginations and obsessions; it was falling under a spell. 'Dites-moi,' she breaks out at last, 'est-ce là le ton de l'amitié? Est-ce celui de la confiance? Qui est-ce qui m'entraine? Faites-moi connaître à moi-même; aidez-moi à me remettre en mesure. Mon âme est bouleversée; sont-ce mes remords? Est-ce ma faute? Est-ce vous? Serait-ce votre départ? Qu'est-ce donc qui me persécute?' Such was her language when Guibert was still absent; but when he returned, when, triumphant with fresh laurels, he besieged her, adored her, when she felt the pressure of his presence and heard the music of his voice, then indeed there was an end of all doubt and hesitation; blinded, intoxicated, overwhelmed, she forgot what should never be forgotten, she forgot Mora, she forgot the whole world.

C'est Vénus tout entière à sa proie attachée!

By a cruel irony, the one event which, in other circumstances, might have come as a release, proved, in Julie's case, nothing less than the final misfortune. Mora died, and his death took away from her for ever all hope of escape from an intolerable situation. For, in the months which followed, it became clear enough that Guibert, whatever else he may have been, was no Mora. Sainte-Beuve, led astray by insufficient knowledge, has painted Guibert as a callous and dunderheaded donkey, a half-grotesque figure, dropping love-letters out of his pockets, and going to the grave without a notion of the tumult he had created. Such a person could never have obtained dominion over Julie de Lespinasse. The truth is that Guibert's character was infinitely better calculated to bring a woman of high intelligence and violent emotions to disaster and destruction. He was really a clever man; he was really well-meaning and warm-hearted; but that was all. He was attractive, affectionate, admirable, everything, in fact, that a man should be; he had, like most men, his moments of passion; like most men, he was ambitious: and he looked forward, like most men, to a comfortable and domestic old age. It is easy to understand how such a character as that worked havoc with Mademoiselle de Lespinasse. It seemed to offer so much, and, when it came to the point, it provided so little – and to her, who asked either for nothing or for all! She had swallowed the bait of his charm and his excellence, and she was hooked with the deadly compromise which they concealed. 'Je n'aime rien de ce qui est à demi,' she wrote of herself, 'de ce qui est indécis, de ce qui n'est qu'un peu. Je n'entends pas la langue des gens du monde: ils s'amusent et ils bâillent; ils ont des amis, et ils n'aiment rien. Tout cela me paraît déplorable. Oui, j'aime mieux le tourment qui consume ma vie, que le plaisir qui engourdit la leur; mais avec cette manière d'être, on n'est point aimable; eh bien! on s'en passe; non, on n'est point aimable, mais on est aimé, et cela vaut mille fois mieux que de plaire.' This was written when Mora was still alive; but, when she had lost him, she discovered soon enough that even passion might go without its recompense from one who was, precisely, a man of the world. 'Ah! mon ami,' she exclaimed to Guibert, summing up her tragedy in a single sentence, 'mon malheur, c'est que vous n'avez pas besoin d'être aimé comme je sais aimer.' No, assuredly, he was never tempted to ask for such dangerous delights. 'Mon ami,' she told him, 'je vous aime, *comme il faut aimer*, avec excès, avec folie, transport, et désespoir.'

Her complete consciousness of the situation made her position more pitiable, but it did not help her to escape. She was bound to him by too many ties; and he, youthful and complaisant, found it beyond his force to break her bondage. Even when she despised him most, her senses fought against her reason, and she lost herself in shame. The phantom of Mora was perpetually before her eyes, torturing her with vanished happiness and visionary upbraidings.

'Oh! Combien j'ai été aimée! une âme de feu, pleine d'énergie, qui avait tout jugé, tout apprécié, et qui, revenue et dégoûtée de tout, s'était abandonnée au besoin et au plaisir d'aimer: mon ami, voilà comme j'etais aimée. Plusieurs années s'étaient écoulées, remplies du charme et de la douleur inséparables d'une passion aussi forte que profonde, lorsque vous êtes venu verser du poison dans mon cœur, ravager mon âme par le trouble et le remords. Mon Dieu! que ne m'avez-vous point fait souffrir! Vous m'arrachiez à mon sentiment, et je voyais que vous n'étiez pas à moi: comprenez-vous toute l'horreur de cette situation? comment trouve-t-on encore de la douceur à dire: mon ami, je vous aime, mais avec tant de vérité et de tendresse qu'il n'est pas possible que votre âme soit froide en m'écoutant?'

His unfaithfulness, and his marriage, were, after all, little more than incidents in her anguish; they were the symptoms of an incurable disease. They stimulated her to fresh efforts towards detachment, but it was in vain. She was a wild animal struggling in a net, involving herself, with every twist and every convulsion, more and more inextricably in the toils. Sometimes she sank into a torpor; existence became a weariness; she drugged herself with opium to escape a pain which was too great to bear. Evening after evening she spent at the opera, drinking in the music of Orpheus, the divine melodies of Gluck. 'Il n'y a qu'une chose dans le monde,' she wrote, 'qui me fasse du bien, c'est la musique, mais c'est un bien qu'on appelerait douleur. Je voudrais entendre dix fois par jour cet air qui me déchire, et qui me fait jouir de tout ce que je regrette: *J'ai perdu mon Euridice.*' But she could never shake off her nightmare. Among her friends, in her charming salon, she would suddenly be overcome with tears, and forced to hurry from the room. Every knock upon the door brought desire and terror to her heart. The postman was a minister of death. 'Non, les effets de la passion ou de la raison (car je ne sais laquelle m'anime dans ce moment) sont incroyables. Après avoir entendu le facteur avec ce besoin, cette agitation, qui font de l'attente le plus grand tourment, j'en étais malade physiquement: ma toux et ma rage de tête m'en avaient avancée de cinq ou six heures. Et bien! après cet état violent, qui n'est susceptible ni de distraction ni d'adoucissement, le facteur est arrivé, j'ai eu des lettres. Il n'y en avoit point de vous; j'en ai reçu une violente commotion intérieure et extérieure, et puis je ne sais ce qui est arrivé, mais je me suis sentie calmée: il me semble que j'éprouve une sorte de douceur à vous trouver encore plus froid et plus indifférent que vous ne pouvez me trouver bizarre.' Who does not discover, beneath these dreadful confidences, a superhuman power moving mysteriously to an appointed doom? a veiled and awful voice of self-immolation?

> Je suis la plaie et le couteau!
> Je suis le soufflet et la joue!
> Je suis les membres et la roue,
> Et la victime et le bourreau!

Her last letters are one long wail of agony. – 'Je ne sais si c'est vous ou la mort que j'implore: j'ai besoin d'être secourue, d'être délivrée du malheur qui me tue.' – 'Mon ami, *je vous aime*. Quand vous verrai-je? Voilà le résultat du passé, du présent, et de l'avenir, s'il y a un avenir! Ah! mon ami, que j'ai souffert, que je souffre! Mes maux sont affreux; mais je sens que je vous aime.' – 'Ah! s'il vous reste quelque bonté, plaignez-moi: je ne sais plus, je ne puis plus vous répondre; mon corps et mon âme sont anéantis. . . . Ah! Mon Dieu, je ne me connais plus.' Yet, in spite of all the pains of her existence she was glad that she had lived. 'J'en mourrai peut-être,' she had written, when she could still hope, 'mais cela vaut mieux que de n'avoir jamais vécu'; and, in the depth of her despair, it was still the same. – 'Ah! ces souvenirs me tuent! Cependant je voudrais bien pouvoir recommencer, et à des conditions plus cruelles encore.' She regretted nothing; she was insatiable. Shattered in body and in mind, she fell at last into complete and irremediable collapse. Guibert, helpless and overwhelmed, hurried to her, declared he could never survive her; she forbade him her presence; the faithful d'Alembert alone watched beside her bed. 'Adieu, mon ami,' she wrote to Guibert, when the end was approaching. 'Si jamais je revenais à la vie, j'aimerais encore à l'employer à vous aimer; mais il n'y a plus de temps.' The wretched man, imprisoned in her ante-chamber, awaited the inevitable hour. With a supreme effort, she wrote him her valediction. She implored him to let her die at last. – 'Ah! mon ami, faites que je vous doive le repos! Par vertu, soyez cruel une fois.' She sank into the arms of d'Alembert, thanking him tenderly for that long kindness, that unalterable devotion; then, begging from him some strange forgiveness, she seemed, for a moment, to be struggling to an avowal of unutterable things. The ghastly secret trembled; but it was too late.

She died on the 22nd of May, 1776, in the forty-fourth year of her life. She was buried quietly in the cemetry of Saint-Sulpice, d'Alembert and Condorcet performing the final rites. For d'Alembert, however, there was one more duty. She had named him her executor; it was his task to examine her papers; and, when he did so, he made a discovery which cut him to the heart. Not a single letter of his own had been preserved among all the multitude; instead, it was Mora, Mora, Mora, and nothing else. He had fondly imagined that, among her friends, his own place had been the first. In his distress, he rushed to Guibert, pouring out his disappointment, his cruel disillusionment: 'Oh! we were all of us mistaken; it was Mora that she loved!' Guibert was silent. The tragic irony was complete. A thousand memories besieged him, a thousand thoughts of past delights, of vanished conversations, of delicious annihilated hours; he was stifled by regrets, by remorse, by vain possibilities; he was blinded by endless visions of a pearl richer than all his tribe; a dreadful mist of tears, of desecration, of horror, rose up and clouded him for ever from his agonized and deluded friend.

> O lasso,
> Quanti dolci pensier, quanto disio
> Menò costoro al doloroso passo!

1906

# The Abbé Morellet

Talleyrand once remarked that only those who had lived in France
before the Revolution had really experienced *la douceur de vivre*.
The Abbé Morellet would have agreed with him. Born in 1727 at
Lyons, the son of a small paper merchant, how was it possible, in
that age of caste and privilege, that André Morellet should have
known anything of life but what was hard, dull, and insignificant?
So one might have supposed; but the contrary was the case. Before
he was thirty this young man, without either fortune or connections, and without taking very much trouble about it, found
himself a member of the most brilliant society in Paris, the close
friend of the famous and the great, with a rosy future before him.
The secret of it was simple: he had shown that he was intelligent;
and in those days a little intelligence went a long way. So, indeed,
did a little – a very little – money. A thousand francs from a
generous cousin had opened Paris to him, by enabling him to go to
the Sorbonne, whence, after five years, he had emerged an Abbé
and an infidel. A chance meeting with Diderot did the rest. The
great *philosophe*, forty years of age and at the height of his
intellectual power, completely captivated a youth whose eager
mind was only waiting for new ideas and new activities. Every
Sunday morning the Abbé scaled the stairs to Diderot's lodging, to
sit entranced for hours, while the Master poured forth the
irresistible floods of his amazing conversation. 'J'ai éprouvé peu de
plaisirs de l'esprit au-dessus de celui-là,' wrote Morellet long
afterwards; 'et je m'en souviendrai toujours.' One can well believe
it. The young man listened so intelligently that Diderot soon saw
he would do; enrolled him among his disciples; introduced him to
all his friends; and set him to write articles for his great
Encyclopædia. *La douceur de vivre* had begun.

Thirty delightful years followed – years of exciting work,

delicious friendship, and ever-growing optimism. The great battle for liberty, tolerance, reason, and humanity was in full swing; the forces of darkness were yielding more and more rapidly; and Morellet was in the forefront of the fight. He wrote with untiring zeal. Besides his Encyclopædia articles, he produced pamphlets in favour of the Protestants, he brought out a *Manuel des Inquisiteurs* exposing the methods of the Inquisition, he translated Beccaria's great work. But his principal interest was political economy. A close friend of Turgot, he was one of the earliest believers in Free Trade. He translated *The Wealth of Nations*; though the cast of his mind contrasted curiously with Adam Smith's. The Abbé, like most of the *philosophes*, preferred the *a priori* mode of argument. The reasons which led him to favour Free Trade are characteristic. The rights of property, he argued, are fundamental to the very existence of civilized society; now to interfere with the freedom of exchange is to attack one of the rights of property; therefore Protection and civilization are incompatible. This extremely complete argument seems to have escaped the notice of Tory Free Traders.

But the Abbé was not merely enlightened and argumentative; he had another quality which was essential in those days if one was to make any figure at all: he was malicious – though only, of course, at the expense of 'the enemies of reason'. Some particularly biting little flysheets of his actually brought a word of praise from the mighty Patriarch of Ferney. 'Embrassez pour moi l'Abbé Mords-les,' wrote Voltaire to a common friend; 'je ne connais personne qui soit plus capable de rendre service à la raison.' This was a testimonial indeed! Morellet's reputation went up with a bound, and he himself declared that the sentence was all he wanted by way of an epitaph.

Only one thing more was needed to make his success complete; and that a kindly fate provided. Palissot, a *protégé* of a certain great lady, the Princesse de Robecq, attacked the *philosophes* in a satirical farce. Morellet, among the rest, replied with a stinging pamphlet; but he was unwise enough to direct some of his sharp remarks, not at Palissot, but at the Princess. This could not be allowed. Madame de Robecq had been the mistress of the Duc de Choiseul, who was all-powerful with Madame de Pompadour and, through her, with the King. A *lettre de cachet* sent Morellet to the Bastille. One can imagine no more striking example of the corruption and tyranny of the *ancien régime* – if only the poor Abbé had been treated properly – thrown into an underground dungeon, let us say, loaded with chains, and fed on bread and water. Unfortunately, nothing of the sort occurred. The victim was given a comfortable room, plenty of excellent food, a bottle of wine a day, provided with writing materials, and allowed all the books he asked for, besides being given the run of the Bastille library, which was especially strong in novels. He spent three months in peaceful study; and returned to liberty with the added glory of martyrdom.

Liberty and martyrdom – one hardly knew which was the pleasanter. In Paris one's mornings passed in reading and writing – the quill dashing over the paper with a heavenly speed; and one's afternoons and evenings were spent in company. There were dinners at d'Holbach's; there were the nightly gatherings in the little rooms of Mademoiselle de Lespinasse; there were lunches with Madame Geoffrin; and everywhere and always the conversation was copious and audacious to an intoxicating degree. Madame Geoffrin, indeed, insisted upon limits. 'Voilà qui est bien!' she used to exclaim, when the talk grew too wild and high. Then the more reckless spirits, headed by d'Alembert, would go out into the Tuileries Gardens, and, sitting under the trees, continue the discourse until the exploded ruins of religions, philosophies, and conventions fell in showers about their ears. If Paris grew too hot or too noisy, there was always, close at hand, Auteuil. There lived Madame Helvétius, the widow of one of the leading *philosophes*, in a charming little villa, with a garden and all the simple pleasures of a country life. A curious *ménage*, highly typical of the nation and the age, was gathered together between those friendly walls. Morellet spent every summer and all his week-ends there; another clever Abbé also had rooms in the house; and so had a younger man, Cabanis, to whom Madame Helvétius was particularly attached. The elements of sentiment and friendship were so perfectly balanced between the four that their harmony and happiness were complete. Year after year the summers waxed and waned in the Auteuil garden, while Morellet lingered there, with peace, wit, kindness, and beauty around him. What was there left to wish for? Well! it would be nice, he sometimes thought, to have a little – a very little – more money. His income – made up of a few small pensions and legacies – was about £100 a year.

A most pleasant interlude was a visit to England, where Morellet spent several months as the guest of Lord Shelburne. Shelburne was a failure at politics (he was a Prime Minister and a man of intellect – a hazardous combination); but he made an admirable host. Garrick and Franklin were asked down to Bowood to meet the Abbé, and then he was carried off on a driving tour all over England. One day, near Plymouth, there was a picnic on the banks of the Tamar. After the meal, as the company lay on the grass, and the evening fell, three country girls made their appearance; on which the Abbé, offering them a basket of cherries, asked them, in his broken English, for a song. They smiled, and blushed; but sing they did, in unison, with the sweetest voices. The description of the scene in Morellet's *Mémoires* reads like a page from the *Vicar of Wakefield*.

Even affluence came at last. The incumbent of a priory, the reversion of which had been given to Morellet by Turgot twenty years before, died, and the Abbé found himself in the possession of a spacious country house, with land, and an income of £600 a year. This was in 1788. In less than a year all was over. The Abbé never lived in his priory. The tempest of the Revolution engulfed both him and it. The rights of property were violated, and the priest was deprived of a sinecure that he was enjoying as a member of a Church in which he disbelieved. Morellet's surprised indignation at this catastrophe – his absolute unconsciousness that the whole effort of his life had been in reality directed towards this very goal – makes comic reading – comic, and pathetic too. For still worse was to follow. The happy *ménage* at Auteuil was broken up. Cabinis and the other Abbé believed in the Revolution; Madame Helvétius agreed with them; and Morellet, finding himself in a minority of one, after a violent scene left the villa for ever. His plight was serious; but he weathered the storm. A revolutionary tribunal, before which he was haled, treated him gently, partly because it transpired in the course of the proceedings that he had been a friend of Turgot, '*ce bon citoyen*'; he was dismissed with a caution. Then, besides saving his own neck, he was able to do a good turn to the *Académie Française*, of which he was the Director. When that body was broken up, the care of its valuable possessions – its papers and its portraits – fell to him. He concealed everything in various hiding-places, from which he drew forth the precious relics in triumph, when the days of order returned.

For they did return; and the Abbé, very old and very tired, found his way, with one or two others, to young Madame de Rémusat's drawing-room. There he sat dozing by the fire, while the talk sped on around him; dozing, and nodding; then suddenly waking up to denounce Monsieur de Chateaubriand and lament the ruin of French prose. He was treated with great respect by everybody; even the First Consul was flattering; even the Emperor was polite, and made him a Senator. Then the Emperor vanished, and a Bourbon ruled once more on the throne of his fathers. With that tenacity of life which seems to have been the portion of the creatures of the eighteenth century, Morellet continued in this world until his ninety-second year. But this world was no longer what it used to be: something had gone wrong. Those agitations, those arrangements and rearrangements, they seemed hardly worth attending to. One might as well doze. All his young friends were very kind certainly, but did they understand? How could they? What had been their experience of life? As for him, ah! *he* had listened to Diderot – used to sit for hours talking in the Tuileries Gardens with d'Alembert and Mademoiselle de Lespinasse – mentioned by Voltaire – spent half a lifetime at Auteuil with dear Madame Helvétius – imprisoned in the Bastille . . . he nodded. Yes! *He* had known *la douceur de vivre*.

1924

# Madame de Lieven

Aristocrats (no doubt) still exist; but they are shorn beings, for whom the wind is not tempered – powerless, out of place, and slightly ridiculous. For about a hundred years it has been so. The stages in the history of nobility may be reckoned by the different barricades it has put up to keep off the common multitude. The feudal lord used armour to separate him from the rest of the world; then, as civilization grew, it was found that a wig did almost as well; and there was a curious transition period (*temp*. Marlborough) when armour and wigs were worn at the same time. After that, armour vanished, and wigs were left, to rule splendidly through the eighteenth century, until the French Revolution. A fearful moment! Wigs went. Nevertheless the citadel still held out, for another barrier remained – the barrier of manners; and for a generation it was just possible to be an aristocrat on manners alone. Then, at last, about 1830, manners themselves crumbled, undermined by the insidious permeation of a new – a middle-class – behaviour; and all was over. Madame de Lieven was one of the supreme examples of the final period. Her manners were of the genuinely terrific kind. Surrounded by them, isolated as with an antiseptic spray, she swept on triumphantly, to survive untouched – so it seemed – amid an atmosphere alive with the microbes of bourgeois disintegration. So it seemed – for in fact something strange eventually happened. In her case, aristocracy, like some viscous fluid flowing along, when it came to the precipice did not plunge over the edge, but – such was its strength, its inherent force of concentration – moved, as it had always moved, straight onward, until it stuck out, an amazing semi-solid projection, over the abyss. Only at long last was there a melting; the laws of nature asserted themselves; and the inevitable, the deplorable, collapse ensued.

Born in 1785, a Russian and a Benckendorf, Madame de Lieven was by blood more than half German, for her mother had come from Würtemberg and her father's family was of Prussian origin. From the first moment of her existence she was in the highest sphere. Her mother had been the favourite companion of the Empress Marie, wife of Paul I, and on her death the Empress had adopted the young Benckendorfs and brought them up under her own care. At the age of fifteen, Dorothea was taken from a convent and married to the young Count de Lieven (or, more correctly, Count Lieven without the 'particule'; but it would be pedantry to insist upon an accuracy unknown to contemporaries) whose family was no less closely connected with the Imperial house. His mother had been the governess of the Emperor Paul's children; when her task was over, she had retained the highest favour; and her son, at the age of twenty-eight, was aide-de-camp to the Emperor and Secretary for War. Paul I was murdered; but under the new Czar the family fortunes continued to prosper – the only change being the transference of the Count de Lieven from the army to the diplomatic service. In 1809 he was appointed Russian ambassador at Berlin; and in 1812 he was moved to London, where he and his wife were to remain for the next twenty-two years.

The great world in those days was small – particularly the English one, which had been kept in a vacuum for years by the Napoleonic War. In 1812 a foreign embassy was a surprising novelty in London, and the arrival of the Lievens produced an excitement which turned to rapture when it was discovered that the ambassadress was endowed with social talents of the highest order. She immediately became the fashion – and remained so for the rest of her life. That she possessed neither beauty nor intellect was probably a positive advantage; she was attractive and clever – that was enough. Her long gawky figure and her too pronounced features were somehow fascinating, and her accomplishments were exactly suited to her *milieu*; while she hated reading, never opening a book except Madame de Sévigné's letters, she could be very entertaining in four languages, and, if asked, could play on the pianoforte extremely well. Whenever she appeared, life was enhanced and intensified. She became the intimate friend of several great hostesses – Lady Holland, Lady Cowper, Lady Granville; she was successfully adored by several men of fashion – Lord

Willoughby, Lord Gower, and (for a short time – so it was whispered) the Prince Regent himself. She was made a patroness of Almack's – the only foreign lady to receive the distinction. Exclusive, vigorous, tart, she went on her way rejoicing – and then there was a fresh development. The war over, the era of conferences opened. In 1818, at Aix-la-Chapelle, where all the ministers and diplomats of Europe were gathered together, she met Metternich, then at the beginning of his long career as the virtual ruler of Austria, and a new and serious love-affair immediately began. It lasted during the four years that elapsed between the Congress of Aix-la-Chapelle and that of Verona; and in Metternich's love-letters – extremely long and extremely meta-physical – the earlier stages of it may still be traced. The affair ended as suddenly as it had started. But this close relationship with the dominating figure in European politics had a profound effect on Madame de Lieven's life.

Henceforward, high diplomacy was to be her passion. She was nearly forty; it was time to be ambitious, to live by the head rather than the heart, to explore the mysteries of chanceries, to pull the strings of cabinets, to determine the fate of nations; she set to work with a will. Besides her native wits, she had two great assets – her position in English society, and the fact that her husband was a nonentity – she found that she could simply step into his place. Her first triumph came when the Czar Alexander entrusted her personally with an overture to Canning on the thorny question of Greece. Alexander's death and the accession of Nicholas was all to the good: her husband's mother received a princedom, and she herself in consequence became a Princess. At the same time Russia, abandoning the traditions of the Holy Alliance, drew nearer to England and the liberal policy of Canning. Madame de Lieven became the presiding genius of the new orientation; it was possibly owing to her influence with George IV that Canning obtained the Premiership; and it was certainly owing to her efforts that the Treaty of London was signed in 1827, by which the independence of Greece became an accomplished fact. After Canning's death, she formed a new connection – with Lord Grey. The great Whig Earl became one of the most ardent of her admirers. Sitting up in bed every morning, he made it his first task to compose an elaborate epistle to his Egeria, which, when it was completed, he carefully perfumed with musk. The precise nature of their relationship has never transpired. The tone of their correspondence seems to indicate a purely platonic attachment; but tones are deceitful, and Lord Grey was a man of many gallantries; however, he was sixty-eight. It is also doubtful who benefited most by the connection: possibly the lady's influence was less than she supposed. At any rate it is certain that when, on one occasion, she threatened a withdrawal of her favours unless the Prime Minister adopted a particular course, she was met with a regretful, an infinitely regretful, refusal; upon which she tactfully collapsed. But, on another occasion, it seems possible that her advice produced an important consequence. When Lord Grey took office, who was to be Foreign Minister? Lady Cowper was Madame de Lieven's great friend, and Palmerston was Lady Cowper's lover. At their request, Madame de Lieven pressed the claims of Palmerston upon the Premier, and Palmerston was appointed. If this was indeed the result of her solicitations, the triumphant Princess was to find before long that she had got more than she had bargained for.

In the meantime, all went swimmingly. There was always some intriguing concoction on the European table – a revolution in Portugal – the affairs of Belgium to be settled – a sovereign to be found for Greece – and Madame de Lieven's finger was invariably in the pie. So we see her, in the Memoirs and Letters of the time, gliding along in brilliant activity, a radiating focus of enjoyment, except – ah! it was her one horror! – when she found herself with a bore. If it was her highest felicity to extract, in an excited *tête-à-tête*, the latest piece of diplomatic gossip from a Cabinet Minister, her deepest agony was to be forced to mark time with undistinguished underlings, or – worst of all! – some literary person. On such occasions she could not conceal her despair – indeed she hardly wished to – even from the most eminent – even from the great Chateaubriand himself. 'Quand elle se trouve avec des gens de mérite,' he acidly noted, 'sa stérilité se tait; elle revêt sa nullité d'un air supérieur d'ennui, comme si elle avait le droit d'être ennuyée.' She only admitted one exception: for royal personages very great allowances might be made. A royal bore, indeed, was almost a contradiction in terms; such a flavour of mysterious suavity hovered for ever round those enchanted beings. She was always at her best with them, and for her own particular royalties – for the

Czar and the whole imperial family – no considerations, no exertions, no adulations could be too great. She corresponded personally with her imperial master upon every twist and turn of the international situation, and yet there were tedious wretches . . . she would not bear it, she would be ruthless, they should be *écrasés* – and she lifted her black eyebrows till they almost vanished and drew herself up to her thinnest height. She looked like some strange animal – what was it? Somebody said that Madame Appony, another slender, tall ambassadress, was like a giraffe, and that she and Madame de Lieven were of the same species. 'Mais non!' said Madame Alfred de Noailles, 'ce n'est pas la même classe: l'une mangera l'autre et n'aura qu'un mauvais repas' – 'One sees Lieven,' was Lady Granville's comment, 'crunching the meek Appony's bones.' Everyone was a little afraid of her – everyone, that is to say, except Lady Holland; for 'Old Madagascar' knew no fear. One day, at a party, having upset her work-basket, she calmly turned to the ambassadress with, 'Pick it up, my dear, pick it up!' And Madame de Lieven went down on her knees and obeyed. 'Such a sight was never seen before,' said Lady Granville.

Lady Holland – yes; but there was also somebody else; there was Palmerston. Madame de Lieven, having (so she was convinced) got him his appointment as Foreign Secretary, believed that she could manage him; he was, she declared, 'un très-petit esprit'; the mistake was gross, and it was fatal. In 1834, Palmerston appointed Stratford Canning ambassador to Russia; but the Emperor disliked him, and let it be known, through Madame de Lieven, that he was unwilling to receive him. Palmerston, however, persisted in his choice, in spite of all the arguments of the ambassadress, who lost her temper, appealed to Lord Grey – in vain, and then – also in vain – tried to get up an agitation in the Cabinet. Finally, she advised the Czar to stand firm, for Palmerston, she said, would give way when it came to the point. Accordingly, it was officially stated that Stratford Canning would not be received in Russia. The result, however, was far from Madame de Lieven's expectations. Palmerston had had enough of female interferences, and he decided to take this opportunity of putting an end to them altogether. He appointed no ambassador, and for months the English business in St. Petersburg was transacted by a *chargé d'affaires*. Then there happened precisely what the wily minister had foreseen. The Emperor could support the indignity no longer; he determined to retort in kind; and he recalled the Lievens.

So ended the official life of the Princess. The blow was severe – the pain of parting was terrible – but, as it turned out, this was only the beginning of misfortune. In the following year, her two youngest sons died of scarlet fever; her own health was broken; stricken down by grief and illness, she gave up the Court appointment with which her services had been rewarded, and went to live in Paris. Suddenly she received a peremptory order of recall. Nicholas, with autocratic caprice, had flown into a fury; the Princess must return! Her husband, seeing that a chance of self-assertion had at last come to him, fell in with the Emperor's wishes. A third son died; and the Prince was forbidden to communicate the fact to his wife; she only learnt it, months later, when one of her letters to her son was returned to her, with the word 'mort' on the envelope. After that, there was hectic correspondence, the Prince at one moment actually threatening to cut off his wife's supplies if she remained in Paris. She would not budge, however, and eventually the storm blew over; but the whole system of Madame de Lieven's existence had received a terrible shock. 'Quel pays!' she exclaimed in her anguish. 'Quel maître! Quel père!'

The instinct which had kept her in Paris was a sound one; for there, in that friendly soil, she was able to strike fresh roots and to create for herself an establishment that was almost a home. Her irrepressible social activities once more triumphed. Installed in Talleyrand's old house at the corner of the Rue de Rivoli and the Rue St. Florentin, with an outlook over the Place de la Concorde, she held her nightly *salon*, and, for another twenty years, revived the glories of her London reign. Though no longer in any official situation, she was still perpetually occupied with the highest politics, was still the terror of embassies, still the delight of the worldly and the great. Still, in her pitiless exclusiveness, she would *écraser* from time to time some wretched creature from another sphere. 'Monsieur, je ne vous connais pas,' she said in icy tones to a gentleman who presented himself one evening in her *salon*. He reminded her of how often they had met at Ems, in the summer – had taken the waters together – surely she must remember him. 'Non, Monsieur,' was the adamantine reply, and the poor man slunk away, having learnt the lesson that friendship at Ems and friendship in Paris are two very different things.

Such was the appearance; but in fact something strange had happened: Madame de Lieven's aristocracy was trembling over the abyss. The crash came on June 24, 1837 – the date is significant: it was four days after the accession of Queen Victoria – when, worn out by domestic grief, disillusioned, embittered, unable to resist any longer the permeations of the Time Spirit, the Princess fell into the arms of Monsieur Guizot. Fate had achieved an almost exaggerated irony. For Guizot was the living epitome of all that was most middle-class. Infinitely respectable, a Protestant, the father of a family, having buried two wives, a learned historian, he had just given up the portfolio of public instruction, and was clearly destined to be the leading spirit of the bourgeois monarchy of Louis-Philippe. He was fifty years old. His first wife had been a child of the *ancien régime*, but he had tamed her, turned her thoughts towards duty and domesticity, induced her to write improving stories for the young, until at last, suddenly feeling that she could bear it no longer, she had taken refuge in death while he was reading aloud to her a sermon by Bossuet on the immortality of the soul. His second wife – the niece of the first – had needed no such pressure; naturally all that could be wished, she wrote several volumes of improving stories for the young quite of her own accord, while reflections upon the beneficence of the Creator flowed from her at the slightest provocation; but she too had died; his eldest son had died; and the bereaved Guizot was left alone with his high-mindedness. Madame de Lieven was fifty-two. It seemed an incredible love-affair – so much so that Charles Greville, who had known her intimately all his life, refused to believe that it was anything but a 'social and political' *liaison*. But the wits of Paris thought otherwise. It was noticed that Guizot was always to be found in the house in the Rue St. Florentin. The malicious Mérimée told the story of how, after a party at the Princess's, he had been the last to leave – except Guizot; how, having forgotten something, he had returned to the drawing-room, and found that the Minister had already taken off the ribbon (the 'grand cordon') of the Legion of Honour. A chuckle – a chuckle from beyond the tomb – reached the world from Chateaubriand. 'Le ridicule attendait à Paris Madame de Lieven. Un doctrinaire grave est tombé aux pieds d'Omphale: "Amour, tu perdis Troie." ' And the wits of Paris were right. The *liaison*, certainly, was strengthened by political and social interests, but its basis was sentimental passion. The testimony of a long series of letters puts that beyond a doubt. In this peculiar correspondence, pedantry, adoration, platitudes, and suburban *minauderies* form a compound for which one hardly knows whether smiles or tears are the appropriate reaction. When Guizot begins a love-letter with – 'Le Cardinal de Retz dit quelque part', one can only be delighted, but when Madame de Lieven exclaims, 'Ah! que j'aurais besoin d'être gouvernée! Pourquoi ne me gouvernez-vous pas?' one is positively embarrassed. One feels that one is committing an unpardonable – a deliciously unpardonable – indiscretion, as one overhears the cooings of these antiquated doves. 'Si vous pouviez voir,' he says, with exquisite originality, 'tout ce qu'il y a dans mon cœur, si profond, si fort, si éternel, si tendre, si triste.' And she answers, 'Maintenant, je voudrais la tranquillité, la paix du cottage, votre amour, le mien, rien que cela. Ah! mon ami, c'est là le vrai bonheur.' La paix du cottage! Can this be really and truly Madame de Lieven?

Yet there was a point at which she did draw the line. After the death of the Prince in 1839, it was inevitable that there should be a suggestion of marriage. But it faded away. They were never united by any other vows than those which they had sworn to each other in the sight of heaven. It was rumoured that the difficulty was simply one of nomenclature. Guizot (one would expect it) judged that he would be humiliated if his wife's name were not his own; and the Princess, though wishing to be governed, recoiled at that. 'Ma chère, on dit que vous allez épouser Guizot,' said a friend. 'Est-ce vrai?' 'Oh! ma chère,' was the reply, 'me voyez-vous annoncée Madame Guizot!' Was this the last resistance of the aristocrat? Or was it perhaps, in reality, the final proof that Madame de Lieven was an aristocrat no longer?

The idyll only ended with death – though there were a few interruptions. In 1848, revolution forced the lovers to fly to England; it also precipitated the aged Metternich, with a new young wife, upon these hospitable shores. The quartet spent a fortnight together at Brighton; until their discreet conversations were ended for ever by the restoration of order; and the *salon* in the rue St. Florentin was opened again. But a new dispensation was beginning, in which there was no place for the old minister of

Louis-Philippe. Guizot stood aside; and, though Madame de Lieven continued to wield an influence under the Second Empire, it was a gradually declining one. The Crimean War came as a shattering blow. She had made it up with the Czar; their correspondence was once more in full swing; this was known, and, when war came, she was forced to leave Paris for Brussels. Her misery was complete, but it only lasted for eighteen months. She crept back on the plea of health, and Napoleon, leniently winking at her presence, allowed her to remain – allowed her at last to re-open, very gingerly, her *salon*. But everything now was disappearing, disintegrating, shimmering away. She was in her seventy-second year; she was ill and utterly exhausted; she was dying. Guizot, a veteran too, was perpetually at her bedside; she begged him at last to leave her – to go into the next room for a little. He obeyed, and she was dead when he returned to her. She had left a note for him, scribbled in pencil – 'Je vous remercie des vingt années d'affection et de bonheur. Ne m'oubliez pas. Adieu, Adieu.' At the last moment, with those simple and touching words, the old grandeur – the original essence that was Dorothea Benckendorf – had come into its own again.

1931

# The Président de Brosses

A charming and sometimes forgotten feature of the world as it used to be before the age of trains and telephones was the provincial capital. When Edinburgh was as far from London as Vienna is to-day, it was natural – it was inevitable – that it should be the centre of a local civilization, which, while it remained politically and linguistically British, developed a colour and a character of its own. In France there was the same pleasant phenomenon. Bordeaux, Toulouse, Aix-en-Provence – up to the end of the eighteenth century each of these was in truth a capital, where a peculiar culture had grown up that was at once French and idiosyncratic. An impossibility today! It is hard to believe, as one whisks through Dijon in a tram, that here, a hundred and fifty years ago, was the centre of a distinct and vigorous civilization – until, perhaps, one leaves the trams, and turns aside into the rue de la Préfecture. Ah! One has come upon a vanished age. The houses, so solid and yet so vivacious, with their cobbled courts and coloured tiles, seem to be withdrawn into an aristocratic resignation. Memory and forgetfulness are everywhere. It is the moment to reflect upon the Président de Brosses.

Dijon, the capital of Burgundy, had become in the eighteenth century pre-eminently a city of magistrates. There the provincial *parlement* assembled and the laws were administered by the hereditary judges, the nobility of the long robe, whose rule was more immediate, more impressive, and almost more powerful, than the King's. Charles de Brosses was born into this aristocracy, and grew up to be a perfect representative of its highest traditions. He was extremely intelligent, admirably conscientious, and crammed full of life. He was at once a wit, a scholar, a lawyer, and a man of the world. He resembled the generous wine of the country in his combination of gay vitality with richness and strength. His tiny figure and his satirical face lost in the forest of a judicial wig might prompt to laughter – 'the corners of one's mouth', said Diderot, 'couldn't help going up when one looked at him'; but he was impressive on the bench; and, late in life, was to prove his patriotism by his intrepid resistance when the privileges of his province were attacked by the royal authority. In his leisure, he devoted himself to every kind of literary and scientific work. A tour in Italy produced a series of amusing letters, which, published posthumously, are still read and remembered; his book on the newly discovered Herculaneum (1750) was the first on the subject; his *Histoire des navigations des Terres Australes* (1756) was of use to both Cook and Bougainville; his *Culte des Dieux Fétiches* (1760) contained a curious speculation on the origin of the religion of Egypt; his *Traité de la formation mécanique des langues* (1765) was the earliest attempt at a science of etymology; and his labours were concluded with an elaborate edition of *Sallust* (1777) upon which he had worked for thirty years. The growth of knowledge had converted his research and his speculations into mere curiosities; but it was natural that the citizens of Dijon should have honoured him as one of their most splendid luminaries, and that the Président de Brosses should have been compared in his day to that other great provincial figure of a previous generation – the Président de Montesquieu. Of course, though Dijon was select and Dijon was magnificent, it had to be admitted that there did exist a higher tribunal, at whose bar taste, learning, and behaviour received their final doom or their crowning approbation: the drawing-rooms of Paris reigned supreme. In those drawing-rooms the Président was well thought of; he had powerful friends at Court; was it not to be expected that at last, in the fullness of time, his worth would be completely recognized and receive its due reward in the highest honour that could fall to a man of his pretensions – a seat in the Academy? A prize, indeed, that it was impossible not to hope for! The promises of other worlds had grown dim and dubious; but here, among the glorious forty, was a definite, an indisputable immortality – and one, moreover, that possessed the singular advantage of being enjoyable here and now, while the eighteenth-century sun still shone on the rue de la Préfecture.

The Président was at the height of his exuberant manhood – he was not yet fifty – when something occurred which had a strange and unexpected effect upon his history. Voltaire, having quarrelled with Frederick the Great and shaken the dust of Potsdam from his feet, had been wandering for some years in uncertainty among the minor states that lay between France and Germany. He had settled for a time at Colmar; he had moved to Lausanne; then he had gone to Geneva and taken a country house in its neighbourhood. But the Calvinism of the townspeople, who frowned at his passion for private theatricals, annoyed him; and his eye fell on the house and territory of Ferney, which was just inside the borders of France, but, lying on the eastern slopes of the Jura mountains, was so remote as to be almost independent of French control and within a drive of the free city of Geneva. This was exactly what he wanted – a secluded abode, where he would have elbow-room for his activities, and from which he could bolt at any moment, if things became too hot for him. Accordingly, in 1758, he bought Ferney, where he lived for the rest of his life; and at the same time he entered into negotiations for the purchase of a neighbouring property – that of Tournay – which belonged to the Président de Brosses. The Président, who already had a slight acquaintance with the great man – his wife, a Crévecœur, was the daughter of one of Voltaire's oldest friends – declared that he would be delighted to oblige him. There was some stiff haggling, for each party prided himself on his business capacity, but eventually Voltaire, for 35,000 francs, became possessed of the domain of Tournay – which included the right to the title of Count – on a life-tenancy. The bargain, obviously, was something of a gamble; the new Comte de Tournay was sixty-four, and, so he declared, on the point of death; but then he had been on the point of death ever since any one could remember. When it was all over, the Président had an uneasy feeling that he had been done. The feeling increased as time went on, and his agent informed him that the estate was being allowed to go to rack and ruin. He complained; but the poet replied with a flat denial, declared – what was quite true – that he had built a theatre at Tournay, and begged the Président to come and see his latest tragedy performed in it. A little later, a new manœuvre began: Voltaire proposed that he should buy the property outright. The Président was not altogether averse; but this time he was far more cautious; as the negotiations proceeded, he became privately convinced that an attempt was being made to cheat him; but he said nothing, and the proposal lapsed. Voltaire, on his side, was none too pleased with his bargain. The land of Tournay was poor, and the Countship had brought with it various responsibilities and expenses not at all to his taste. He was vexed; and his vexation took the form of bothering the Président, in letter after letter, with a multitude of legal questions upon points connected with the property. The Président was also vexed; but he answered every letter and every question with extreme civility.

In this way two years passed – two years during which the Président published his *Culte des Dieux Fétiches* and Voltaire his *Candide*. The old creature at Ferney was at last beginning to settle down to the final and by far the most important period of his immense and extraordinary career. Free, rich, happy, with his colossal reputation and his terrific energy, he was starting on the great adventure of his life – his onslaught upon Christianity. Meanwhile his vitality and his pugnacity were satisfying themselves in a multitude of minor ways. He was belabouring Rousseau, torturing Fréron, annihilating le Franc de Pompignan; he was corresponding with all the world, he was composing half a dozen tragedies, he was writing the life of Peter the Great, he was preparing a monumental edition of Corneille. When, in the midst of these and a hundred other activities, he received a bill for 281 francs from a peasant called Charlot Baudy for fourteen loads of wood from Tournay, he brushed the matter on one side. More bother from Tournay! But it was ridiculous – why should he pay for wood from his own estate? And besides, he remembered quite well that the Président, before the sale was completed, had told him that he could have as much wood as he wanted. He did nothing, and when Charlot Baudy pressed for the money, refused to pay. Then, early in 1761, a letter arrived from the Président. 'Agréez, Monsieur,' he began, 'que je vous demande l'explication d'une chose tout-à-fait singulière.' Charlot Baudy, he continued, had, *before the sale of Tournay*, bought from the Président the cut wood on the estate; Baudy had now sent in his account of what he owed the Président, and had subtracted from it the sum of 281 francs for wood supplied to M. de Voltaire; his reason for this was that M. de Voltaire had told him that the wood was a gift from the Président. 'Je vous demande excuse,' the letter went on, 'si je vous répète un tel propos: car vous sentez bien que je suis fort éloigné de croire que vous l'ayez tenu, et je n'y ajoute pas la moindre foi. Je ne prends ceci que pour le discours d'un homme rustique fait pour ignorer les usages du monde et les convenances; qui ne sait pas qu'on envoie bien à son ami et son voisin un panier de pêches, mais que si on s'avisait de lui faire la galanterie de quatorze moules de bois, il le prendrait pour une absurdité contraire aux bienséances.' The sarcasm was clear and cutting, and the Président proceeded to give his own account of what had occurred. He distinctly remembered, he said, that Voltaire, at the time of the negotiations about Tournay, had in the course of conversation, complained of a lack of firewood, and that he had thereupon recommended Baudy as the man who would supply Voltaire with as much as he wanted. That was all; the offensive notion of a present had never entered his head. 'J'espère,' he concluded, 'que vous voudrez bien faire incontinent payer cette bagatelle à Charlot, parce que, comme je me ferai certainement payer de lui, il aurait infailliblement aussi son recours contre vous; ce qui ferait une affaire du genre de celles qu'un homme tel que vous ne veut point avoir.'

It was obvious to anyone in his senses that the Président was right: that his account of the matter was the true one, and that, as he had said, the only reasonable thing for Voltaire to do was to pay Baudy the money – the miserable sum of money! – and finish the business. But Voltaire was not in his senses – he never was when even the most miserable sum of money was concerned. He could not bear to think of parting with 281 francs. It was monstrous; the land and everything on it was his; the wood had been given him; he would not be set down; and this wretched man had dared to be ironical! At any rate, he had had the wood and burnt it, and the Président de Brosses might do what he liked. Accordingly, in his next letter, he airily dismissed the subject. 'It is no longer a question,' he said, 'of Charles Baudy and four loads of wood' – and proceeded to discuss an entirely different matter. The Président replied in detail, and then reverted for a moment to Baudy – 'Four loads – read *fourteen*; you dropped a figure; we call this a *lapsus linguae*'; – and he begged Voltaire once more to avoid the painful publicity of a lawsuit. Voltaire made no reply; he hoped the whole thing was over; but he was wrong. In June, the Président sued Baudy for 281 francs, and in July Baudy sued Voltaire for the same sum. The cases came on at the local court, and were adjourned.

And now the fury of the frantic old desperado flamed up sky-high. Seizing his pen, he poured out, in letter after letter to all the lawyers in Dijon, his account of what had happened – the swindling to which he had been subjected – the insults to which he had been exposed. To a particular friend, the Président de Ruffey, he sent a long formal statement of his case, followed by a private sheet of enraged argumentation. As for his enemy, he was no longer a président – the little bewigged monster – he was a fetish. He would see to it that the nickname stuck. 'Le Fétiche,' he shrieked, 'demande de l'argent de ses moules et de ses fagots . . . Le misérable m'accable d'exploits.' He had put up Baudy, who was a man of straw, to do his dirty work. 'Songez qu'il faisait cette infâmie dans le temps qu'il recevait de moi 47 mille livres! . . . Qu'il tremble! Il ne s'agit pas de le rendre ridicule: il s'agit de le déshonorer. Cela m'afflige. Mais il payera cher la bassesse d'un procédé si coupable et si lâche.' Finally he addressed the Fetish himself in a letter composed in his most magnificent style. 'Vous n'êtes donc venu chez moi, Monsieur, vous ne m'avez offert votre amitié, que pour empoisoner par des procès la fin de ma vie.' In great detail he went over the whole dispute. With singular violence, and no less singular obtuseness, he asserted the hopelessly contradictory propositions, both that the wood was his own and that the Président had given it him; he hinted that his enemy would make use of his position to pervert the course of justice; and he ended with threats. 'S'il faut que M. le Chancelier, et les Ministres, et tout Paris, soient instruits de votre procédé, ils le seront; et, s'il se trouve dans votre Compagnie respectable une personne qui vous approuve, je me condamne.'

The Président's moment had come – the testing moment of his life. What was he to do? It was still not too late to withdraw, to pay the money with a shrug of the shoulders and put an end to this fearful hubbub and this terrifying enmity. For a short space, he wavered. It was true that Voltaire was the greatest writer of the age, and perhaps he deserved some allowances on that score. In any case, he was an extremely dangerous antagonist – a man who had made mincemeat of all his literary opponents and fought on equal terms with Frederick the Great. But no! It was intolerable! His Burgundian blood boiled, and the proud traditions of aristocracy and the judicial habits of a lifetime asserted themselves. 'Là-dessus on dit': –

so he explained later to a friend – 'c'est un homme dangereux. Et à cause de cela, faut-il donc le laisser être méchant impunément? Ce sont au contraire ces sortes de gens-là qu'il faut châtier. Je ne le crains pas. ... On l'admire, parce qu'il fait d'excellents vers. Sans doute il les fait excellents. Mais ce sont ses vers qu'il faut admirer.' And so, taking Voltaire's letter, he wrote upon the margin of it a reply, in which he not only rebutted his arguments but told him exactly what he thought of him. Point by point he exposed the futility of Voltaire's contentions. He showed that there was actually a clause in the lease, by which the cut wood on the estate was specifically excepted from the sale. He offered to drop the matter if Voltaire would send him a receipt in the following terms: 'Je soussigné, François-Marie Arouet de Voltaire, chevalier, seigneur de Ferney, gentilhomme ordinaire de la chambre du Roi, reconnois que M. de Brosses, président du Parlement, m'a fait présent de . . . voies de bois de moule, pour mon chauffage, en valeur de 281 f., dont je le remercie.' He pointed out that otherwise he had nothing to do with the business, that Voltaire owed the money to Charlot Baudy, and that it was indeed extraordinary to see 'un homme si riche et si illustre se tourmenter à tel excès pour ne pas payer à un paysan 280 livres pour du bois de chauffage qu'il a fourni.' His incidental remarks were nothing if not outspoken. 'En vérité,' he wrote, 'je gémis pour l'humanité de voir un si grand génie avec un cœur si petit sans cesse tiraillé par des misères de jalousie et de lésine. C'est vous-même qui empoisonnez une vie si bien faite d'ailleurs pour être heureuse.' As for the suggestion that he would bring undue influence to bear upon the case, – 'il ne convient pas de parler ainsi: soyez assez sage à l'avenir pour ne rien dire de pareil à un magistrat'. 'Tenez vous pour dit,' the letter concluded, 'de ne m'écrire plus ni sur cette matière ni surtout de ce ton. Je vous fais, Monsieur, le souhait de Perse: *Mens sana in corpore sano.*'

It is difficult indeed to imagine the scene at Ferney while Voltaire was deciphering, on the edges of his own letter, this devastating reply. But there was worse to follow. A note came from the Président de Ruffey, in which, with infinite politeness, he made it clear that in his opinion Voltaire had no case, and that he had better pay. At the same time Ruffey wrote to Madame Denis, Voltaire's niece, advising her to give the money privately to Baudy. Madame Denis had not the courage to do so; she showed the letter to her uncle, who, in a dictated reply, still tried to keep up an appearance of self-confidence. 'Je ne crains point les Fétiches,' he added in his own hand. 'Et les Fétiches doivent me craindre.' And again, at the bottom of the paper, he scribbled, 'N.B. Il n'y a qu'une voix sur le Fétiche.' But such screams were useless; the game was up. The Président's letter remained unanswered; Voltaire swallowed in silence the incredible affront; and when, a little later, the Président, feeling that he could afford to be magnanimous, informed a common friend that he would cancel his account with Baudy if Voltaire gave 281 francs to the poor of Tournay, the great man was glad enough to fall in with the suggestion.

The Président had triumphed; but could he really have supposed that he would escape from such an antagonist unscathed? The sequel came ten years later, when the Président Hénault died and left a seat vacant at the Academy. There was a strong movement in favour of electing the Président de Brosses. There appeared to be no other very suitable candidate; his friends rallied round him; and d'Alembert, writing to Voltaire from Paris, assured him that there was every likelihood that 'ce plat Président' would be chosen for the vacant place. The serious feature of the case was that the old Maréchal de Richelieu, who, after a lifetime of fighting and gallantry, amused his decrepitude by making his influence felt in affairs of this kind, supported him. What was to be done? Voltaire was equal to the occasion: his letters flew. At all costs the Fetish must be kept out. He wrote repeatedly to Richelieu, in that tone of delicate cajolery of which he was a master, touching upon their ancient friendship, and spinning a strange tale of the perfidies committed by 'ce petit persécuteur nasilloneur', until the Maréchal melted, and promised to withdraw his support. Finally Voltaire despatched to d'Alembert a signed declaration to the effect that he would himself resign from the Academy if Brosses was elected. This settled the matter, and no more was heard of the candidature of the Président. It seems likely that he never knew what it was that had baulked him of the ambition of his life. For 281 francs he had lost the immortality of the Academy. A bad bargain, no doubt; and yet, after all, the transaction had gained him another, and in fact a unique, distinction: he would go down to history as the man who had got the better of Voltaire.

1931

# A Bibliographical Note

*Landmarks in French Literature* (1912) was Lytton Strachey's first book. Other books published during his lifetime were: *Eminent Victorians* (1918); *Books and Characters: French and English* (1922); *Pope* (1925); *Elizabeth and Essex: A Tragic History* (1928); and *Portraits in Miniature and Other Essays* (1931). Following his death in 1932, his brother and literary executor James Strachey published *Characters and Commentaries* (1933); *Virginia Woolf and Lytton Strachey: Letters* (1956), with Leonard Woolf; and *Spectatorial Essays* (1964). In 1948 some of his essays – including many of those contained in this volume – were regrouped by James Strachey into two volumes, *Biographical Essays* and *Literary Essays*, as part of the Uniform Edition of the Collected Works of Lytton Strachey. At the time of his death Strachey had been collaborating with Roger Fulford on *The Greville Memoirs* which were published, edited by Ralph and Frances Partridge, in eight volumes (1937–8).

After James Strachey's death in 1967, the executorship passed to his wife Alix Strachey. In 1969 Lytton Strachey's 'entertainment' *Ermyntrude and Esmeralda* was published with an introduction by Michael Holroyd, who also edited *Lytton Strachey by Himself: a Self-Portrait* (1971). *Lytton Strachey: The Really Interesting Question and Other Papers* (1972) was edited by Paul Levy. Alix Strachey, who died in 1973, had created the Strachey Trust, a registered charity to which she gave all literary manuscript material and the Stracheys' copyright. Since her death the Trust has administered the literary estate. At the time of writing, the Trustees are: Lord Annan, Quentin Bell, Lucy Norton (Chairman), Michael Seifert and Dorothea Vaughan; and Michael Holroyd and Paul Levy, who together act as literary executors. Ann Wilson is the Trust's secretary. The principal aims of the Trust are to promote high standards of cataloguing and to encourage accessibility to scholars of manuscript collections such as its own, part of which is now in the British Library.

Michael Holroyd
Paul Levy

March 1979

# Index